W9-BGD-935

WITHDRAWN

The **AMA**
Dictionary of
Business and Management

The **AMA**
Dictionary of
Business and Management

George Thomas Kurian

American Management Association

New York • Atlanta • Brussels • Chicago • Mexico City • San Francisco
Shanghai • Tokyo • Toronto • Washington, D. C.

Bulk discounts available. For details visit:
www.amacombooks.org/go/specialsales
Or contact special sales:
Phone: 800-250-5308
E-mail: specialsls@amanet.org
View all the AMACOM titles at: www.amacombooks.org
American Management Association: www.amanet.org

This publication is designed to provide accurate and authoritative information in regard to the subject matter covered. It is sold with the understanding that the publisher is not engaged in rendering legal, accounting, or other professional service. If legal advice or other expert assistance is required, the services of a competent professional person should be sought.

Library of Congress Cataloging-in-Publication Data

Kurian, George Thomas.
    The AMA dictionary of business and management / George Thomas Kurian.
        p. cm.
    Includes bibliographical references and index.
    ISBN-13: 978-0-8144-2028-7
    ISBN-10: 0-8144-2028-1
    1. Management—Dictionaries. 2. Business—Dictionaries. I. Title. II. Title: Dictionary of business
        and management.
    HD30.15.K894 2013
    650.03—dc23

                                                                                    2012032937

© 2013 George Thomas Kurian.
All rights reserved.
Printed in the United States of America.

This publication may not be reproduced, stored in a retrieval system, or transmitted in whole or in part, in any form or by any means, electronic, mechanical, photocopying, recording, or otherwise, without the prior written permission of AMACOM, a division of American Management Association, 1601 Broadway, New York, NY 10019.

The scanning, uploading, or distribution of this book via the Internet or any other means without the express permission of the publisher is illegal and punishable by law. Please purchase only authorized electronic editions of this work and do not participate in or encourage piracy of copyrighted materials, electronically or otherwise. Your support of the author's rights is appreciated.

About AMA
American Management Association (www.amanet.org) is a world leader in talent development, advancing the skills of individuals to drive business success. Our mission is to support the goals of individuals and organizations through a complete range of products and services, including classroom and virtual seminars, webcasts, webinars, podcasts, conferences, corporate and government solutions, business books and research. AMA's approach to improving performance combines experiential learning—learning through doing—with opportunities for ongoing professional growth at every step of one's career journey.

Printing number
10 9 8 7 6 5 4 3 2 1

650
KUR

29.95

181

8/2/13

The **AMA**
Dictionary of
Business and Management

A

A1 In life and marine insurance, rating given to person or property in perfect condition.

AAA Prime rating given to securities by Standard and Poor's.

AAP AFFIRMATIVE ACTION PROGRAM

Abandonment 1. Final stage in a product life cycle when the decision is made to discontinue it. 2. Relinquishing a product to a third party with or without a settlement or compensation.

Abandonment option Choice of terminating an investment before its scheduled closing date.

ABB ACTIVITY-BASED BUDGETING

ABC ACTIVITY-BASED COSTING

ABC AUDIT BUREAU OF CIRCULATION

Abilene paradox Theory that some decisions ostensibly based on consensus are counterproductive because they are founded on misperceptions and poor communications. Proposed by JERRY HARVEY, Professor Emeritus of Management, George Washington University, in 1974.

Abnormal return Rate of return for a risk greater than that required or expected by analysts.

Above-the-line 1. Entries in a profit-and-loss account that are within the ordinary activities of business. 2. Entries in a balance sheet dealing with revenue, as opposed to capital. Compare BELOW-THE-LINE. 3. Advertising through television, radio, newspapers, and Internet.

Abreaction channel Mechanisms for employees to express dissatisfaction with their work or their superiors.

Absence culture Corporate culture in which absenteeism is condoned.

Absenteeism Unauthorized leave from work, especially repeatedly.

Absolute cost advantage Cost of producing

particular products as influenced by certain advantages, such as cheap labor or abundant natural resources.

Absolute cost barrier Built-in obstacle to entry into a new market, such as the advantage held by established or large firms.

Absolute market share Per capita income. See RELATIVE SHARE.

Absolute monopoly Severe form of monopoly in which production and distribution of a product or service is in the hands of a single corporation.

Absolute performance standard Theoretical standard of performance, such as ZERO DEFECT, against which actual performance may be judged.

Absorption costing Accounting process in which overhead costs of production are apportioned on the basis of seven elements: unit, weight, or volume; labor hours; machine hours; direct labor costs; direct material costs; prime costs; and standard hours.

Abusive dismissal Termination of an employee that is technically legal in some countries but violates accepted standards of fairness and equity.

Accelerated depreciation Rate of depreciation of assets that is faster than useful-life basis.

Acceleration principle Relationship between a change in output and the level of investment spending. The capital to output ratio is known as the ACCELERATOR.

Accelerator 1. Company that supplies office space, marketing space, and infrastructural services. 2. Capital-output ratio that indicates changes in output and level of investment.

Acceptance Agreement to the terms of a bill of exchange certifying that the person on whom it is drawn accepts the conditions of the bill, denoted by the person's signature.

Acceptance bonus Bonus paid to a new employee upon beginning a job; part of a Golden hello.

Acceptance sampling QUALITY CONTROL technique that uses statistical methods to examine a sample before acceptance of a batch.

Acceptance theory of authority Principle that defines AUTHORITY in terms of its acceptance by subordinates and not as inherent in the office.

Accession rate Measure of the number of new employees joining a firm over a given period.

Accident analysis Use of ERGONOMIC analysis techniques to identify causes of accidents and potential hazards in the workplace, so as to create a safer working environment.

Accord and satisfaction Legal device defining a contractual obligation and the satisfaction and discharge of that obligation under the law of tort.

Account 1. A statement of transactions. 2. In advertising, marketing, and public relations, a client from whom a commission or fee is obtained in return for services.

Account executive Professional in an advertising, marketing, or public relations agency responsible for liaising with a client and implementing the client's business program.

Account reconciliation Procedure for ensuring reliability of accounting records by verifying authorized amounts and actual payments.

Accountability 1. Relationship in which each party is responsible for the discharge of assumed responsibilities in compliance with proper legal and ethical standards. 2. Clear presentation of financial information that makes it possible to identify the legitimacy of transactions.

Accountant Trained professional in a corporation or business responsible for collating, recording, analyzing, and communicating financial information.

Accounting controls 1. Procedures for monitoring the accuracy and integrity of accounts and their compliance with accepted regulations and practices. 2. Procedures ensuring that expenditures and costs conform to projections and plans.

Accounting event Internal or external transaction or charge, either credit or debit, recognized as a valid entry in an account.

Accounting period Time frame of an account, usually a month, quarter, or year.

Accounting process Act of recoding, preparing, and analyzing financial transactions for the benefit of accountants and auditors.

Accounting rate of return Ratio in accounting that expresses profit before interest and taxation, usually for the accounting period as a percentage of the capital.

Accounts payable Amount owed by a business, person, or supplier, classified as a CURRENT LIABILITY in the balance sheet.

Accounts receivable Amount owed to a business by customers for invoice amounts classified as current accounts in the balance sheet.

Accretion Growth or increase in value.

Accrual Estimate in an account of a liability not supported by an invoice at the time the account is prepared. It is classified as a CURRENT LIABILITY in a balance sheet. In *accrual accounting*, revenues are credited when earned and expenses are debited when incurred.

Acculturation Process of adapting to, functioning, and flourishing in new, foreign cultural and societal environments, especially without long preparation, and dealing on equal terms with those who have different cultural mores.

Accumulated depreciation. Total depreciation written off the cost or valuation of a fixed asset since it was first brought into the balance sheet. Also known as *aggregate depreciation*.

Accumulated dividends Dividends not paid to the shareholders but carried forward to the next balance sheet.

Achieved penetration Extent to which a product or service has gained market acceptance, expressed as a percentage or ratio of actual customers to potential customers.

Achievement culture Organizational culture that fosters achievement, a sense of accomplishment, and a positive attitude toward success.

Achievement motivation theory Principle that defines achievement as exhibiting certain social and personal characteristics, such as devotion to the task at hand, acceptance of responsibility, desire for professional growth, proper motivation, ability to interact positively with peers, expertise and training, ability to multitask, and espousal of ethical standards and values.

Acid test ratio Financial proportion of liquid assets to current liabilities, which shows how far a company is able to meet its debt obligations.

Ackoff, Russell Lincoln (1919–2009) Pioneer of operations research and systems, organizational theorist and consultant, author of *Ackoff's Fables: Irreverent Reflections on Business and Bureaucracy* (1957) and *Introduction to Operations Research* (1957). He was Anheuser-Busch Professor Emeritus of Management Science at Wharton School, University of Pennsylvania.

Acquisition See ACQUISITION MANAGEMENT

Acquisition management Acquiring and managing an established product or company as a means of growth and diversification, thereby overcoming the disadvantage in time that growth by internal development presents. This is a painless way to enter a new market that may be difficult otherwise to penetrate. In industries where COMPETITIVE ADVANTAGE is held in assets and reputation, and back orders are built up over time, acquisitions can help to achieve a strong market position immediately. Foreign companies especially find it easier to acquire domestic companies as a way of breaking into unfamiliar markets. Financially acquisitive growth is attractive for a publicly traded company if its price-earnings ratio is high relative to that of the target company because it enhances the acquirer's earnings per share; also, it is positive when the goodwill element of the acquisition costs is treated as reserves rather than as an asset. However, acquisition presents substantial risks, with failure rates approaching 50%. The success of an acquisition strategy depends on two factors: the acquisition must create or add value, and the acquired company must be successfully integrated into the parent company. The purchase value of an acquisition typically includes a bid premium of 30 to 40% over the market value of the target company, which makes it difficult for the acquisition to be financially viable. Many acquisitions fail because the perceived benefits of increased market share fail to meet the estimated profit margins, turnover, or cash flow, and fail to meet the additional costs of integration.

There are four mechanisms that achieve value creation and offset the downside: (1) Resource sharing, by which operating costs are combined and rationalized, leading to cost reductions through economies of scale and scope. (2) Skills transfer in production technology, financial controls, and distribution and expansion of cross-company pool of expertise. (3) Enlargement of size, which creates market dominance in sales and expertise; increased bargaining power over suppliers, bankers, and customers; reduction of competition; and use of tax credits. (4) Restructuring by closing down surplus capacity, reducing head office staff, and rationalizing unprofitable product lines. Another form of restructuring is through UNBUNDLING, whereby parts of the business that are unprofitable are spun off. In many instances, acquisitions fail because the planned values cannot be realized owing to organizational issues. Key personnel may depart and clashes of ORGANIZATIONAL CULTURES may lead to mistrust, lack of communication, or poor control systems. The degree of integration and success will determine the degree of strategic interdependence between the acquirer and the acquired. It is also necessary to preserve the autonomy of the acquired company in order to retain its distinctive character and culture.

There are three types of acquisitions integration: (1) full consolidation of operations, organization, and culture of both companies so that there are no boundary lines; (2) partial consolidation in which the autonomy of the acquired company is retained while strategic capabilities are interchanged; and (3) full autonomy of the acquired company, which becomes a stand-alone subsidiary. There are five ingredients for successful integration: (1) Mutual understanding of the strengths and weaknesses, history, culture, and management style of the two companies so that the values of each part are not destroyed. (2) Cultivation of a shared vision and camaraderie by employees of both companies that is strong enough to overcome the natural distrust accompanying the changes. (3) Willingness to share data and information and skills. (4) Recognition of the extent of the post-acquisition changes and willingness to confront the problems and opportunities that such changes present. (5) Management communicates openly with employees about the cost-benefits of integration.

Acquisitive society A cultural group that places a premium on the acquisition and possession of material things as the path toward happiness and fulfillment. See CONSPICUOUS CONSUMPTION.

Across the board Characterization as applicable uniformly and without distinction to all participants.

Action-centered leadership Technique of management development devised by leadership thinker JOHN ADAIR, which trains leaders by practical problem solving.

Action learning Management development technique devised by business thinker R. G. Revans, which focuses on group process and solution of real problems encountered in corporate settings.

Action research Work that furthers the study of organizational processes by influencing the activity being studied and controlling the input and output under investigation. It is based on the premise that the act of investigation itself changes the nature of the subject being studied.

Active management Management style in which managers are involved in initiating corporate bonding, setting goals, and motivating colleagues.

Active partner Stakeholder who provides capital and who contributes skills to the management of the company. Active partners are also often involved in day-to-day operations.

Activity Operation in an organization for which costs are incurred. The operation may be at several levels, such as to produce a product, operate a business unit, or market goods to customers. Each activity is a unit of budgeting, management, or costing.

Activity analysis Process of identifying appropriate output measures as activities, resources, and other cost drivers and determining their effects on the costs of making a product or providing a service. This is one of the three techniques first propounded by business guru PETER DRUCKER for discovering the optimum organizational structure for a corporation; the other two were DECISION ANALYSIS and RELATIONS ANALYSIS.

Activity-based budgeting (ABB) Accounting procedure that identifies the costs involved in running each sector of a business.

Activity-based costing (ABC) Method of costing products that links overall cost to the total cost of all activities that contribute to their manufacture. It is designed to control INDIRECT COSTS and to reflect actual rather than paper costs. The method assigns costs to products based on resources actually consumed and efforts actually expended. It identifies costs for each unit of task, such as machine setup or job scheduling. As a result, ABC is a component of the strategic planning process, and unlike conventional accounting, calibrates future costs instead of simply measuring past history. It identifies areas for savings and cost reduction through streamlining processes and activities, and it measures cost drivers. While ABC assigns material costs to products in the same manner as conventional accounting, it does not treat direct labor and direct materials as elements that generate overhead. Rather, it premises that products incur indirect costs because they consume resources and these are treated as distinct elements, not as a function of direct costs. In a traditional cost system, costs are related to volume and are triggered by individual units, but in ABC, batches rather than individual units are the bases of measurement; for example, doubling the volume does not proportionately double the number of machine setups. Purchasing is another cost driven by batches whose costs are allocated in traditional accounting by material costs; in ABC, costs are directly related to the number of purchase orders and are allocated in proportion. It thus reflects ECONOMIES OF SCALE, taking into account materials handling, setups, warehousing, and other factors. In addition, ABC assigns BELOW-THE-LINE costs, such as sales, marketing, R&D, and administration, as divided by class of customer. That is, customer costs vary substantially as a result of the type of customer, order size, service levels, product size, and distribution channel and territory. Cost-reduction policies can thus be generated based on the average number of units per customer order, number of locations, type of sales promotion, pricing strategies, returns, channels of distribution, number of sales calls, and speed of bills payment. Pareto analysis (see PARETO RULE) is used to separate customer-driven and product-driven costs.

Because ABC uses more cost pools and assigns costs to a broader range of factors, it can reflect the complexity of costs more accurately. ABC assigns key manufacturing and business process costs to activity centers. First-stage cost drivers are assigned to products. The analysis of second-stage cost drivers is more rigorous, where costs are proportional to the batches produced and, in the case of design engineering, to the products themselves. Activity centers may be product driven or customer driven. They may be homogenous processes, as in an assembly line, or business processes, such as marketing. In ABC, second-stage drivers such as direct labor costs, material costs, and machine hours are supplemented by setup times, inspection costs, warehouse costs, and sales calls. ABC also distinguishes among hierarchical product-driven costs at three levels: individual, batch, and market or product. Customer-driven activities are distinguished at four levels: (1) order level, including order entry, shipping, billing, and freight; (2) customer level, including sales force, credit and collections, and service; (3) market level, including R&D, advertising, promotion, and marketing; and (4) enterprise level, including pensions and management.

ABC is generally applied to manufacturing, but it is becoming important in the service sector as well. It is growing critical in capital-intensive industries where time-based costing is considered representative of cost utilization and labor costs are assigned to the process rather than the product. Capital costs and change-over costs tend to be high in capital-intensive industries. Because fixed costs are high in capital-intensive industries, profitability is determined by high-capacity utilization. In such cases, variable pricing is called for and the cost of excess capacity should not influence pricing decisions. Large fixed costs are annually assigned to production lines rather than spread over all departments. In some process industries, logistics costs can skew overall costs. Costs to specific customer segments will vary widely. Customer sales volume, location, high-capacity utilization, limited production flexibility, and product mix also affect logistics costs. By allocating indirect costs more accurately, ABC identifies profitable opportunities and permits exit from unprofitable activities. Thus, the key elements in ABC are cost drivers. Because ABC leads to a significant rethinking of policies and overall corporate strategy, it is more realistic and simpler than traditional costing systems.

Activity-based management Management based on analysis of the various activities that contribute to the running of the company.

Activity ratio Financial ratio based on the relationship of sales revenue to assets, showing how well the assets are being used.

Activity sampling Work-sampling technique in which observations of workers, processes, and machines are made and analyzed over a period of time. This technique is used by industrial engineers to determine the efficiency of each step in a large operation.

Actualization-atmosphere factors Motivational elements, encompassing favorable working conditions, job security, and remuneration.

Actuals Real costs rather than estimated costs.

Actuarial return RETURN ON INVESTMENT as measured by discounted cash-flow analysis. Also known as *internal rate of return*.

Adair, John (1934–) British academic and leadership theorist. Visiting professor at the University of Exeter (1990–2000) and Chair of Leadership Studies at United Nations Staff College, Turin. Author of *How to Grow a Leader: Seven Key Principles of Effective Leadership Development* (2006), *Effective Teambuilding: How to Make a Winning Team* (1987), *The John Adair Handbook of Management and Leadership* (2004), *Leadership and Motivation: The Fifty-Fifty Rule and Eight Key Principles of Motivating Others* (2007).

Adair, John Eric Management expert known for his three-circle model of leadership, representing the task, the team, and the individual, known as ACTION-CENTERED LEADERSHIP. He was Professor of Leadership Studies at the University of Surrey (1969–1984).

Adams, J. Stacey *See* EQUITY THEORY.

Adams, Scott Cartoonist and creator of the DILBERT PRINCIPLE.

Adaptive control Form of self-regulation in an industrial process, designed to ensure continuous performance at optimum level through a changing environment.

Adaptive expectation In MACROECONO-MIC theory, forecasts of future values based on past values.

Adaptive isomorphism Experimentation with new products and processes to catch up with technology or meet emerging markets.

Adaptive management Style of management that is flexible and supple in modifying a company's goals and plans to take advantage of changing environments and market conditions.

Added value See VALUE ADDED

Add-on Accessory or replacement part of a product sold to a customer.

Adhocracy Organizational structure characterized by an absence of bureaucratic rigidities, enabling managers to think and act out of the box. Term coined by futurist ALVIN TOFFLER.

Adjustable-rate mortgage (ARM) Mortgage for which the interest rate is adjusted at periodic intervals to reflect prevailing rates of interest in the money market.

Adjustable-rate share Type of preferred stock whose interest rate is linked to Treasury bill interest rates.

Adminisphere Department of a company that deals with administrative matters.

Administered price Set by the seller, a price that is independent of market conditions.

Administered vertical marketing system Marketing scheme in which a major retail chain acts as the captain, coordinating marketing activities at all levels, including planning and management.

Administrative management Traditional school of management associated with business thinker HENRI FAYOL and sociologist MAX WEBER. It emphasizes the importance of formal structure and hierarchy.

Administrative receiver Person appointed by a court to administer and manage all the assets of a company, including the power to sell assets. Also known as *administrator*.

Adopter Consumer who adopts an innovation introduced by a corporation.

Adoption curve Graph showing the rate at which a new technology is embraced by consumers.

Adoption of new products Process by which consumers adopt new products and services, align them with meeting their needs, and make them part of their work life and leisure.

Adoption theory Principles behind the diffusion of innovations over time, including the time frame for their acceptance, varying with innovators, early adopters, and laggards.

ADR ALTERNATIVE DISPUTE RESOLUTION

ADR AMERICAN DEPOSITORY RECEIPT

Ad tracking research Market research that periodically measures the impact of an advertising campaign, including brand awareness.

Advanced manufacturing technologies (AMT) High technology adapted for manufacturing such as COMPUTER-AIDED DESIGN.

Adventure In business, a speculative commercial enterprise.

Advertising Promotion of ideas, goods, or services through a commercial medium with an identified sponsor. The purpose of advertising is to inform, promote brand awareness, and create confidence in the product or service offered. An *advertising campaign* is a systematic and orchestrated program with stated strategy, objectives, and budget.

Advocacy Promotion of a better public image, or the building of customer good-will by linking a product or service with a well-known cause or movement that enjoys public support.

Affective That which deals with an attitude

or response based on emotion and desire, rather than on objective analysis.

Affiliate 1. Company associated with another company through common ownership. 2. In broadcasting, a local station that carries the programs of a national network.

Affinity card Credit card issued to a member of a group that carries with it certain advantages.

Affirmative action program (AAP) Procedures to achieve or remedy an imbalance in hiring and employment as applied to minorities and women. Often mandated by government, it sometimes includes quotas governing the percentage of minorities and women represented in an organization.

AG (Aktiengesellschaft) Abbreviation used in German-speaking countries to designate a publicly traded company.

Age analysis Breakdown of outstanding ACCOUNTS PAYABLES, divided by the time the accounts have been overdue.

Age and life-cycle segmentation In market research, a demographic breakdown of the customer base by age, gender, and marital status.

Age discrimination Action showing bias against older people and senior citizens when providing services or recruiting employees. As an attitude, termed *ageism*.

Agency relationship Relationship in which

a principal engages an agent to perform some official duty or service on his or her behalf and delegates the necessary authority for this purpose. The costs of monitoring and bonding in such a relationship are known as *agency costs*. When the interest of a principal and an agent collide, it may lead to an *agency problem*. Agents may be either *special agents* or *general agents*, depending on the scope of their authority and purview. See also AGENCY THEORY.

Agency shop Requirement that nonunion employees in a bargaining unit pay the union a sum equivalent to union fees and dues, even if they are not members of the union.

Agency theory Delegation of responsibility from one party to another, and the relationship between the delegator and the delegate; see also AGENCY RELATIONSHIP. Such relationships exist between managers and shareholders, employers and employees, professionals and their clients, and politicians or civil servants and citizens. Delegation need not be explicit, and may cover a wide range of transactions. There are costs associated with delegation, including: (1) monitoring costs incurred by the principal to regulate the agent's conduct; (2) bonding costs to insure against mala fides; (3) residual costs, including loss against actions by the delegate that cause loss; and (4) communication costs incurred to maintain the flow of information between the delegator and the delegate.

Information asymmetries inhibit effective delegation in two ways: (1) information may be withheld by the agent deliberately to increase his or her own value; or (2) information may be hidden by the agent by contrarian actions. The former is known as *hidden information* and the latter as MORAL HAZARD. These factors play a part in the most common agency relationship between shareholders and management, where the delegators are too dispersed to exercise effective control and the delegates or managers have extraordinary discretion to pursue policies that may be against the interests of the delegators. Managers may take unwarranted risks, build personal empires, and build up expense accounts. To reduce the temptation to do so, shareholders may introduce SHARE OPTIONS and PROFIT-SHARING schemes as incentives for managers to perform better.

Agenda Items to be discussed in a business meeting or goals included in a plan of work or other nature.

Agent 1. Person or company authorized to act on behalf of another. 2. Vector of an action that is carried out, as in *agent of change*.

Agglomeration economies Benefits occurring when a large number of consumers live in close proximity or in clusters.

Aggregate demand The sum of demand for all goods and services in an economy at a particular time, a key concept in

KEYNESIAN ECONOMICS. It comprises investment, government expenditure, and imports less exports.

Aggregate planning Efficient planning process designed to produce the optimum output at the right costs within the best lead time. It contains long-term targeted sales forecasts, production levels, inventory levels, and customer backlogs, and is designed to satisfy the demand forecast at optimum cost. Aggregate planning begins with a determination of demand in relation to current capacity. Demand may be increased through pricing, promotion, back ordering, and new demand creation. It may also be increased through other means such as hiring, overtime, part-time or casual labor, inventory, subcontracting, and cross-training. Aggregate planning strategies include a LEVEL-OUTPUT STRATEGY that maintains a steady production rate and a CHASE DEMAND STRATEGY that matches SUPPLY AND DEMAND period by period.

Aggregate supply Total supply of all goods and services in an economy, as determined after DEREGULATION, COMPETITION, and unrestricted labor supply.

Aggressive In management or investment, a willingness to take high risks to realize higher than average gains.

Agile development Process of development that is not rigid, quickly adapts to changing circumstances, and incorporates implementation.

Agile manufacturing Production system that meets the demands of customers by adopting flexible schedules without sacrificing quality or incurring additional costs. It emphasizes customer satisfaction and the establishment of flexible supply pipelines.

Agility Organizational ability to respond with flexibility and speed, as a source of competitive advantage; recommended by business writer TOM PETERS and professor ROSABETH MOSS KANTER.

Agreement corporation Firm that conducts international banking transactions that are exempt from normal banking and ANTITRUST laws; Also called *edge corporation*.

AI ARTIFICIAL INTELLIGENCE

AIDAS Acronym for attention, interest, desire, action, and satisfaction, regarded as components of effective communication and marketing.

Alderfer, Clayton (1940–) American psychologist who developed Maslow's Hierarchy of Needs by categorizing the hierarchy into his ERG theory (Existence, Relatedness, and Growth) in his book *Existence, Relatedness and Growth: Human Needs in Organizational Settings* (1972). He further developed his ideas in *The Five Laws of Group and Intergroup Dynamics* (2005).

Alienation In human resources management, source of employee dissatisfaction resulting from any of several factors: (1) powerlessness, or the inability to influence work conditions; (2) isolation, or the absence of human interaction during working hours; (3) meaninglessness, or the absence of recognition for work well done; (4) low self-esteem, resulting from lack of individual worth; (5) loss of identity with corporate culture or brand; (6) lack of prospects, or the sense that there is little chance for advancement within a group; and (7) lack of equality, or discrimination based on factors extraneous to work.

A-list Top names in an industry or profession.

All-inclusive income concept In accounting, inclusion of all items of profit and loss in an earnings statement.

Allocation base In management accounting, cost-allocation basis used to assign costs to each cost object.

Allotment Method of distributing unissued shares in a limited company in exchange for a contribution of capital.

Allowable marketing costs Optimum marketing cost under which a healthy or desirable profit margin can be maintained.

Alpha-release First stage in release of a product or service in which lead users and company employees participate.

Alternative dispute resolution (ADR) Avenue for settling business disputes in foreign countries other than through their legal systems, including ARBITRATION, MEDIATION, and CONCILIATION.

Altman, Edward (1941–) Professor of Finance at Stern School of Business at New York University. He is best known for his development of *Z*-score for predicting bankruptcy, which he published in 1978. His other books include *Corporate Financial Distress and Bankruptcy* (2005) and *Recovery Risk* (2005).

AMACOM Publishing division of the American Management Association.

Amalgamation Merger of two or more companies under one of several scenarios, such as: (1) the dissolution of an existing company and the formation of a new one, (2) the acquisition of one company by the other, and (3) the straightforward merger of two companies to form a new company with a new name.

Ambit claim Exaggerated demands on an ARBITRATION board to leave room for subsequent concessions.

American depository receipt (ADR) Receipt issued by a bank that may be traded as a security in the financial market.

American option Financial OPTION that can be exercised until the expiry date.

Amortization In accounting, a form of depreciation in which the annual amount deemed to waste away from a FIXED ASSET is treated as an expense. In the case of a lease, the cost is divided by the number of years of its term and is treated as an annual charge against profit. GOODWILL may be amortized as debt and front-end fees charged for a loan. In mortgages, interest payments are divided on a sliding scale by which they take precedence over the principal in the repayment schedule.

AMT ADVANCED MANUFACTURING TECHNOLOGIES

Analysis Set of accepted procedures that examines issues as a whole and in part, using mathematical techniques, setting expectations, and creating ratios to determine whether the expectations have been met.

Analyzer strategy Strategy in strategic management that is less risky than prospector strategy. It analyzes emerging markets for possible opening before entering them.

Angel investor Backer in a high-risk enterprise, such as startups or theater.

Angyal, Andras (1902–1960) Hungarian-born American management specialist who coined the term biosphere, which he described in terms of interlocking systems governed by autonomy and homonomy. Author of *Foundations for a Science of Personality* (1941).

Annual account Audited financial statement of a corporation, by law published annually and including profit and loss, balance sheet, cash-flow statement, director's report, and auditor's report.

Annual general meeting Obligatory meeting of all the shareholders of a company for approving the annual report and voting on proposals.

Annual hours Practice of averaging employees' working hours over a year rather than the traditional number of hours per week or month.

Anomaly In financial markets, abnormal returns that influence the prices of many financial obligations, such as DERIVATIVES.

ANSI American National Standards Institute

Ansoff, Igor (1918–2002) Russian-American mathematician and father of Strategic Management. Professor of Industrial Administration at Carnegie Mellon University (1963–68) and Professor of Management, Vanderbilt University (1968–73). Ansoff is known for his research in environment turbulence, contingent strategic success paradigm, and real-time strategic management. Author of *Strategic Management* (2007) and *Corporate Strategy* (1965).

Ansoff matrix Classification device for four basic marketing strategies, developed by mathematician IGOR ANSOFF: (1) market penetration, (2) market extension,

(3) product development, and (4) diversification.

Antagonistic cooperation Temporary cooperation between two parties who are normally rivals.

Antitrust laws Any of several laws passed by the U.S. Congress making illegal any restraints on trade and any monopolies that inhibit or interfere with FREE TRADE and COMPETITION.

App Application for a computer program.

Applied research Market research aimed at solving a specific business problem that will lead to a better understanding of the way a market works, how it responds to a particular strategy, and how to reduce uncertainty.

Apprenticeship programs First developed in Germany, these are on-the-job training programs of four or five years' duration, during which participants are also enrolled in school. The coursework is equal, rather than supplemental, to the on-the-job training, and often there is compensation for the work or the promise of employment following completion of the training. Apprenticeships are distinguished from *internships*, which are more common in the United States and are unpaid, shorter-term on-the-job training programs, sometimes with the prospect of employment afterwards but no guarantee of it.

Approach-approach conflict A situation in which a person faces two potentially satisfying but incompatible goals.

Appropriate technology Low-level technology that is feasible and applicable to lesser developed countries that lack the infrastructure necessary to sustain higher-tech operations.

Appropriation 1. Allocation of net profits in an account after determining its costs and expenses. 2. Allocation of payments to a particular debt out of several existing debts.

A priori segmentation Process of dividing markets on the basis of conventional assumptions rather than on market research.

Arbitrage Financial operation that takes advantage of a difference in interest rates or commodity prices between one market and another. It is nonspeculative because the trader, or *arbitrageur*, enters into the transaction only when there is a clear differential in price and both prices and rates are known.

Arbitrary allocation Cost assignment in which the costs are based on variables that cannot be controlled.

Arbitration Settlement of a civil dispute using an *arbitrageur* or *arbitrator* or tribunal. The judgment of an arbitrator may be either binding or nonmandatory.

Argyris, Chris (1923–) American business theorist, Professor Emeritus at Harvard

Business School, and a Thought Leader at Monitor Group. He is best known for his seminal work in the area of learning organizations. In his book *Action Science* (1985) he advocated solutions to practical problems by generating new knowledge. Other terms developed by Argyris includes actionable knowledge, ladder of inference, and double loop learning. His books include *Flawed Advice and Management Trap: How Managers Can Know When They are Getting Good Advice and When They Are Not* (2000), *On Organizational Learning* (1993), and *Personality and Organization: The Conflict Between the System and the Individual* (1957).

ARM Adjustable-rate mortgage

Arm's length Characteristic of a transaction in which the parties are unrelated and neither party receives any special terms or preference.

Article In law, part of a document that governs the status of a corporation, association, or professional body, which details the rights, duties, powers, and privileges of the members and the officers, the authorized share capital, and the conduct of meetings.

Articles of Association Numbered clauses in a document serving as the constitution of an organized group, stipulating the conditions, purposes and procedures governing the group.

Articulated accounts Accounts prepared

under the double bookkeeping system in which the retained earnings in the Profit-and-loss account equals the increase in the net worth of the business.

Artificial intelligence (AI) Computer software that exhibits or mimics intelligent human behavior, including a capacity to learn, reason, analyze, discern relationships between facts, and communicate ideas. AI is divided into two categories: (1) knowledge representation systems, also known as Expert systems, that capture and encode expert knowledge; and (2) systems that create new knowledge by extrapolating data and patterns.

ASA Attraction-selection-attrition

ASCII American Standard Code for Information Interchange, a standard code for the transfer of information between computers.

Ascribed status Social status that a person enjoys outside his or her professional circle.

A shares Most important class of Ordinary shares. Compare B shares.

Aspirational brand Product or product line that lends prestige to its users and sets them apart as connoisseurs.

Aspirational group Reference group in market research consisting of peers who have common interests and aspirations.

Assembly line Means of mass production invented by industrialist HENRY FORD, based on the ideas of management thinkers FRANK GILBRETH and F. W. TAYLOR. It dominated manufacturing in the first half of the 20th century and helped to reduce dependence on skilled craftsmen.

Assertiveness training Courses designed to help employees develop potential abilities, exercise initiatives, enhance self-esteem, articulate cogent ideas, and exercise boldness in translating vision into action. It uses behavior modification to enable people to overcome inhibitions.

Assessment center Human resources program by which employee behaviors and abilities are evaluated, including planning and organizing, leadership and communication, tolerance for stress, and initiative. Participants are assessed while engaging in such activities as IN-BASKET TRAINING, leadership group discussions, ROLE-PLAYS, interviews, and management games.

Asset Tangible or intangible possession that has VALUE in economic terms and can be listed on the positive side of a BALANCE SHEET. For example, securities and funds are generally backed up by assets.

Asset management 1. Management of the financial assets of a company to maximize RETURN ON INVESTMENT. 2. Investment service offered by banks and other institutions for wealthy customers.

Asset stripping Acquisition or takeover of a corporation whose shares are valued below their real worth and whose subsequent sale of these assets is done without regard to the wishes of shareholders, employees, suppliers, or creditors.

Asset substitution effect Situation in which the major portion of a risky investment is borne by bondholders rather than shareholders.

Asset value Total value of a company's ASSETS less its LIABILITIES, divided by the number of ORDINARY SHARES in issue.

Assignment Act of transferring a property, material interest, benefit, or right.

Assumpsit Common-law action to recover damages for BREACH OF CONTRACT.

Assurance 1. Conveyance of a property and the instrument by which it is conveyed. 2. In the U.K., insurance.

Asymmetric information Information possessed by one party to a transaction that is not available or accessible to the other.

At call Money lent on a short-term basis that must be repaid on demand.

Atkinson system Wage incentive plan allowing payment of 1.3% for each 1% of production, with a 5% step bonus on completion of the task, with only base wage when production drops below 75% of target.

At limit Instruction to a broker to buy or sell shares of stock, commodities, or currencies at a specified price.

Attachment 1. Proceeding that authorizes a creditor to secure an amount due from a debtor on the basis of a judgment. 2. Data file embedded in an e-mail message.

Attention management Method of ensuring that employees are focused on their tasks and are in tune with organizational goals.

Attitude Mindset or perspective that determines behavior and conduct. An attitude may be COGNITIVE (involving perception or thinking), BEHAVIORAL (involving measurement of behavioral responses), or AFFECTIVE.

Attraction-selection-attrition (ASA) Characteristic of management culture in which individuals are attracted to an organization that has value systems comparable to their own and in which organizations select employees based on similar compatibility. As a result, employees who do not conform to this management culture are attrited.

Attribution Theory of leadership that pays attention to the performance and behavior of employees and learns what motivates them. Attributions are critical to management because perceived causes of behavior influence judgments and actions. Thus, leaders determine whether success or failure is due to causes that are within the indi-

vidual's control. Attribution is a three-stage process: (1) the behavior is observed over a period of time; (2) the behavior is deemed intentional and deliberate; and (3) the behavior is caused by external or internal factors. The assessor then examines the behavior for three key elements: consistency, distinctiveness, and consensus.

Attrition 1. In human resources, the decline in employment through retirement and resignation rather than dismissal or layoff. 2. Gradual decline of equipment and machinery through wear and tear.

Audience Total population who can access and receive a particular mode of communication and is receptive to its message.

Audience research In the communications industry, research concerned with the goal of discovering audience interests, tastes, and habits.

Audit Independent examination of the financial state or health of an organization, usually on the basis of accepted accounting principles, policies, regulations, standards, rules, or controls. Audits may be external or internal. Generally, audits are conducted by licensed professional or chartered auditors.

Audit Bureau of Circulation Organization representing advertisers and advertising agencies, charged with scrutinizing and verifying the circulation of newspapers and periodicals.

Audit trail Sequence of documents, files,

and other records examined during an AUDIT, showing the legitimacy of transactions.

Auditing by rotation Pattern of auditing in which parts of a company are subject to in-depth AUDITS every three years.

Autarky Policy of economic self-sufficiency advocated by a country's nationalists to discourage imports and investments abroad.

Authoritarian management Style of management that emphasizes discipline and obedience to a person of superior rank, rigid adherence to tradition, highly personal and undemocratic methods, and low tolerance for consensus.

Authority Right derived from legitimacy to command others to act in a desired fashion.

Authority of knowledge Right to issue orders, held by a person most intimately involved in a situation or with most knowledge about its details.

Authority of situation Right to issue orders, held by a person closest to an emergency situation.

Authorized capital Shares that a new company is allowed to issue under the terms of its ARTICLES OF ASSOCIATION.

Autocratic management Leadership style involving unquestioned authority and personal decision making; there are no efforts made to synthesize or integrate opposing viewpoints. Opposite of DEMOCRATIC MANAGEMENT.

Autogestion Management by a committee of workers.

Automatic stabilizer Trigger mechanism in fiscal policy that kicks in automatically when certain targets are reached. It counterbalances the undesirable feedback effect of changes in economic activity.

Automation Independent performance by machines of tasks that are traditionally done by humans.

Autonomous work group (AWG) Form of work organization in which workers have limited autonomy and manage their affairs without direct supervision of management.

Autonomy Degree to which a job provides an employee with the discretion and independence to schedule his or her work. Managers tend to have increased autonomy in decentralized organizations. Increased autonomy gives workers a feeling of greater responsibility for their outcomes and thus greater motivation and sense of accomplishment. The degree of autonomy is governed by the CORPORATE CULTURE and the management style of the boss.

Avant-garde New and original, as in the fine and performing arts.

Avoidable costs Expenses incurred as a result of a management decision, usually involving risk, rather than costs that are normal to business operations.

Avoidance Risk-management strategy that eliminates or reduces political risks by calibrating the possibilities of political instability.

Avoidance conflict resolution Strategy that ignores the causes of a conflict and instead focuses on controlling its fallout.

AWG Autonomous work group

B

B2B Business to business, denoting direct trading without intermediaries.

B shares Category of ORDINARY SHARES with limited voting power.

B2C Business to consumer.

Babbage, Charles (1792–1871) Patron saint of operations research and management science. His inventions include a mechanical calculator, a computer, and a punch-card machine. His most successful book, *On the Economy of Machinery and Manufacturers* (1835), described the tools and machinery used in English factories. By analyzing the operations, he was able to suggest improvements. Babbage was also an advocate of the division of labor and of PROFIT SHARING.

Baby bond U.S. bond with a low face value.

Baby boomer Person born during the immediate World War II period, especially in the later 1940s and 1950s; considered as a discrete demographic group.

Baby Wagner acts State and territorial laws based on the federal Wagner-Connery Act of 1935, dealing with labor representation procedures and unfair labor and management practices.

Backdoor financing Procedure by which U.S. government agencies borrow directly from the U.S. Treasury.

Backflush accounting Method of costing a product based on minimum inventory and sales. Costs are allocated after actual costs are determined, and there is no separate accounting for WORK-IN-PROGRESS.

Backscratching Reciprocity in granting favors.

Backselling Sales promotion in marketing whereby a product or service is promoted at a point outside the selling chain.

Backward integration Process of adding more items to a company's portfolio by moving further back along the SUPPLY CHAIN and eliminating intermediaries.

Backwardation Situation in which the spot price of a commodity is higher than the FORWARD PRICE.

Bailout Financial aid given to a corporation by a government or institution to help it avoid collapse.

Bait and switch Deceptive retail practice of advertising low-priced products to lure customers to a store, only to let them know that the advertised products are out of stock and persuading them to buy higher-priced substitutes.

Balance of payments National accounts representing all transactions with the outside world, divided into current account and capital account. The former includes the trade account, which records the balance of imports and exports. Overall, the accounts must always be in balance. A deficit or surplus requires purchase or sale of foreign currencies, monitored by the INTERNATIONAL MONETARY FUND.

Balance of trade National accounts that represent a country's trading position, including VISIBLES (commodity exports and imports) and INVISIBLES (services).

Balance sheet Statement of the total assets and liabilities of a corporation in a fiscal period. The first part shows the FIXED ASSETS and LIABILITIES, and the second part shows how they have been financed. The two parts must be in balance. The balance sheet represents the accounting equation of a company that satisfies the formula that Assets = liabilities + equity.

Balanced score card (BSC) Management evaluation on the basis of both financial and nonfinancial criteria. Developed by business professors and writers ROBERT KAPLAN and DAVID NORTON in 1992, it evaluates performance on four levels: (1) financial, including costs and operating profits; (2) customer satisfaction, including market shares; (3) internal business, including development of new products and markets; (4) learning and growth curve, including employee satisfaction, productivity, and value. Of these, the first is a LAGGING INDICATOR and the others are LEADING INDICATORS.

The score card provides a mechanism for management to examine the business from four perspectives: (1) customer—How do customers perceive the firm? (2) internal—What are the firm's strengths? (3) learning and innovation—How can value be created or upgraded? and (4) financial—How will stock prices react? BSC forces management to look at the operation comprehensively and to optimize output; it integrates available information and simplifies and highlights performance data such as quality, teamwork, capability, and innovation. It places corporate vision and strategy in foremost position, and managers are typically involved in the design of BSCs, rather than accountants and financial executives. Each score card pits perspectives against measures and goals, and pairs strategy with implementation, as follows:

Financial Perspective		Internal Business Perspective	
Goals	*Measures*	*Goals*	*Measures*
Survival	Cash Flow	Productivity	Value Added

Financial Perspective		Internal Business Perspective	
Goals	*Measures*	*Goals*	*Measures*
Success	Sales Growth	Cut Waste	
Prosperity	Market Share	Capital Intensity	
		Design Productivity	Engineering Efficiency

Customer Perspective		Innovation	
Goals	*Measures*	*Goals*	*Measures*
New Products	% Sales	Technology Leadership	New Product Design
Speed of Response	On-time Delivery	Product Efficiency	Revenue per Employee
Preferred Supplier	Customer Satisfaction	Motivation	Staff Attitudes
Market Share			

Baldridge, Malcolm (1922–1987) Secretary of Commerce under President Reagan. The Malcolm Baldridge Award is named after him.

Baldridge award The Malcolm Baldridge National Quality Award is given annually by the U.S. Department of Commerce to corporations and other organizations that have excelled in quality in six categories: manufacturing, service, small business, health care, education, and nonprofit. The criteria include leadership, strategic planning, customer and market focus, measurement analysis, knowledge management, workforce focus, process management, and results. Named after a former U.S. Secretary of Commerce.

Balloon payment Irregular or large installment of a loan repayment.

Band Trading range of a commodity or currency, marked by ceilings and floors or upper and lower limits.

Bandcurve chart Breakdown graphic that separately magnifies the details of some of the elements in the chart.

Bandwidth Total spread of a workday under a flexible hours system.

Bank Financial institution that takes deposits and extends loans on a commercial basis. It also provides money transfers and a number of other services. Banks are supervised by a CENTRAL BANK, which sets the terms and interest rates and oversees fiscal solvency.

Bank of England Central bank of the U.K., a branch of the Treasury established under the U.K. Banking Act of 1979.

Bank of International Settlements (BIS) Bank that acts as a mechanism supporting the financial operations of Central Banks in international monetary transactions. It is headquartered in Switzerland. Founded on 1930, it is one of the world's oldest financial organizations.

Bankruptcy Legal state of a delinquent creditor who is unable to repay loans and has declared insolvency.

Bankruptcy Reform Act Act of Congress in 1978 giving bankruptcy court judges greater powers and making it easier to file petitions. It also reformed tests of the ability to repay. Under CHAPTER 11, a company can apply to a court for protection from its creditors while undergoing reorganization.

Banque d'Affaires In French-speaking countries, the type of bank that handles both the business of a merchant bank or an investment bank and a clearing bank.

Bar code Universal product code, or UPC, consisting of an array of parallel rectangular bars and spaces, printed on a product or package for sale in a retail outlet. An optical scanner or reader reads the code at the checkout and displays the pricing information on a screen.

Barnard, Chester (1886–1961) American management expert who made contributions to the CLASSICAL SCHOOL OF MANAGEMENT. He was particularly interested in the functions of the executive, which he defined in his book *Functions of the Executive* (1938). He developed the ACCEPTANCE THEORY OF AUTHORITY, which states that authority is legitimate only if accepted by subordinates.

Barnard's unit Idea developed by management expert CHESTER BARNARD that an organization should be made up of small departments of 10 or fewer members.

Bargaining Negotiations of two or more parties with different targets and expectations, with the goal of arriving at a mutually satisfactory settlement through rational discussion.

Bargaining zone Area of overlap in the interests of two negotiating parties within which BARGAINING can occur.

Barnevik, Percy Swedish-born business executive, former chairman of Asea Brown Boveri, who introduced the term MATRIX MANAGEMENT.

Barometer stock Widely held security, such as a BLUE CHIP, regarded as an indicator of the state of the market.

Barriers to entry Factors that prevent or inhibit competitors from entering a market and competing with established producers. These may include artificial road blocks, red tape, subsidies, patents, control of distribution networks, ECONOMIES OF SCALE, and brand loyalties. One of PORTER'S FIVE FORCES, barriers to entry put potential entrants at a disadvantage. These are additional costs that must be incurred by new entrants, which give existing firms an unfair advantage.

There are three types of deterrents: structural obstacles, risks of entry, and reduction of incentives. There are natural barriers, such as existing MONOPOLIES, and there are barriers based on size. Size-independent barriers include subsidies, tariffs, trade restrictions, anti-dumping rules, quotas, regulatory policies, licensing, special tax breaks, restrictions on pricing, favorable location, proprietary information, and restricted access to banking, raw materials, and other inputs, as well as regulations governing technologies and know-how and reduced access to distribution channels and markets. Other barriers include regulations governing safety, language, product standards and testing, accreditation, and plant safety. Access to raw materials can be limited by competitors' tying up suppliers through long-term contracts, and labor costs can be driven up through artificially high union demands. New firms may find it difficult to compete with established firms because of policies that militate against economies of scale. There are certain industry characteristics that affect the survivability of new entrants. For example, high industry concentration makes incumbents more powerful and the price of failure higher for new entrants. For new entrants to leapfrog over older firms, they need to have a technological edge and knowledge of what makes the markets tick.

Barriers to exit Factors that make it difficult for a corporation to exit a country because of legal requirements that discourage CAPITAL FLIGHT.

BARS BEHAVIORALLY ANCHORED RATING SCALES

Barter Trade in which goods and services are exchanged without the intermediation of money.

Barth, Carl Georg Lange (1860–1939) Norwegian-American mechanical engineer who popularized the industrial use of compound slide rules.

Barth system Term used in WORK STUDY developed by Norwegian-American engineer CARL BARTH, in which payment due is calculated on the basis of standard times per unit of work.

Bartlett, Christopher Professor of Business Administration, Harvard Business School. Author of *The New Global Business Manager* (2002), *New Game, New Rules: Developing Manager for a Competitive World* (2000), *Companies, Cultures and Transformation to the Transnational* (1999); and *Managing Across Borders: The Transnational Solution (reissued 1988), named as one of the 50 most important books of the century.*

Base currency Money used as the basis for an exchange rate, as, for example, the U.S. dollar.

Base year First of a series of years in an index.

Basket of currencies Group of selected currencies used to determine the value of another currency.

Basle Convergence Accord 1968 agreement reached by the GROUP OF 20 and enacted through the BANK OF INTERNATIONAL SETTLEMENTS governing capital adequacy. The group recommended that banks have specific liabilities covering a minimum of 8% of their capital at risk. The accord was updated by Basle II (2004), which set new conditions for assessing risk and disclosing risk-related information.

Bata system Participative system of management developed by Bata Shoe Company in the 1920s.

Batch production Manufacturing process in which products are made in batches rather than continuously, and production is carefully scheduled to maximize utilization of capacity and minimize capital locked up in WORK-IN-PROGRESS.

Bathtub curve A graph showing the failure rate of machinery, which takes the shape of a bathtub, with three phases: (1) a burn-in or startup phase; (2) a normal phase in which the machinery is at peak performance; and (3) a wear-out phase at the end of its design life.

BATNA BEST ALTERNATIVE TO A NEGOTIATED AGREEMENT

Bayesian methodology Statistical analytical technique, named after British mathematician Thomas Bayes, used in forecasting, which treats the best estimate or probability as a firm certainty.

BCM BUSINESS CONTINUITY MANAGEMENT

Beachhead demand In collective bargaining, a demand made not in hope of gaining immediate acceptance but for use in future bargaining.

Bear Reference to a market in which the prices are falling. A person who sells or does not buy when prices are falling is con-

sidered *bearish*. A *bear dealer* sells SHORT by buying at lower prices certain commodities, currency, or securities that have already been sold at higher prices. Contrast BULL.

Bear hug Approaches by a company to the board of another company that an offer is about to be made for its shares. A friendly bear hug is known as the *teddy bear hug*.

Bear raid Practice among unscrupulous stock traders to spread false rumors relating to a sell-off of stock in order to bring down its price.

Becker, Gary Stanley (1930–) American economist, professor of economics and sociology at the University of Chicago. He won the Nobel Memorial Prize for Economics in 1992 and was awarded the Presidential Medal of Freedom in 2007. He was one of the first economists to branch out into sociology. He argued that many types of human behavior are rational in that they maximize utility. He is also among the foremost exponents of human capital and is credited with the theory of Rotten Kids.

Bedeian, Arthur Management professor at Louisiana State University and a historian of management. His best–known publication is *Management Laureates: A Collection of Autobiographical Essays* (1992).

Beer, Anthony Stafford (1926–2002) British theorist and professor at Manchester Business School, best known for his work in the fields of operational research and management cybernetics. He was a visiting professor at 30 universities He was the first to apply cybernetics to management, defining cybernetics as the science of effective management.

Behavior Characteristic conduct of a person, group, or corporation in response to a set of circumstances, including motivation, expectation, attitudes, and actions.

Behavioral attitude Amalgam of beliefs, tendencies, and feelings that influence behavior.

Behavioral economics Economic research based on the behavioral sciences, such as sociology and psychology, to explain and predict economic behavior.

Behavioral finance Study of the psychological factors in financial decision making, and on the overall market outcomes and ways in which these decisions deviate from the rational pursuit of self-interest. It covers a range of cognitive and emotional biases affecting decision making, including errors in judgment in estimating probable outcomes, underreaction and overreaction, and an inability to assess market anomalies and uncertainties.

Behavioral observation scale Measure used in assessing the performance of employees, in which workers are evaluated on the basis of how well they perform under stress.

Behavioral school Management theory that relies heavily on psychology, particularly drive and motivation and especially in times of change and stress. It developed out of the HAWTHORNE STUDY experiments of the early 1930s, which linked workers' attitudes with productivity. It describes the workplace as a social system dependent on collaboration among its participants. Important in such a system are improved means of communication, leadership, motivation, and group behavior. The thinkers who helped to develop this school of management thought were MARY PARKER FOLLETT, CHESTER BARNARD, ABRAHAM MASLOW, KURT LEWIN, RENSIS LIKERT, and Keith Davis. The growth of the behavioral sciences during the 1940s also helped the theory to gain a larger following.

Behavioral theory of the firm Principle, developed by economist RICHARD CYERT and business professor JAMES MARCH, that a business organization is a coalition of different interest groups representing a variety of ideas, whose members are constantly bargaining for power. The colliding interests make decision making an uncertain exercise.

Behaviorally anchored rating scales (BARS) Measure to evaluate the job performance of employees. It involves breaking up a large task into constituent smaller parts, each with a range of possible behaviors that are then ranked on a scale calibrated from ineffective to excellent.

Behaviorism Branch of social psychology

dealing with human behavior in response to defined stimuli.

Beige book Report on the current economic climate, prepared by the FEDERAL RESERVE BOARD.

Belbin, Meredith (1926–) British theorist and researcher known for his work on management teams. He was visiting professor at Henley Management College in England. He is best known for his book, *Management Teams* (1981). He was the first to describe an effective team with eight members among whom were the investigator, shaper, evaluator, and finisher.

Belbin group Team of workers in a corporation that addresses a specific task, working in competition with other similar groups. Named after Meredith Belbin, who studied work groups.

Bell, Daniel (1919–2011) American sociologist, futurist, and professor emeritus of Harvard University, known for his studies on post-industrial society. He was one of the leading intellectuals of the latter half of the 20th century. His best-known works are *The End of Ideology* (1960), *The Coming of the Post-Industrial Society* (1973), and *The Cultural Contradictions of Capitalism* (1976).

Below-the-line 1. In accounting, the entries in a PROFIT-AND-LOSS statement that separate items relating to profit and loss from those that show distribution of profits and sources of financing. 2. In national accounts, transactions relating to capital as opposed to revenue. 3. In advertising, expenditures in which no commission is payable to an agency.

Benchmark job Job used as a reference point in setting remuneration, retirement, benefits, and compensation packages.

Benchmarking Comparative process of identifying the best practices in relation to products both within an industry and outside of it, and using them as desirable reference points and goals. It is part of TOTAL QUALITY MANAGEMENT. Such benchmarking is usually applied to customer satisfaction, cost reduction, and productivity and effectiveness. There are 10 generic categories for designing benchmarks: (1) customer service performance; (2) product/service performance; (3) core business process performance; (4) support processes and service performance; (5) employee performance; (6) supplier performance; (7) technology performance; (8) new product and innovation performance; (9) cost performance; and (10) financial performance.

Benchmarking should create uniform standards that are consistent with corporate culture and achieve the corporation's strategic objectives. It is supported by actions to collect actionable data. The information should be collected on a RADAR CHART, sometimes called a *spider chart*. In addition to careful design, benchmarking should be accompanied by management support, training for the project team, management information systems, appropriate information technology, and adequate resources. In the 1970s, Xerox pioneered a 12-step benchmarking process in five phases, as follows:

1. Phase 1 *Launch Planning* Identify what to benchmark, identify comparative companies, and determine data collection methods.

2. Phase 2 *Organize Analysis* Determine current performance gap, project future performance levels.

3. Phase 3 *Reach-out Goals* Establish functional goals and communicate them to the staff and gain their acceptance.

4. Phase 4 *Assimilate Action* Develop action plans and implement them, monitor progress, recalibrate benchmarks.

5. Phase 5 *Act Maturity* Integrate practices into processes.

Benchmarking may be integrated with REENGINEERING in seven steps:

1. Identify value-added strategic processes from the customer's perspective.

2. Map and measure existing process to identify areas of improvement.

3. Implement the easy ones.

4. Benchmark for best practices to develop solutions, approaches, designs, and innovative alternatives to the existing system.

5. Develop alternative approaches where existing processes are unsatisfactory.

6. Redesign processes.

7. Make provision for continuous reimprovement.

Beneficial interest Right to enjoy the USUFRUCTS of a property in addition to a legal ownership.

Benefit segmentation Dividing a market on the basis of the benefits expected by consumers from a product.

Benefits realization Translation of projects into perceived benefits for its users.

Bennis, Warren Management guru and exponent of *leadership theory* and *group dynamics*, especially SENSITIVITY TRAINING and T-GROUPS.

Bertrand, Joseph Louis Francois (1822–1900) French mathematician who is also noted as an economist. In the field of economics he revised the oligopoly theory, specifically the Cournot Competition Model, using prices rather than quantities as strategic variables showing that the equilibrium price was simply the competitive price.

Bertrand competition Situation that occurs in an OLIGOPOLY whereby companies producing undifferentiated or homogeneous products compete against each other in terms of price. Named after Joseph Bertrand.

Best alternative to a negotiated agreement (BATNA) In a collective bargaining situation, when industrial action would be more beneficial to either management or the union than would be settling the dispute.

Beta coefficient Measure of the volatility of a stock, indicative of its associated risk.

Beta testing Trial run of a product in the field, under conditions that approximate the actual market conditions.

Beta version Trial version of a product that allows customers to test it and provide feedback to the manufacturer.

Beveridge curve Ratio between total unemployment and total job vacancies. Named after Albert Beveridge, historian and U.S. senator from Indiana.

BHAG Big, hairy, audacious goal

Bid defense Defensive tactic against a hostile takeover attempt. As the number of hostile bids to take over companies have increased in the post–World War II era, so have defensive tactics against such attempts, as follows:

Lockup strategies. There are three types. In the first variant, a White knight is given the right to purchase authorized but unissued shares of the target company, thus increasing the cost of acquisition to a hostile bidder. In the second variant, the *asset lockup*, the white knight has the right to purchase a particularly attractive asset. In the third variant, the *stock lockup*, a major shareholder is asked to buy shares in the open market to prevent a hostile bidder from gaining a controlling share.

The self-tender defense. A firm undertakes a tender offer for its own shares, which are then retired as treasury stock. This is especially effective against the two-tier or front-end loaded hostile takeover, in which a raider acquires majority control and then forces the remaining shareholders to sell out for an undisclosed amount. The *self-tender* is usually for fewer shares than the hostile bid because of legal constraints. Self-tenders are used in conjunction with other defenses, such as Golden parachutes. Staggered board elections also discourage raiders and give the firm an advantage of time. Self-tenders raise the cost to an aggressor.

The Kamikaze defense. There are a number of Kamikaze defenses, all of which involve the loss or sale of attractive assets. In a Scorched-earth policy, all or most of a company's good assets are sold; this is done when the offer is below the market price. In the *sale of crown jewels approach*, key assets that are of interest to the raider are sold. In the *fat man strategy*, the target company itself purchases the assets sought by the hostile bidder. The Poison pill is a lethal dose for the aggressor; the company issues stock dividends to the target's stockholders with special redemption and conversion features that reduce the raider's ability to control the board. To be effective, the authorization of a large block of blank-check preferred stock must be authorized by the stockholders. The common stock dividend can be converted into shares of the acquirer.

The employee benefit plan. This defense consists of four methods. A company may use the stock held in benefit plans to assist a LEVERAGED BUYOUT. Or, the employee plan can refuse to render its shares or tender them only to a friendly bidder. The plan may also buy the target company's stock and the plan's surplus assets may be used to shore up the defense.

Many companies have certain amendments to their articles and by-laws that deter undesirable bids, called SHARK RE-PELLENTS. Among the most widely used are: (1) STAGGERED DIRECTORSHIPS under which the board of directors is divided into three groups, each of which comes up for reelection once in three years. As a result, it will take up to five years to gain control of the board. (2) Limited dismissal or size, in that board members may be removed only for a specific cause and not by majority vote; or the size of the board may be limited to prevent a raider from packing that board with its nominees at a single annual meeting. (3) Fair-price amendments are used to protect shareholders who have not tendered their stock in the first step of a merger, so that they can obtain a fair price in the second round. (4) GOLDEN PARACHUTE

agreements designed to protect senior executives can add costs to the bidder. Some companies issue bonds that are convertible with shares of common stock; another tactic is relocation to a more friendly state, like Delaware.

Bifurcation Divestment of part of a business to enable the principals to concentrate on the remaining part.

Big bath Worst year for a company in terms of financial losses.

Big-bath accounting Corporate strategy of taking a large write-off or writing off unprofitable lines in one quarter to report higher earnings in the next quarter.

Big Board New York Stock Exchange.

Big business Colloquial term for large corporations that represent the corporate sector and act as the dominant part of an economy. Contrast SMALL BUSINESS.

Big, hairy, audacious goal (BHAG) Very ambitious, long-term objective consistent with a company's core values and purposes that serves to galvanize all resources in its pursuit. Term coined by JIM COLLINS and Terry Porras, of Stanford University.

Bigelow plan Wage-incentive approach that provides for a step bonus between the minimum wage and the standard wage, with 1% additional salary for each 1% additional output.

Bilateral dependency In collective bargaining, the phenomenon in which labor and management are dependent on each other to survive, even when their immediate interests collide.

Bilateral monopoly Contract between one monopoly seller and one monopoly buyer.

Bill of exchange Unconditional written order authorizing the payment of a specified sum of money to a third party

Bill of lading Receipt listing goods shipped signed by an agent of the shipper or issued by a common carrier.

BIMBO Buy-in management buyout

Biological asset Living plants or animals considered an asset on a balance sheet.

Biotechnology Use of biological organisms, cells, and systems in technological or machine-driven processes.

Bird in hand In finance, the preference on the part of investors for dividends rather than capital gains.

Black box Element in a system not observable to a researcher or an observer, which controls other elements or inputs. For example, the psychological motives of a consumer are not quantifiable or observable to market researchers.

Black capitalism Entrepreneurship among black people as a solution to depressed economic conditions.

Black economy Economic activity outside of the national accounts and that yields no taxable revenues. Also termed *underground economy*. See also Black market.

Black Friday Friday following Thanksgiving, which marks the beginning of the Christmas holiday shopping season; reference is to stores being "in the black" because of the high volume of sales.

Blackhole engineering Design or assembly of complex machinery in which the original designer leaves blanks where he or she expects outside specialists or suppliers to supply the missing design.

Black knight Person or corporation making a Hostile bid.

Black leg Nonunion employee who refuses to join a strike. Also *scab*.

Black market Unregulated and untaxed market outside normal market oversight, populated by Rogue traders.

Black Monday Either of two Mondays, October 28, 1929, or October 19, 1987, marked by extremely large one-day drops in prices on the New York Stock Exchange.

Black swan Event that is improbable under normal circumstances but not impossible.

Blake, Robert R. (1918–2004) Management guru, author of *The Managerial Grid* (1964). He developed the BLAKE-MOUTON MANAGERIAL GRID model, which conceptualizes management in terms of leadership styles.

Blake-Mouton managerial grid Scale of managerial behavior, leadership, and performance developed by management experts ROBERT R. BLAKE and JANE S. MOUTON. Management is measured on a 9-point scale along two dimensions: productivity and interaction with people. There are a total of 81 possible styles, ranging from LAISSEZ-FAIRE to AUTHORITARIAN and COUNTRY CLUB.

Blamestorming Concerted efforts to allocate responsibility in the case of a blunder or disaster.

Blanchard, Ken (1939–) American management expert. His book, *One-Minute Manager* (co-authored with Spencer Johnson), sold millions of copies. He wrote 30 other books, including *Raving Fans: A Revolutionary Approach to Customer Service* (1993), *Leadership and the One-Minute Manager: Increasing Effectiveness Through Situational Leadership* (1985), and *Whale Done: The Power of Positive Relationships* (2002).

Blanket Relating to situations or activities with broad scope, covering an entire industry, such as *blanket coverage, blanket agreement*, or *blanket policy*.

Blau, Peter Michael (1918–2002) Austrian-born American sociologist and theorist, professor at Columbia University. He is associated with theories describing upward mobility, occupational opportunities, heterogeneity, and population structures. Blau Space is named after him. His books include *Bureaucracy in Modern Society* (1956), *American Occupational Structures* (1967), *On the Nature of Organizations* (1974), and *Inequality and Heterogeneity: A Primitive Theory of Social Structure* (1977).

Blau typology Technique used by sociologist PETER BLAU to classify formal organizations on the basis of the answer to "Who benefits?" It distinguishes four types of benefits: (1) mutual, as in clubs and political parties; (2) business, as in banks and shops; (3) service, as in hospitals and schools; and (4) commonweal, as in fire and police services.

Block release Form of a training program in which employers permit employees to take time off with full pay to undergo training.

Blow-off top Rapid increase in stock price, followed by an equally sharp drop in price.

Blue chip stock ORDINARY SHARE of the most highly rated companies in a stock market. Name derives from the color of the highest value chip in poker. These stocks are regarded as virtually unsinkable.

Blue collar Relating to workers on the ground, often engaged in menial labor, as distinguished from executive office personnel, or WHITE COLLAR.

Blue-sky law Law providing for state regulation and supervision of investment securities and involving licensing and registration.

Blue-sky research Theoretical high-risk research aimed at discovering or establishing fundamental principles rather than innovations. It involves a high degree of uncertainty, but may yield some profitable breakthroughs.

Board of directors Group of elected or nominated persons charged with the governance, supervision, or management of an institution or company.

Body corporate Corporation consisting of a group of persons considered a distinct entity, such as shareholders of a company.

Body language Nonverbal communication through facial expressions, gestures, eye contact, and body movements, also known as *kinesics*. Some gestures convey different meanings depending on cultural context.

Body shopping Practice whereby a consultancy supplies people to work on a temporary contract basis in lieu of permanent employees.

Boehm's spiral model Development model adopted as part of strategy for new product development. Named after Barry Boehm, American software engineer.

Bogey Informal standard set at a low level, often used by labor unions to restrict output.

BOGO The sales offer of "Buy one, get one free."

Boiler room Part of an organization where day-to-day business is transacted.

Boilerplate Part of the text of a document that can be used repeatedly in drawing up similar documents, with suitable modifications.

Boldfaced Used to describe conspicuous and unapologetic action or language.

Boll weevil Nonunion worker.

Bolton, Alfred (1926–2007) Born in Canada, Bolton was a management historian and worked with researcher Ron Greenwood in a seminal study of the Hawthorne experiment; see HAWTHORNE STUDY.

Bond Type of financial security with a nominal value, on which interest is paid until it is redeemed, at which point the nominal value is returned to the holder with a premium. See also BABY BOND, GILT-EDGED BOND, PERFORMANCE BOND.

Bonus 1. Extra payment to employees or others in recognition of work well done, or as an extraordinary compensation at the end of a special term. 2. Extra money distributed to shareholders outside of the proceeds or dividends.

Bonus culture Corporate culture that thrives on excessive bonuses, even when the company suffers losses.

Book value Worth of a company calculated as its total Assets less Intangibles and Liabilities.

Bootstrap 1. Leveraged buyout by a Private equity firm. 2. Takeover strategy in which a two-tiered offer is made to the shareholders of a target company. 3. Company started with little capital that meets its operating costs out of its revenues.

Borderless world Globalized world in which national regulations and barriers do not inhibit multinational business activities, and where businesses are free to follow profitable opportunities wherever they find them.

Boston matrix Performance analysis and assessment tool for business units in large, diversified corporations, developed by Boston Consultancy Group. It parlays market shares and growth rates to develop an overall business strategy, and identifies the most profitable units in a company. The matrix divides units into four categories: (1) Cash cows, which are mature businesses or products with low growth rates. Typically they generate substantial cash flow, which is used to support investment in other areas.

(2) Stars, which are businesses or products that exhibit high rates of growth and are beginning to generate substantial revenues. (3) Question marks, which are products or businesses that have a low market share and doubtful prospects of growth and that face extraordinary competitive pressures. (4) Dogs, which are questionable businesses that operate against considerable headwinds and face an uncertain future.

Bottom-fishing Investment strategy of buying up low-priced shares in order to flip them at a profit when the circumstances are more favorable.

Bottom-up Relating to an approach that relies heavily on input from the bottom tier of management and makes strategic decisions and identifies opportunities based on lessons learned at the ground level.

Bottom-up design *See* Top-down or Bottom-up design.

Boulton, Matthew (1728–1809) Associate of inventor James Watt, who helped develop the first steam engine, and a partner in the engineering firm Boulton, Watt and Sons.

Boulwarism In industrial relations negotiations, a fixed and unyielding position taken by management on what are reasonable concessions to be made to the unions; name derives from that of a General Electric executive.

Boundaryless organization Organizational structure in which there is a deliberate effort to deemphasize hierarchic boundaries and barriers, and to empower employees, create cross-functional teams, and delayer responsibilities.

Bounded rationality Ability to make complex decisions on the basis of incomplete and fluid knowledge. It deviates from the model of self-interest, in that it accepts what is possible and feasible as an alternative to what is ideal and perfect.

Box-Jenkins model Forecasting technique that feeds back data from earlier forecasts to refine later ones. Named after analysts George Box and Gwilym Jenkins and described in their *Time Series Analysis: Forecasting and Control* (1970).

Box store Retail store that sells a limited assortment of groceries in their original boxes or cartons at lower prices. Large electronics stores selling televisions and computers are known as *big-box stores.*

Boyatzis, Richard Eleftherios (1946–) Dean, Case Western Reserve University. He has published numerous books on emotional intelligence, behavior change, and competencies. Author of *The Competent Manager: A Model for Effective Performance* (1982).

Boycott Concerted effort by an aggrieved group against a business or political entity by discouraging economic activity, such as buying and selling, thereby applying economic pressure to achieve a stated goal.

Bracket creep Transition from one income group to the next higher group as a result of income growth; refers to federal income tax brackets.

Brain drain Emigration of skilled professionals from developing countries to developed countries, thus draining the available talent from the former.

Brainstorming Free-ranging group discussion in which the purpose is to explore the terrain rather than to erect structures. It creates a buccaneering atmosphere in which participants are emboldened to think outside the box and exercise uninhibited actions. The goal is to generate as many ideas as possible without evaluating them. Technique originally developed by advertising executive ALEX OSBORN. Compare DELPHI TECHNIQUE.

Brand Trade name of a product that is promoted as a handle by which consumer loyalties are created. Brands are part salesmanship, part psychology, and part media seal of approval. They are ultimately about quality, reliability, and trust, and they reinforce the bonds between consumer and manufacturer.

Brand loyalty Attachment to a particular product marketed under one name. Brand loyalty often reduces competitiveness by discouraging consumer desire to experiment with new products.

Brand management Marketing of one or

more BRANDS and their images as distinct from the products.

Brand mark Unique glyph or graphic symbol that often identifies a BRAND.

Brand personality Creation of a man, woman, or animal to represent a corporate image, as in the case of the Colonel for fast-food enterprise KFC.

Brand recognition Extent to which consumers can identify a BRAND with the associated products and recall it readily when they need it.

Brand value Worth of a BRAND to its owner, based on its market penetration and the BRAND LOYALTY it enjoys. This often appears in company balance sheets as an INTANGIBLE.

Branding equity Corporate equity derived from the brand name as an ASSET, apart from its physical assets.

Breach of contract Failure by one party to a contract to perform the obligations as detailed in the contract. A statement that a contract or any of its clauses will be breached in the future is called a *repudiation breach* or *anticipatory breach*.

Breadth of market Theory that the health of a market is measured by the relative value of items that are going up or down in price.

Breakeven In management accounting, the separation of FIXED COSTS and variable costs to determine the optimum production, sales, or level of activity at which the business begins to be profitable.

Breech, Edward (1909–2006) British management historian who popularized the theories of HENRI FAYOL and F. W. TAYLOR. Author of *Principles* and *Practice of Management* (1953).

BRIC The four largest emerging economies: Brazil, Russia, India, and China.

Brick and mortar Relating to businesses with physical facilities and structures, as distinguished from an Internet business.

Brick by brick Form of forecasting based on an unsophisticated sampling of the opinions and views of salespersons and customers.

Bridge loan Short-term loan that spans the time gap between the purchase of one asset and the sale of another.

Briggs, Katherine Cook (1875–1968) Management specialist who, along with daughter Isabel Briggs-Myers (1897–1980), developed the *Myers-Briggs type personality test,* commonly used to evaluate applicants for employment.

Bright lights and trumpets Celebrity status accorded highly paid corporate executives.

Brinkmanship Act of taking risks routinely to outsmart opponents and gain difficult objectives.

Broadbanding Pay structure consisting of a small number of pay bands or scales, each applicable to a given level of performance, skill, or achievement.

Broker Agent who acts as a middleman between two principals in a transaction.

Broking Buying and selling on behalf of others.

Brown goods In retailing, goods such as televisions, radios, and stereos.

Brownlow committee U.S. committee appointed by President Franklin D. Roosevelt in 1937 that advocated for the first time the application of management principles to public administration.

BSC BALANCED SCORE CARD

Bubble Unstable financial situation, in which prices are artificially inflated through IRRATIONAL EXUBERANCE.

Bubble economy Period of economic activity marked by IRRATIONAL EXUBERANCE and wild and uncontrolled SPECULATION.

Bucket shop 1. Negative term for an organization that operates at the fringes or outside the mainstream to offer commodities, CREDIT-DEFAULT SWAPS, securities, or contracts at a discount. 2. In the U.K., a positive term for a shop selling discounted airline tickets.

Buddy system Management practice of assigning an experienced employee to train a novice.

Budget A quantitative statement or structured plan for money management, reflecting accurately the financial state of an entity in a given fiscal period. From medieval English meaning "wallet" or "leather purse." Budgets are subject to AUDIT. They are prepared by accountants, and budgetary control is exercised by a group of financial professionals. Budgets may be of several kinds, such as *capital budget* and *cash-flow budget*. Budgets allow corporations to better utilize and anticipate the financial resources available to them. They enable accountants and managers to compare estimates with ACTUALS, and thus plan for the imponderables in operating a corporation.

Budgetary control Methodical control of operations through establishment of standards and targets regarding income and expenditure and continuous monitoring of performance against them.

Buffering Practice of isolating external or internal operations from exogenous uncertainties, a technique used in CONFLICT MANAGEMENT.

Buggins's turn U.K. idiomatic expression describing promotions and rewards based on seniority alone.

Built-in obsolescence Design of a product so that it has a limited lifetime and needs to be replaced within a short time.

Built-in stabilizer Fiscal mechanism that is triggered automatically by every downturn as a way to mitigate the market's downward plunge.

Bull Reference to a market in which prices are steadily rising, driven by profits and favorable economic reports. People who buy when prices in the market are rising are termed *bullish*. A *bull dealer* trades up in expectation of growth. Compare BEAR.

Bulling the market When a speculator trades to push prices upward artificially.

Bumping Demotion of a senior employee, which in turn leads to the dismissal of a junior employee.

Bundling Marketing strategy of incorporating similar products into a single package, targeted to a specific customer base. As a competitive strategy, marketers may bundle a newer or less successful product with a stronger one, resulting in cost savings.

Bureaucracy Organizational mode that relies on a cadre of managers and directors selected on the basis of their expertise to run administrative affairs and provide leadership. Bureaucracy is characterized by permanence and stability, experience, precedent, and impersonal decision making.

Bureaucratic management Management that is steeped in AUTHORITARIAN philosophy and run on the basis of hierarchy, order, discipline, and precedent.

Bureaupathology Underbelly of bureaucracy characterized by red tape, inability to make quick decisions, and hesitancy to take advantage of emerging opportunities; also by passing the buck, resistance to change, reliance on rules and regulations rather than innovation, and confused response to uncertainties.

Bureausis Resistance to BUREAUPATHOLOGY on the part of customers.

Burnout Work-related psychological condition characterized by emotional exhaustion, decreasing efficiency, and loss of interest in meeting professional goals and making rational decisions. The situation is brought on by unrelenting pressure of work, in which the subject finds no personal fulfillment.

Burns, James MacGregor (1918–) Historian, political scientist, expert in leadership studies. His trailblazing book, *Leadership,* introduced two types of leadership: transactional leadership and transformational leadership.

Burns, Tom (1913–2001) British sociologist noted for his study, *The Management of Innovation* (1961).

Business agility Ability of a business to adapt rapidly and cost efficiently to changes in the business environment. It incorporates ideas of flexibility, balance, adaptability, and coordination.

Business buy behavior Factors governing the decision to buy equipment, services, products, and raw materials; these include cost, loyalty to regular suppliers, the emergence of better brands or suppliers, and the need to meet new needs.

Business continuity management (BCM) RISK MANAGEMENT plan to avoid possible disruptions resulting from unforeseen breaks in administrative personnel, including death of key managers, national calamities, terrorism, and sabotage. Emergency plans must specify the sequence of steps to be taken to restore normalcy. Business continuity and disaster recovery planning can demand a great deal of resources. The average annual cost of computer network downtime was $42,000 in 2011. OUT-SOURCING has become a standard practice to add flexibility to the SUPPLY CHAIN and avoid disruptions.

Business cycle Repeating mode or pattern in business history, whereby upturns are followed by RECESSIONS and gains are followed by losses. Cycles introduce uncertainty in business plans because they have different durations.

Business game Management training program consisting of exercises designed to build business skills, encourage participants to develop problem-solving and decision-making abilities, hone ideas and abilities, and bond with other members of the team.

Business interruption policy Insurance policy that pays claims for financial losses resulting from exogenous factors such as fire, flood, or riots.

Business-level strategies Three generic strategies popularized by MICHAEL PORTER in the 1980s: The low-cost strategy emphasizes lower costs, although not necessarily lower prices. The differentiation strategy focuses on development of a unique product for which it can charge a premium price, It focuses quality, innovation, and sensitivity to customer needs. The third strategy focuses on serving the needs of a limited group.

Business plan Detailed scheme setting out the stated mission of a business. It is the first step before incorporation and before raising capital and securing loans. It also forecasts activity volumes, cash flows, and anticipated profits. The U.S. Small Business Administration recommends that a business plan include four main elements: (1) overview, (2) marketing analysis, (3) financial plan, and (4) management plan.

A business plan should provide the following details.

1. Personal details on the founder, owner, partners, and directors and their qualifications and experience.

2. Structure of business—that is, whether it is a corporation, partnership, or proprietorship.

3. Business activities and details of the product or service.

4. Commencement date.

5. Objectives, especially in terms of sales and profits.

6. Information on prior history and antecedents.

7. Number of employees and anticipated staff requirements and their salary ranges and possible sources of manpower.

8. Products and services offered, pricing policy, and competing products and services. Information on the market for the product or services in the context of the competition. Testing of products for quality.

9. Existing market for the product or services, whether it is growing (sunrise) or declining (sunset) or static and seasonal.

10. Names of competitors, their pricing policy, and strengths and weaknesses. Quality of the competition and ideas on how to overcome their advantages.

11. Ideas on marketing the product or service and costs of doing so including budgets for advertising, promotion, and public relations.

12. Marketing opportunities and their costs, including names of potential suppliers and their terms.

13. Real estate costs involved in setting up offices and facilities, whether lease, purchase, or rent.

14. Nature of the real estate, whether it is storage, office, or retail space, and the proposed location with information on local and municipal zoning laws.

15. Manufacturing equipment for production, including purchase price and depreciation. Cost of servicing and the nature of the acquisition, whether lease, rent, or purchase.

16. Trading equipment, including vans and cars, their value and purchase, rent, or lease terms.

17. Sales forecasts on monthly, quarterly, and annual basis, including sales prices and agency discounts. Comparative sales data on industry-wide basis from government and private business experts.

18. Sources of funds, such as sales of stocks, loans, and debts with long-term and short-term projections.

19. Cash-flow projections for at least three years.

20. Convincing projections showing when and at what stage the business will be self-sustaining.

Business process reengineering Approach to organizational CORPORATE RESTRUCTURING based on a radical reassessment of the reasons the business exists. It asks the questions, "What are its core competencies?" and "What are its strengths in terms of the market and its products and services?" It seeks to reinvent the business, taking advantage of the information technologies that allow simultaneous processing of tasks that were conventionally done sequentially. It links inputs and outputs more rationally so as to enhance efficiency and productivity and the learning curve of employees. The essential elements of reengineering are:

1. Initiation from the top from someone with a vision

2. Leadership

3. New value system that focuses on adding value for the customers

4. Rethinking the way people perform their work

5. Emphasis on cross-functional work teams

6. Enhanced information dissemination

7. Training

8. Involvement of all participants

9. Rewards based on results

Business school Graduate school for business management and related disciplines, commonly awarding a master's degree in business administration.

Business strategy Protocol statement outlining the plans, principles, and policies of managing a business. It sets the direction of the firm and seeks to maximize the internal competitive advantages and strengths. It specifies the ways in which this is done, whether through internal growth (expansion of existing products) or through innovation or external growth (mergers and acquisitions).

Business structure Legal form of a company as defined in its charter. Business could be a sole proprietorship, a partnership, a private company, or a public limited company.

Business system The quality of the business environment as governed by the political and economic philosophy of a nation. In most capitalist countries (see CAPITALISM), this system is called the FREE MARKET system, in which there are minimum regulations and state control, and where the market is self-governing and makes its own structural adjustments.

Bust Severe decrease in stock prices and business activity, as part of a business cycle.

Buy-back Act of buying back the shares of a company from an investor, for purposes of CORPORATE RESTRUCTURING or to remove the threat of a HOSTILE BID.

Buyer's market Market in which there is an oversupply of goods and where the prices for them are falling.

Buyers' remorse Emotional response involving confusion or regret on the part of a buyer in a sales transaction that was based on poor information or misleading advertisements.

Buy-in Purchase of more than 50% of a company by an outside group, with intentions of a full takeover.

Buy-in management buyout (BIMBO) Buyout in which the management of the company invests in the venture along with VENTURE CAPITALISTS, who exercise managerial control.

Buying on margin Purchase of an asset by paying the margin, or initial down payment, and borrowing the balance from a bank or broker.

Buyout Acquired rights or ownership to a company or product through monetary compensation in full; buyouts can be by employees, management, or outsiders.

Buzz group In market research, an informal group, of not more than four or five persons, chosen from a larger group to discuss ideas developed during larger sessions.

Buzzword Term for a fashionable but overused word or expression that describes a current idea or concept.

Byham, William C. (1936–) American organizational psychologist. He is the co-author of *Zapp: The Lighting of Empowerment*. He promoted the use of the Assessment Center Method for the selection of managers.

C

Cabinet crowd Section of the bond trading unit of the New York Stock Exchange that handles active bonds.

Cadbury report In the U.K., the report of the 1992 Cadbury Committee on the financial aspects of corporate governance. The report established a Code of Best Practice that has influenced management thinking.

Caesar management Autocratic, power-oriented corporate leadership.

Cafeteria benefit Employee fringe benefit, such as food from the company cafeteria.

Cafeteria plan Flexible benefits package offered to employees that enables them to customize their benefits by selecting among alternative options.

Call center Office that handles large number of incoming and outgoing calls for telephone sales, customer service, or market research.

Call option Option that gives the holder the right but not the obligation to buy a stock at an agreed-upon price at any time up to a given date or the expiration of the contract. It is the opposite of PUT OPTION.

Campaign Series of organized actions with a set goal, especially in advertising, sales, marketing, and public relations.

Cannibalization Market anomaly in which the increased sale of one brand results in the decreased sale of another related brand.

Canvass To interview a large number of people together to garner their opinions on a particular subject without any filters, especially used in market research.

CAP Code of Advertising Practice

CAP COMMON AGRICULTURAL POLICY

Cap and trade Environmental policy tool that imposes a mandatory cap on emissions while allowing polluters some flexibility in how they comply.

Capability gap The difference between capabilities in house and those actually needed to accomplish a task.

Capacity costs Fixed costs of running a business.

Capacity planning Process used to determine how much capacity is optimum for any given output and for the efficient use of material and personnel. In the short term, capacity planning concerns issues of scheduling labor shifts and balancing resource capacities. It also involves unexpected cycles of demand.

Capital 1. Total value of the ASSETS of a company less its LIABILITIES. 2. Total paid-up shares of a company. 3. In economic theory, the financial factor in production as distinct from its HUMAN CAPITAL, or labor; the latter usage is considered exploitative in Marxist philosophy.

Capital account 1. Account in corporate financial records showing the cumulative subscription of the shareholders or partners, considered as part of the net assets of a company. 2. Account in the financial records noting expenditures on such material assets as land, buildings, and machinery.

Capital budgeting Appraisal of a range of investment projects to determine their financial returns.

Capital flight Transfer of currency from one country to another to escape taxation or political instability.

Capital gain Increase in the value of an ASSET between the time it was bought and the time it is sold.

Capital gains tax Tax on gains achieved through a realized increase in VALUE—for example, from the sale of stock or a home—most often at a different rate than tax on earned income.

Capital market Exchange in which money is raised by governments and corporations. The capital market is populated by private investors, HEDGE FUND managers, insurance companies, pension funds, and merchant banks. Capital markets are a feature of FREE MARKET economies.

Capital movement Transfer of capital between countries, as governed by exchange controls and regulations. It consists of both long-term and short-term transfers; the latter are speculative and take advantage of temporary movements in exchange rates and interest rates.

Capital structure Balance between ASSETS and LIABILITIES, especially the composition of the assets and borrowings. The assets may be FIXED (tangible or intangible), or CURRENT (stock, debt, or credit), while the borrowings may be long or short term, fixed or floating, secured or unsecured. Ideally, the capital structure should be in balance.

Capitalism Economic system in which the means of production are owned by private individuals rather than the state. Contrast with COMMAND ECONOMY.

Capitalist 1. Pertaining to CAPITALISM. 2. Individual who invests money in a company in return for part ownership and some of its profits, without participating in its management.

Capitalization 1. Amount representing the total financial investment of a company. 2. Structure of the *capital investment*—that is, the extent to which it is divided into ORDINARY or PREFERRED shares or into shares and loans. 3. Conversion of the reserves into capital by a scrip issue. 4. Accounting practice of treating capital as fixed expenditures.

Captive market 1. Group of consumers who are obliged to buy a product or service because there are no comparable alternatives. 2. Passive or involuntary audience, especially of a broadcast or theatrical program.

Carbon credit Environmental reward that can be exchanged between industrial firms. The credit is based on the amount of harmful gases emitted and consequent penalties for exceeding those quotas. Also referred to as CAP AND TRADE.

Career anchor Pattern of skills, interests, and value developed early in a person's career that directs the trajectory of his or her career. Term coined by management professor EDGAR H. SCHEIN.

Career development Establishment of a career path directed by clearly defined goals and including development of the skills and attitudes to achieve those goals. Also *career management*.

Career ladder Recognized upward path of promotion and advancement within a company.

Career path Sequence of jobs that a person holds or plans to hold during a career.

Carrying costs Expenses of maintaining an inventory, including OPPORTUNITY COSTS, wastage, and insurance.

Cartel Association of independent companies that conspire to set the prices of products or services they own or offer. Cartels are illegal in most developed countries, although there are numerous ways in which the law can be circumvented. Different from an OLIGOPOLY, a cartel represents COLLUSION rather than mere cooperation. Such collusion may be overt, as in the case of the Organization of Petroleum Exporting Countries (OPEC), or it may refer to price synchronization. A cartel may be, in principle, profit maximizing or market sharing. *Profit-maximizing cartels* maximize the aggregate profits of all firms by making the same pricing and output decisions. The distribution of the market between the firms is determined by marginal cost considerations, and agreement is reached between the firms as the redistribution of profits, with the firms producing the most output and the lowest-cost firms making payments to the higher-cost firms in order to reduce the incentive of the latter to expand the output. *Market-sharing cartels*, on the other hand, allow each member to retain a certain segment, defined in terms of either market share or geographic area. This division is governed by historic patterns or the power and influence of each member.

A successful cartel must be able to defend itself against threats from buyers and suppliers. In addition, the cartel must ensure that each member adheres to the terms of the agreement and retaining membership is more profitable than leaving it. This is difficult when cartel-operated MONOPOLIES face inelastic demand or when members face the temptation to exceed their quotas to increase profitability. Excessive cheating can destroy a cartel. On the other hand, a number of factors can increase the stability of a cartel. These include cycles of growth and prosperity when the regulations regarding pricing and output are less onerous, limited membership as fewer members are more manageable, a slow process of innovation and change, similarity and symmetry in the producers' cost functions, production of more essential items that are more price-inelastic, marketing of more homogeneous products, marketing of a smaller number of products, and the availability of uniform price information.

Cartels affect the sector in which they operate in three ways: They alter the structure of influence, they are more efficient in the allocation of resources, and they are more efficient in production. In a cartel, weaker firms have a disproportionate influence because they can upset the delicate balance of power. In principle, the collusion among cartels is socially undesirable and illegal, but they can survive across national boundaries where they face less political stigma. They reduce the forces of competition, constrain production below the optimal levels, and raise prices. In short, they gain obscene profits and encourage political corruption in the highest levels of office. Because they have less competition, they have no incentive to be efficient or to reduce costs.

Cascade 1. Series of events or transactions that build momentum with time and constitute a continuum. 2. In production, multiple operations in which each stage is the output of the previous one.

Cascade briefing Technique of top-down communication through an organizational pyramid.

Case study Management training method based on real-life situations. Unlike business games, case studies have no action component, but they encourage people to believe that every problem has a solution waiting to be discovered. Case-study analysis offers multiple solutions to a given problem and introduces ways in which real life impinges on theory.

Cash cow Marketing situation in the BOSTON MATRIX, in which a product with a steady income stream may be used to generate cash for investment.

Cash crop Agricultural produce that is sold in the market, as opposed to one that is consumed by the producer. Compare Sub-sistence crop.

Cash flow 1. Movement of cash in and out of a business, consisting of inflows and outflows. Cash flow is liquidity that enables an uninterrupted ability to meet financial requirements. 2. Net income from a transaction after meeting expenses. Typical cash flow takes into account payments from customers, cash from investment activities, and cash from financing activities. *Cash flow statements* facilitate decision making by providing an accurate mirror of the profitability and financial health of the company.

Cash trap Strategic position of a business that spends all the cash it generates and has little or no reserves to be transferred to shareholders. Such a business exhibits a low share value and high capital intensity in markets with low product differentiation.

Cash with order Fully paid-up purchase order.

Cashless society Society in which economic transactions are carried out and registered electronically with the help of credit or debit cards, without recourse to paper currency or specie.

Casualization Process of reducing full-time employees in favor of temporary staff who do not get fringe benefits or pensions.

Catalyst Managerial role identified by management guru Peter Drucker, in which

the manager is also a cheerleader and motivator-in-chief.

Catch-22 An inherently contradictory situation that cannot be solved. From Joseph Heller's novel of the same name.

Catchment area Geographical region from which a recruitment or sales program draws most of its participants and that therefore is treated as a valuable asset.

Category discounter Aggressive *off-price retailer* that offers branded merchandise in certain products at heavily discounted prices. Category discounters are popular with consumers but are bringing the death of mom-and-pop stores.

Category killer Brand that achieves such complete domination in a market that it becomes synonymous with the category itself, for example, Xerox (copier) or Kodak (film).

Causal quantitative model Forecasting technique that uses a causal relationship between two or more variables to create a growth model for products. The technique relies heavily on mathematical techniques such as Regression analysis.

Cause-effect diagram Also known as a Fishbone chart or *Ishikawa diagram*, from its inventor Kaoru Ishikawa, the cause-effect diagram generates lists of specific possible causes of a problem, as part of a Total Quality Management process. It involves four steps: (1) identifying the problem; (2) identifying the main categories of possible causes; (3) identifying the most likely causes under each of these categories; and (4) diagramming the steps to discover possible linkages among these categories and their solutions.

Cautious shift Tendency of employees to be more cautious when working in a team than when working on their own.

Caveat emptor (*Latin*, "Let the buyer beware") Principle that places the burden on the consumer to verify the credentials of a product before purchase.

Caveat venditor (*Latin*, "Let the seller beware") Principle that places the burden of the conditions of sale and the quality of the merchandise on the seller.

Cellular manufacturing Process that produces families of parts in a single line, cell of machines, or production units within a large factory that has complete responsibility for producing a family of like parts or products. The cell is self-contained or standalone, and although the machines are dissimilar, they are placed in close proximity to one another. This enables a continuous flow-line with resulting high productivity.

Cellular organization Organization comprising a number of independently run companies linked by common management or interests.

Census tract Small geographical and demographic unit of about 100 households with common socioeconomic characteristics.

Center of gravity Ideal location for warehousing and manufacturing based on transport costs.

Central bank Bank established by a national government for purposes of generating, implementing, and overseeing monetary and fiscal policy. The bank supervises the commercial banking system, sets the interest and discount rates, determines the size of the national debt, prints money, controls the money supply, holds the country's reserves of gold and foreign currency, manages dealings with other central banks, conducts negotiations with the INTERNATIONAL MONETARY FUND, manages national accounts, accepts deposits from and grants loans to commercial banks, manipulates the exchange rates, periodically reports on the economic and financial health of the nation, and acts as lender of last resort to the government and the banking system. In the United States, the central bank is known as the FEDERAL RESERVE BOARD; in the U.K. as the BANK OF ENGLAND, and in the EUROPEAN UNION as the EUROPEAN CENTRAL BANK.

CEO CHIEF EXECUTIVE OFFICER

Certificate of deposit Negotiable certificate issued by a bank for a specified period of years with competitive interest rates.

CFO Chief financial officer

Chaebol Large family-owned conglomerate in South Korea. Similar to the Zaibatsu of Japan. Samsung, founded in 1938, is the oldest of the four largest groups. About 30 chaebol control about 40% of the Korean economy. There are three types of chaebol. In the first type, the ownership is direct and complete, and the founder and his family own all of the group. In the second type, the family controls a holding company that, in turn, owns affiliated subsidiaries, as in the case of Daewoo. In the third type, there are interlocking directorates and foundations that link companies through shares, as in Samsung. As chaebol have evolved, there has been a gradual move from the first type to the third type. Even where there is no direct ownership, more than 30% of the executives are from the founding family. Unlike the Japanese Keiretsu, chaebol have neither powerful trading companies nor financial services or institutions.

Chain of command Flow of authority down from the top to the bottom along demarcated organizational lines. The concept is usually depicted on an Organizational chart that identifies superior and subordinate relationships in a structured hierarchy. The duties and responsibilities are clearly defined and each subordinate reports to only one superior. Originally a military principle, it was adapted to business by management innovator Henri Fayol. Also called *Scalar chain*; see also Scalar principle.

Chainsaw consultant Outside expert brought in to reduce or rationalize the labor force; see also Rationalization.

Chairman Usually refers to the chairman of the board, the highest title and rank in a corporate hierarchy, with generally no day-to-day responsibilities.

Chamber of Commerce Voluntary organization in a territorial unit, such as a town or city, representing the interests of the participating businesses, especially with regard to the local authority.

Champy, James A. American management guru and a leading authority on reengineering, organizational change, and corporate renewal. He is the former chairman of Dell Services. His books include *Reengineering the Corporation* (1994), *Reengineering Management* (1995), *Fast Forward* (1996), and *Arc of Ambition* (2001).

Chandler, Alfred D. Jr. (1918–2007) Professor of Business History at Harvard Business School. He wrote extensively on the scale and the structure of modern corporations and redefined economic history in terms of industrialization. He received a Pulitzer Prize for *The Visible Hand: The Managerial Revolution in American Business* (1977). His other books include *Managerial Hierarchies* (1980), *Scale and Scope* (1990), and *Shaping the Industrial Century* (2005).

Change agent Person or institution charged with the task of suggesting or implementing changes in the structure and conduct of a business and its business practices.

Change management Art and science of promoting innovation in management practices through the introduction of new ideas and techniques.

Channel Trade and distribution path or avenue, consisting of wholesalers and retailers who enable the flow of merchandise from point A to point B.

Chaos theory Theory originally developed by mathematicians and later adapted by behavioral scientists. It posits that underneath the apparent disorder and unpredictability of human behavior there is an underlying order and rhythm, and that events have a dynamism and fluidity that lend themselves to creativity. The theory can be applied to management and organizational structure as an attempt to harness chaos under conditions of radical change and to seize opportunities that this change presents.

Chapter 7 Statute of the BANKRUPTCY REFORM ACT (1978), governing liquidation of assets that provides for a trustee appointed by a court to make management charges, secure additional finances, and operate the business to prevent further bleeding.

Chapter 11 Statute of the BANKRUPTCY REFORM ACT (1978), governing the reorganization of partnerships, corporations, and municipalities, as well as private com-

panies. Unless the court rules otherwise, the debtor remains in full control of the operations, even as debtors and creditors negotiate the restructuring of the debt, payments, and loans.

Chapter 13 Statute of the BANKRUPTCY REFORM ACT (1978), governing the repayment of debt by individuals over a period of time.

Charge Legal or equitable interest in property granted to a debtor, giving that person priority over unsecured creditors.

Charge what the traffic will bear Pricing based not on the production costs but on the demand for the product and the willingness of buyers to acquire it.

Chargeable assets In the U.K., India, and Commonwealth countries, property not specifically designated as exempt from CAPITAL GAINS. Exempt assets in these countries include automobiles, principal residences, individual savings accounts, National Savings Certificates, life insurance policies, and GILT-EDGED SECURITIES.

Charisma Quality or aura of a leader who is able to not merely manage people but also inspire them, using his or her ability to communicate ideas and generate excitement.

Charismatic management Management based on the AUTHORITY invested in a person with CHARISMA and other leadership qualities.

Charter To hire a whole ship or aircraft for a specified period or for a specified voyage or flight.

Chase demand strategy Approach to aggregate planning that matches supply and output with fluctuating demand, giving the manufacturer lower storage costs and the ability to respond to the time-sensitive needs of customers.

Cheap money Monetary policy of keeping interest rates artificially low to spur economic activity in times of RECESSION and to reduce the costs of borrowing and investment.

Cherry picking 1. Selection of the cream of the crop, leaving aside products of inferior quality. 2. Selection of an upmarket segment to offer a service or package superior to current offerings and thus provide competitive advantage; companies such as Harley Davidson offer the desired bells and whistles to make their products stand out from others.

Chicago Board of Trade Exchange for trading in commodities and financial futures, founded in 1848 and owned since 2007 by the CHICAGO MERCANTILE EXCHANGE.

Chicago Mercantile Exchange Major FUTURES and OPTIONS market for trading in financial and commodity contracts, founded in 1919.

Chicago School Group of neoclassical economists, including MILTON FRIEDMAN and HERBERT SIMON, who at one time taught at the University of Chicago.

Chief executive officer (CEO) Business official ranking below CHAIRMAN and above all others in a corporation.

Chief financial officer (CFO) Highest-ranking executive in charge of finance, reporting to the CHIEF EXECUTIVE OFFICER.

Chief operating officer (COO) Highest-ranking operations executive, responsible for production, distribution, and personnel, reporting to the CHIEF EXECUTIVE OFFICER.

Chinese wall Information barrier between parts of a business, erected to avoid conflicts of interest.

Choice criteria Critical attributes in evaluating consumer products, especially in relation to available options. These criteria reflect consumer desires and expectations, as well as past experiences.

Choice-shift effect Change in opinion, or effect thereof, produced by participation in a group discussion on courses of action that are more extreme or riskier.

Chronic unemployment Recurring and periodic unemployment lasting for periods of more than six months.

Churning Brokerage practice of encouraging investors or clients to change their portfolios frequently in order to generate more commissions and agency fees.

CIFCI Cost, insurance, and freight, plus commission and interest, which are costs appearing on a BILL OF LADING.

Cinderella business Business, or a division of a business, that has demonstrable potential but does not receive adequate resources for growth. This neglect occurs most often during mergers and acquisitions, when certain parts of a company are left out of the budget process.

Circuit breaker In finance, a method of suspending trading in a particular market when certain extreme price fluctuations take place, instituted by the New York Stock Exchange in 1987.

Classical school of management A group of experts in administrative management and organizational behavior, including CHESTER BARNARD, MARY PARKER FOLLETT, F. W. TAYLOR, and LYNDALL URWICK. It is the oldest school of management, dating back to the 1880s, and it covers three fields of management: SCIENTIFIC MANAGEMENT, ADMINISTRATIVE MANAGEMENT, and BUREAUCRATIC MANAGEMENT, all concerned with efficiency.

Scientific management began in the late 19th century and was spearheaded by F. W. Taylor, FRANK and LILLIAN GILBRETH, and HENRY GANTT. It was the first attempt to apply scientific principles to a systematic study of work methods and change the mindset of employees in favor of efficiency. It called for the selection of the best methods for accomplishing each individual task. Among its organizing principles were (1) scientific recruitment of workers based on their training and aptitudes; (2) genuine cooperation between management and workers based on mutual self-interest; and (3) fair performance standards and implementation of pay for performance incentives. It also called on management to take complete responsibility for planning.

Administrative management is associated primarily with HENRI FAYOL. In contrast to scientific management, which is concerned more with jobs and performance, it provides a general theory of management and is concerned with the theoretical groundwork. According to Fayol, management consists primarily of several layers of functions, such as planning, organizing, commanding, coordinating, and controlling. He distinguished these functions from the more traditional tasks, such as accounting, finance, production, and distribution. Fayol presented 14 principles of management, stressing unity of command, direction, centralization, initiative, and team spirit.

BUREAUCRATIC MANAGEMENT, associated with MAX WEBER, focuses on ideal forms of management. Unlike organizations based on personal ties and loyalty, Weber proposed a bureaucratic organization characterized by division of labor, hierarchy, formal rules, and impersonal selection and promotion of employees.

Clawback Money, usually bonuses or grants, reclaimed by government or other entities, when deemed to have been paid out without justification.

Clayton Antitrust Act Key legislation passed in 1914, placing restrictions on mergers and acquisitions and barring individuals from holding directorships on the boards of competing companies.

Clean float Monetary policy that allows a country's currency to fluctuate in the foreign exchange markets without interference. Compare MANAGED FLOAT.

Clear days Full days, referred to in a contract, excluding the starting and ending days.

Clearing bank Member bank of a CLEARINGHOUSE, which routes checks and directs financial traffic.

Clearinghouse Centralized source for settling accounts between members of a financial network.

Clicks and bricks Business that combines traditional retailing in a physical location with an Internet presence through a website and/or social media.

Clique In business, informal group within a larger organization that is protective of its interests and excludes outsiders.

CLO COLLATERALIZED LOAN OBLIGATION

Cloning In management, tendency in education to train managers who hold identical opinions, preferences, and approaches and who are unwilling to stand out from others.

Closed corporation Public corporation in which all the stock is held by a few shareholders or by members of a family.

Closed economy Economy that neither imports nor exports, and is therefore free of exogenous influences. Primarily a theoretical model, as this is almost impossible today. See also AUTARKY.

Closing bell Signal to mark the end of a trading session at a stock exchange. Compare OPENING BELL.

Closure Process of bringing a meeting to an end by taking a vote on a motion to do so.

Club culture See CORPORATE CULTURE.

Cluster chain Informal communications chain in which information is passed along on a selective, need-to-know basis.

Cluster sampling Method of selecting a sample from a target group, utilizing clusters rather than random choices, an effective technique when sampling a whole population is expensive or impractical.

Clustering Tendency identified by management expert MICHAEL PORTER for companies in the same industry to cluster together in the same geographic locality.

Clutterbuck, David British authority on learning and coaching programs and visiting professor at Sheffield Hallam University. His books include *Coaching At Work* (2005) and *The Situational Mentor* (2004).

Coacting group People who act to reach the same goal, without recognizing or communicating their mutual interest.

Coalition bargaining Bargaining in which two or more unions present a common front in negotiating for their employers.

Coalition building Act of forming temporary alliances among nontraditional allies in an organization to achieve a common goal. Coalitions help us understand behavior in complex organizational structures. Their principal features are that they (1) act as a group, (2) have a common purpose, (3) are independent of the organization, and (4) have an external focus.

Coalition power Degree of influence that results when a number of persons, institutions, or groups act together.

Coase, Richard (1910–) British-born American economist and Professor of Economics at the University of Chicago. He won the Nobel Memorial Prize for Economics in 1991. He is best known for his two articles, "The Nature of the Firm" (1937) and "The Problem of Social Cost" (1960). The first introduces the concept of transactional costs and the second suggests that well-defined property rights could overcome EXTERNALITIES, known as the COASE THEOREM.

Coase theorem Economic principle developed by British economist RICHARD COASE, dealing with TRANSACTION COSTS, EXTERNALITIES, and government regulation. It holds that government regulation of EXTERNALITIES increases social costs, such as pollution and income disparity, and that the most efficient economic outcomes are produced in a society in which there are well-defined property rights, there is perfect competition, and there are minimal transaction costs.

Co-branding Arrangement between two or more companies whereby they jointly promote their products using their logos together.

Cobweb theory SUPPLY AND DEMAND analysis that reflects disruptions in the supply of goods and services, following extraordinary incidents such as a strike.

COD Cash on delivery.

Code of conduct Set of guidelines denoting ethical principles and standards of professional and employee behavior. The code has no legal standing, but it may be cited in a court proceeding regarding, for example, sexual harassment.

Cognitive attitude Positive or negative

evaluation of people, objects, events, and ideas based on empirical or factual knowledge derived from the cognitive faculties.

Cognitive dissonance In business, the conflict between a consumer's expectations of a product and its actual performance, which may influence buying decisions.

Cohort effect In advertising and marketing, the common characteristics of people in a similar age group, reflecting their similar life experiences and expectations.

COLA Cost of Living Adjustment

Colgate doctrine U.S. Supreme Court decision in 1919, later incorporated into the Robinson-Patman Act (1936), recognizing the right of a seller to choose dealers on the basis of a set of criteria and to refuse to sell to others without giving further reasons.

Collar In business, an arrangement or sale by which the maximum price (cap) and minimum price (floor) are fixed in advance.

Collateralized debt obligation (CDO) Structured financial instrument consisting of a bond or note backed by a pool of fixed-income assets. A different class of the instrument, known as a Tranche, has varying levels of credit risk based on cash flows from the pool.

Collaterized loan obligation (CLO) See Collaterized debt obligation.

Collective bargaining Negotiations between employers and employees regarding wages and terms of employment when employees are represented by a labor union.

Collective-effort model In psychology, a theory that working on a task as part of a group tends to weaken individual motivation, as it diminishes the subjective value of the goal and the expectation that an individual's actions can materially change the outcome.

Collins, Jim American writer and business consultant. He is the author of such best-selling titles as *Good to Great, How the Mighty Fall,* and *Built to Last.*

Collusion In antitrust law, an agreement between two parties for an improper purpose that prejudices a third party, as when two firms reach a clandestine agreement excluding competitors from a market.

Collusive duopoly Form of Duopoly in which producers collude to fix prices and thus form a virtual monopoly.

Collusive effects of research Idea held by business theorist Chris Argyris that research programs develop an unconscious bias toward reinforcing existing beliefs and practices while discounting unorthodox ideas.

Comfort letter Statement from an accounting firm to a company preparing a public offering that the unaudited financial statements in the prospectus conform to GENERALLY ACCEPTED ACCOUNTING PRINCIPLES.

Command and control organization Traditional organization with a rigid and multilayered hierarchy, with emphasis on top-down communication and centralized decision making.

Command economy Economic system in socialist countries whereby the productive sectors are controlled or owned by the state, and the right to own private property is severely curtailed. Also termed *planned economy*. Compare FREE MARKET.

Commercial bank Privately owned bank that provides a full range of financial services to individuals and firms. It may also compete with MERCHANT BANKS and INVESTMENT BANKS. Its services are regulated by the CENTRAL BANK.

Commercial bill Bill of exchange other than a U.S. Treasury bill.

Commercial paper Any relatively low-risk, short-term borrowing instrument, maturing at 60 days.

Commission Payment made to an intermediary, such as an agent, broker, or salesperson, usually as a percentage of the goods sold.

Commitment theory In psychology, a theory of cognition that explains why people tend to make commitments without thinking deeply about what such commitments entail.

Commodity 1. Economic good or article of commerce shipped for delivery. 2. Goods that are *fungible*, meaning they are not differentiated by producer, such as agricultural items (soft commodities like corn) or resources (hard commodities like copper); generally, prices for fungible goods are universal, determined by global supply and demand.

Commodity broker Broker who deals in COMMODITIES, either independently or on behalf of principals in a commodity market.

Commodity market An exchange where COMMODITIES are traded, as in London, Chicago, and New York. Some commodities have markets in their countries of origin; for example, tea is traded in auctions after it has been inspected for quality. However, most commodities are simply classified according to conventional standards before trade. COMMODITY BROKERS trade in both FUTURES and ACTUALS. Most futures trading is through clearinghouses that handle OPTIONS trading.

Common agricultural policy (CAP) Policy adopted under the auspices of the EUROPEAN UNION to support free trade within the COMMON MARKET and to protect farmers in member states. The European Commission fixes a threshold price below which produce may not be imported and sets an intervention price at which the EU buys surplus produce to maintain a target price, which is considered an average fair price. It also governs the sale of agricultural products to non-member countries. CAP also subsidizes the modernization of farms.

Common law Legal system dating back to Anglo-Saxon times and still used in the U.K. and in countries with Anglo-Saxon antecedents, such as the United States. It is also called *case law* because it is based on judicial precedent, as distinguished from legislation or statutory law.

Common market Economic association of nations formed to remove trade barriers among its members.

Communication The sharing of information by oral, written, or nonverbal means. The key element in communication is clarity—that is, the receiver of the communication acknowledges the same meaning as intended by the sender. This is not always the case, however, because language in itself does not always have the exact words to convey the intended ideas. Also, every person has a perceptual filter through which words are passed; this filter may sometimes skew the meaning or alter the context, while non-verbal signals may add nuances or suppress meaning. These problems are exacerbated by cultural differences.

Communications management Manage-ment and integration of all channels of communication within an organization, ensuring the free and seamless flow of information across all levels.

Communicator credibility Receiver's determination of the trustworthiness and expertise of a communicator regarding the content of a message sent.

Company Commercial enterprise. A company may be private, public, limited, joint-stock, chartered, or registered, whether incorporated or not. Companies are supervised and regulated by government authorities and their structure is well defined in law. See also CORPORATION.

Company town Geographical area whose economy is dominated by a single employer.

Comparability Accounting principle and tool that requires financial information be presented in a manner that enables comparison with similarly structured companies.

Comparable worth Any two or more things of equal value. In regard to employment, this principle mandates equal pay for equal work, for both men and women and for employees of different national or racial backgrounds. The doctrine extends to pay, title, and privileges.

Comparative advantage Competitive edge in production and marketing that is gained through efficiency in manufacturing and specialization in specific areas, which other countries or companies cannot claim.

Compensation Payment for work consisting of remuneration including salary increases, bonuses (paid or deferred), perquisites, stock options, added life insurance, medical benefits, and the like.

Compensation package Grouping of COMPENSATION items, including salary, benefits, bonuses, and allowances.

Compensatory consumption Tendency of people with relatively limited incomes to splurge on luxury items, creating an illusion that they are materially well-off.

Competency Skills, talent, or traits deemed adequate for performance of a given task. To avoid discrimination, competency is defined as bias-free.

Competency bundle Theoretical concept of a company as a conjunction of technological, cultural, and managerial competencies.

Competition In business, a situation in which companies producing similar products and services try to gain business from the same potential customers. A *competitive market* inhibits the natural tendency toward formation of MONOPOLIES and keeps prices down.

Competition analysis Assessment of a company's strengths and weaknesses, as well as of its competitors, forming the firm's marketing strategy.

Competitive advantage Edge a company has in reaching its target audience because of its marketing strategy or natural superiority. Three generic strategies through which companies gain such an advantage are cost leadership, DIFFERENTIATION, and focus. Cost advantages accrue from EFFICIENCY; differentiation is achieved through attention to the quality of the product, quality of service, creation of a distinct image, and innovation; focus directs all efforts toward maximizing marketing efforts.

Competitive intelligence Information that has been analyzed and is therefore ready for use in decision making. Information becomes intelligence only when and after it is analyzed and prioritized. It is the link between raw information and business strategies based on information.

Competitiveness 1. Ability of a company to produce and sell products similar to those produced by other companies. 2. In world trade, the ability of an economy to maintain exports, supply increasing aggregate demand, and outperform other countries' economies. See also COMPETITIVE ADVANTAGE.

Completion risk Inherent possibility in financing a construction project that it will not be completed.

Complex adaptive system Application of CHAOS THEORY that overrides conventional human controls in a system, in favor of more intuitive and natural ones. That is, organizations that are subject to too much control run the risk of failure.

Complexity theory Variant of CHAOS THE-ORY whereby the natural progression of random events is toward complexity rather than simplicity. Used in business as a way to encourage innovative thinking and real-time responses to change by allowing business units to self-organize. The belief is that business moves in nonlinear fashion with little continuity. However, this view is not a theory for all organizations. Companies that embrace complexity may also lose some of the stability found in traditional systems.

Compliance State of being in accordance with all legal requirements and obligations; also, the department in a business that ensures operations are compliant with all applicable laws.

Composite demand Situation in which a product's demand is shared by different groups who need it for different reasons.

Comptroller Financial director of a company or group of companies.

Compulsory arbitration Process whereby disputes between companies or organizations are referred to a third party, whose decision is binding and may not be appealed.

Compulsory liquidation Court-directed elimination of a company on the basis of a special resolution by its directors, stating that the company is unable to meet its debt obligations. The court then appoints a provisional liquidator or a receiver to negotiate with creditors and distribute assets.

Computer-aided design (CAD) Use of computers to draw up designs for machinery operations, tools, architectural plans, and the like. In conjunction with virtual reality and computer simulations, CAD allows potential customers to view products in their beta stage and to test them before investing in plants and materials. CAD usually works in conjunction with *computer-aided manufacturing* (CAM). Both systems are designed to work in all steps of a typical product life cycle and involve both a design phase and an application phase.

Computer-integrated manufacturing system Common operating system combining COMPUTER-AIDED DESIGN, computer-aided manufacturing, and information-processing systems.

Concentrated segmentation Identification of the most promising segment of a market on which to focus marketing and promotion efforts. Also termed *niche marketing*.

Concentration 1. Existence of a large group of companies engaged in the same business in the same geographical area. 2. Use of many resources on a single project.

Concentration ratio Ratio that indicates

the relative size of firms in relation to their industry as a whole. The four-firm concentration ratio, which consists of the market share (expressed as a percentage) of the four largest firms in an industry, is the most commonly used concentration ratio.

Concept test In market research, technique used to assess the reaction of consumers to a new product or a proposed change to an existing product.

Conciliation In labor relations, effort to bring two opposing sides together by finding common ground and making appropriate mutual concessions.

Concurrent control Management of the performance of an operating system at every stage of a process, in contrast to a Feedback control system in which management is not initiated until the process is complete.

Concurrent engineering Conducting development processes in parallel rather than sequentially, as a way to reduce lead time and control cost. In doing so, each stage can be run earlier and will provide feedback that can optimize the preceding stage.

Conditionality Terms under which the International Monetary Fund provides Balance-of-payment support to member states, usually to solve an underlying structural problem in the economy.

Confidence Belief supported by facts that a certain action will be followed by certain results, as in consumer confidence.

Confidentiality clause Section in an employment contract that stipulates certain types of information to which employees have access but may not transfer it or pass it on to nonemployees.

Conflict management Control or resolution of intramural conflicts on the basis of any of three philosophical approaches: (1) Traditionalist, whereby all conflict is viewed as inherently destructive and should be avoided at all cost. (2) Behaviorist, whereby conflicts are viewed as inevitable and should be harnessed positively. (3) Interactionist, whereby conflicts are signs of organizational vitality and should be encouraged. The principal avenues of conflict management or resolution are avoidance, competition, accommodation, compromise, and collaboration.

Conflict of interest Situation in which a person has discrete responsibilities that impinge negatively on the others. The conflict may be between an employee and a firm, or between two firms one of which is competing with the other for the same outcome or resources. In such cases, the person makes full disclosure or recuses him- or herself.

Conglomerate Diverse and disparate group of companies under a common holding company. In most cases, the individual companies have unrelated businesses. Conglomerates often lack a clear strategic focus and the operating subsidiaries are thus unable to derive synergy from their combined operations.

Conjoint analysis Statistical technique to determine the relative importance that consumers attach to salient attributes of products and the associated utility they expect to derive from them. The technique is based on the finding that consumer products must meet certain felt or well-defined needs in the simplest and most economical manner.

Consensus management Process of overcoming or ending conflicts by reducing the margin of disagreement and finding common ground.

Conservatism In business forecasting, the prudent anticipation of trends and outcomes that errs on the side of abundant caution.

Consistency In accounting, one of four fundamental concepts, requiring that each item within an accounting period be treated in the same manner and subject to the same principles so as to give a true and fair view of the company's financial state. Consistency is key to the comparability of financial statements.

Consolidated Regarding financial statements, the combination of accounts of several related or jointly owned companies so as to present an integrated balance sheet.

Consortium Combination of two or more organizations or entities on a temporary or ad hoc basis for the achievement of common goals.

Conspicuous consumption Purchasing and using multiple products and services to impress others and signal social status.

Constable, John U.K. management consultant and co-author with Roger McCormick of *The Making of British Managers* (1987).

Constraint Circumstance or limiting factor that prevents an organization from achieving a higher level of performance.

Constructive conflict Theory developed by management thinker Mary Parker Follett that industrial disputes involving relatively minor issues can uncover more important problems.

Constructive dismissal Involuntary termination of an employee, which is technically described as voluntary so as to minimize legal consequences.

Consultant Outside expert brought in to offer independent professional advice on a project or on some aspects of corporate management.

Consultative management Style of management that stresses the need to consult with associates before making company-wide decisions.

Consumer 1. Person or group who spends money to acquire goods that are for sale in regular trade channels. 2. Relating to a consumer or consumers, as in *consumer credit*, *consumer goods*, *consumer advertising*, CONSUMER PROTECTION, *consumer research*.

Consumer durable Manufactured product, such as a car or an appliance, that has a relatively long useful life extending over a number of years.

Consumer protection Attempt to safeguard consumer interests in terms of quality, price, safety, and compliance with laws relating to health, truth in advertising, and packaging.

Consumer rights Protections granted by law to consumers regarding purchases, as well as guarantees regarding quality, price, and safety; considered part of fundamental human rights.

Consumerism Movement that places the interests and safety of the consumer ahead of the interests and profits of the manufacturer, and that emphasizes quality and durability of consumer goods.

Consumption Demand for acquisition of goods and services that are produced and marketed within a given economy. Consumption is limited by product supply and available disposable income of purchasers.

Content validity In education, the extent to which the content of a training program has real-life application.

Contingency school of management Developed in the 1960s by JOAN WOODWARD, Paul Lawrence, Jay Lorsch, and FRED FIEDLER, this was an attempt to build flexibility into a management system so that it is able to meet unplanned situations, challenges, and crises calling for different responses. It applies management principles to individual situations based on such variants as environment, personality, and situational peculiarities. There are no universal principles of management, but each situation is unique and must be addressed independently.

Contingent Relating to an event or outcome that is dependent on the occurrence of another event.

Contingent strategic success Theory developed by mathematician and business thinker IGOR ANSOFF to explain why a company can be successful in one area and unsuccessful in another area.

Contingent theory of leadership Developed by management thinker FRED FIEDLER, a theory that leadership is effective only when compatible with the work situation and there is a correlation between leadership style and organizational culture. *Task-oriented leadership* is effective in both favorable and unfavorable situations, while *relationship-oriented leadership* is effective in more LAISSEZ-FAIRE situations.

Contingent worker Nonpermanent worker hired for task-specific purpose. Includes temporary workers, contract workers, college interns, part-time or seasonal employees, and consultants.

Continuity program Offer of inducements to customers to remain loyal, such as airline frequent-flyer programs.

Continuous flow manufacturing (CFM) Integrated production system that remains constant throughout, utilizing minimum stock levels.

Continuous improvement Management effort to improve quality and services, reduce costs, and eliminate waste, as distinguished from sporadic efforts to do same. See also KAIZEN.

Continuous learning Belief that learning is open-ended and never completed; stresses the need to regularly replenish and refine one's skills and knowledge, through either formal or informal learning.

Continuous processing Method by which high volume is continuously produced in a dedicated plant; for example, in a cement operation or electric generating plant, where shutdowns are expensive and wasteful. These operations are largely automated, requiring few personnel.

Contra preferentem From Latin, regarding the interpretation of documents; a principle that, in case of doubt or ambiguity, the law is interpreted as against the party that drafted the agreement.

Contract Legally binding oral or written agreement stipulating the conditions of an exchange between two or more parties, usually for a consideration specified in the terms. The parties to a contract must be legally and mentally competent to sign the agreement, and the contract may be voided in cases of misrepresentation or mala fides. Contracts may be for property or for services, including employment.

Contractarian theory From management development, a view of the company as the nexus of contractual relationships.

Contractual vertical marketing System in which different levels of distribution or production join together for greater economies of scale.

Contribution Share of the cost of a transaction borne by one of the producers; the total contribution is the sum of all the unit contributions.

Control chart One of the seven basic tools of quality control that determines the stability of a manufacturing or business process. Also, *Shewhart chart* or *process-behavior chart*.

Control process Method to determine whether tactical goals or operational plans are being met within a given time and what adjustments should be made to fine-tune them if not.

Controllability In management, the concept that managers are responsible only for controllable costs and investments.

Labor costs and entitlements are beyond the control of managers, and thus are not factored into an evaluation of managerial performance.

Controller Chief accounting executive concerned with financial reporting, taxation, and auditing; also COMPTROLLER.

Controlling interest Ownership of a substantial bloc of shares in a company, which enables that shareholder or group of shareholders to have the decisive voice in company matters.

Convergence In business, the increasing interdependence among communications platforms and formats, including computers, telecommunications, and social media.

Convergent marketing Strategy by which a number of goods are sold through the same channels using the same promotional mix.

Convergent thinking Method of thinking along conventional lines in an effort to find the best solution to a problem; distinguished from DIVERGENT THINKING.

Cooke, Morris (1872–1960) Champion of efficiency in nonindustrial organizations and instrumental in extending management efficiency to professions as disparate as teaching and urban government. His book *Our Cities Awake* (1919) was responsible for a movement to reduce waste in municipal government.

Cooking the books In accounting, deliberate misrepresentation of financial income or expenditure to create illusory profits in violation of traditional reporting practices.

Cooling-off period Time granted for parties engaged in negotiations to reformulate a response after the initial response has failed to gain acceptance.

Cooper, Cary (1940–) Canadian-born British psychologist and Professor of Organizational Psychology and Health at Lancaster University Management School. He is the editor of the *Blackwell Encyclopedia of Management* (2004), *Leadership and Management in the 21st Century* (2004), and *Employee Morale: Driving Performance in Challenging Times* (2009).

Copyright Legal protection for the owner or originator of an original work, which extends to licensing the work for use by others. Copyright covers many forms of INTELLECTUAL PROPERTY, including books, artwork, drama, film, media broadcasts, speeches, magazine articles, and music compositions and performances, as well as computer programs. Protection is granted by the copyright acts in various countries, as well as the International Copyright Convention, and extends beyond a country's borders. Terms vary worldwide, but in the U.S., copyright protection lasts for 75 years beyond the author's lifetime.

Core competency Unique or distinctive capability that endows a business with a strategic and competitive advantage over its rivals and defines its principal mission. The core competency is the basis for competitive capabilities and sustainable competitive advantage. If the advantage is technological, it may be protected by patents if it is vulnerable. The concept of the core competency is associated with RESOURCE-BASED theory, which regards companies as bundles of resources that can be configured to provide specific competitive advantages. The theory addresses a number of issues, such a diversification, and covers changes in the competitive environment, including from globalization, deregulation, and technological change—factors that are eroding traditional sources of competitive advantage.

Core competencies have well-defined characteristics. They convey functionality to the consumer and are unique to the firm; they are sustainable, they are products of innovation and learning; and they are generic. There are three types of core competencies: (1) market access, which links the firm with its customers; (2) integrity, which enhances quality; and (3) functionality, which confers distinct consumer benefits. *Technological core competencies* focus on objective capabilities, while *institutional core competencies* focus on managerial processes. The core competencies are broken into four elements: employee or human knowledge and skills; technological expertise; managerial systems; and corporate values and norms. When companies have few unique advantages and have to work within the same parameters and environments as other organizations, it is the configuration

and application of these core advantages that distinguish leaders. Thus, the concept of core competencies is useful to identify company strengths and to plan diversification, so as to preserve the will to compete, to sharpen focus, to build strategic alliances that complement the core competencies, and to balance company strategy with core objectives and mission statement. To manage core competences well, leaders must transcend the individual STRATEGIC BUSINESS UNITS (SBUs) and inform and support the company's overall mission, because there is potential for conflict between SBU goals and company goals.

Core job competency Key job characteristics that define a well-motivated employee, including skills, identity, significance, autonomy, and feedback.

Core process Set of linked horizontal activities that take an input and transform it into an output of economic value. In traditional businesses organized by functional departments like production, procurement, logistics, sales, marketing, and accounts, work flows upward for approval and downward for action. This bidirectional flow leads to natural inefficiencies that increase as more cogs are added to the system. Core process, on the other hand, removes unnecessary organizational layers and adopts a cross-functional horizontal mode.

Also known as REENGINEERING, core process reduces the organization to three to five critical processes that determine competitive success. The process focuses on (1) product design and development, (2) procurement, (3) logistics, (4) manufacturing, and (5) shipping. Each process involves a number of key activities that cut across traditional functional layers, either generic or industry specific. The purpose is to yield breakthrough improvements, optimize interdependent activities, and eliminate unnecessary functions. For example, it should define performance requirements by benchmarking. It should include a diagnostic study to seek out the causes of inefficiency and identify the opportunities for change. It should involve Process mapping, an analysis of existing information and technical systems architecture. Prioritization is essential. Finally, management has to develop a vision and a set of specific change initiatives, both long term and short term.

Core time Under flexible work arrangements, the period during which all employees must be present at the workplace.

Core value In management, an aspect of a corporation's activities upon which everything else is anchored.

Corner office Executive suite in a corporate office reserved for the top-echelon personnel.

Corpocracy Corporate bureaucracy.

Corporate anorexia Malaise that affects a business after a severe Downsizing and period of cost cutting. The company's com-

petitive edge may be compromised by the elimination of competent personnel.

Corporate brand licensing Licensing of trademarks, trade names, and goodwill for a fee or royalties.

Corporate culture Complex of attitudes, practices, beliefs, norms, and ethical standards held by a corporation and its executives, which colors and governs behavior. The culture determines what kinds of behavior and lifestyles management will accept and what they will proscribe.

Corporate governance Manner in which a company is governed internally and the nature of managerial accountability vis-à-vis the shareholders and general public. Important to corporate governance is the Chain of command and the way in which authority is dispersed. Corporate governance differs from firm to firm and from country to country, with varieties characteristic of each system. It may be individual or collegiate, confrontational or cooperative, selfish or social, legalistic or bound by traditions of honor and obligation, short term and impatient or long term and patient, and rigid and hierarchical or flexible and open. The key element in corporate governance is the role of the Chief executive officer or the Chairman. Also important is the role of the unitary executive board, which comprises most nonexecutive members with only a supervisory role. Day-to-day management is exercised by an executive committee.

Corporate image Way in which a corporation is perceived by the public and the markets. Public relations is used to create a persona or image that is helpful in marketing goodwill. A corporate image is always damaged by scandals, and therefore these have to be downplayed or avoided. On the other hand, a corporation tries to hitch its image to popular movements, such as the environment, to enlarge its constituency.

Corporate plan Document that maps out the future of a corporation and is used to formulate strategies for achieving desirable goals in the context of economic realities.

Corporate profitability matrix A device for delineating cost by customer group. Prices are determined not merely by costs, and different customer segments may be best served by adopting a flexible cost structure. Normal accounting systems do not reveal the differences in costs between different customer groups; however, ACTIVITY-BASED COSTING does. The costs may be allocated on the basis of variations in presale, production, distribution, and after-sale service cost. Two common customer groups used for drawing up a cost-profitability matrix are *carriage trade* at the very high end and *bargain basement* at the low end. Costs also vary according to whether the sale is aggressive or passive.

Corporate raider Predatory entrepreneur who buys up a substantial number of shares of a vulnerable target company, with the intention of taking it over and CANNIBALIZING it or forcing a CORPORATE RESTRUCTURING by which the target company becomes a satellite of the predator's company.

Corporate responsibility Corporation's social, moral, and ethical responsibilities to the public. Part of CORPORATE GOVERNANCE, this covers responsibilities beyond the stockholders and connotes the subordination of purely economic interests to the broader obligations of the environment, customers, and local communities.

Corporate restructuring Implementation of an alternate business strategy following a period of poor performance and increased dissatisfaction on the part of shareholders. The restructuring may consist of DIVESTMENT or DOWNSIZING and a change in the core business.

Corporate strategy Plan establishing the direction of a company and its position in the market, as well as ways in which it fulfills its public responsibilities.

Corporate transformation The orchestrated redesign of the genetic architecture of a corporation. The concept considers the corporation as an evolving organic entity. The model for corporate transformation consists of four major transformational activities: (1) reframing, or refocusing self-perception and mission; (2) restructuring, or reevaluating corporate fitness for competitive activities; (3) revitalization, or harmonizing the corporation with the new environment through recommitment to goals; and (4) renewal, or boosting the morale of employees and reinvigorating their striving for excellence.

Twelve steps lead to total transformation and rebirth: (1) mobilize; (2) create a new vision and a sense of shared purpose that permeates the organization; (3) build a measurement system to benchmark progress; (4) create an economic model that translates ideas into value; (5) allow physical infrastructure to reflect the new realities; (6) redesign the work architecture; (7) achieve a market refocus on growth; (8) create new businesses through cross-fertilization of ideas; (9) exploit information technology; (10) create a reward structure and remove demotivators; (11) encourage learning as an ongoing process; and (12) learn to adapt and use change itself as a catapult to attain the desired goals.

Corporate veil Immunity from a firm's debt obligations, enjoyed by its shareholders.

Corporation A legal entity, operated by persons authorized to conduct a specific business, to raise money for this purpose, and to acquire or sell property. A corporation may be a sole corporation or a limited liability company, and may be public or private. Corporations are taxed at different rates from individuals. See also COMPANY.

Corporation de facto CORPORATION that carries on its business activities despite an ill-defined legal status.

Corporation de jure CORPORATION that is in full compliance with all legal and statutory requirements.

Corporatism Replacement of owners of a private company with professional managers.

Corruption Prevalence and tolerance of unethical practices as the standard for financial gain, especially involving bribery.

Cost accounting Branch of accounting that provides financial information to corporate decision makers. Also termed *managerial accounting*.

Cost allocation Process of assigning the overall costs of a product or service on the basis of cost drivers. Two systems are used for assigning costs: (1) traditional, which focuses on FIXED COSTS; and (2) ACTIVITY-BASED COSTING, which focuses on variable costs. Traditional systems include ABSORPTION COSTING and MARGINAL COSTING.

Cost-benefit analysis Technique used in capital budgeting that takes into account the estimated costs incurred by a proposed investment, as well as its estimated benefits to the bottom line. Such benefits may be monetary or they may be intangible, as in the case of increased goodwill.

Cost control Technique or device to ensure

that operating costs do not keep rising without discipline and that they remain within acceptable limits.

Cost convention Accounting protocol used for recording the costs to be charged against profits for an accounting period. The convention may be based on historic costs, current costs, or replacement costs.

Cost cutting Action to reduce the amount of money spent on corporate operations or on the provision of products and services. This may lead to layoffs, reductions in amenities and bonuses, and/or salary freezes and rollbacks.

Cost driver In ACTIVITY-BASED COSTING, any factor, such as the number of units, number of transactions, or duration of transactions, that drives up costs. This factor determines the allocation of costs to that particular activity.

Cost-effectiveness The degree to which any commercial activity is viable, in terms of its corresponding expenditures of time, money, and energy.

Cost object Item or unit that is treated separately for COST ALLOCATION.

Cost of capital Return on investment compared to the cost (interest rate) an organization has paid to secure capital. This is used as a HURDLE RATE in calculations of discounted cash flows.

Cost of living adjustment (COLA) Increase in government assistance as a result of rises in the COST OF LIVING INDEX, based on current market prices for selected goods and services.

Cost of living allowance Additional pay offered to employees who work in places away from home, especially in foreign countries.

Cost of living index Official government index showing increases in the average cost of basic consumer goods and food, relative to the same costs in a base year.

Cost of quality Any of four categories of costs associated with maintaining quality and standards, either as mandated by government or voluntary to gain market acceptability: (1) prevention costs, including training, planning, process controls, and market research; (2) appraisal costs, incurred in inspection, testing, and quality audits; (3) internal failure costs, incurred in recalls, repairs to defective products, and downtime; and (4) external failure costs, incurred as a result of consumer complaints, including investigations, replacement, and warranties.

Cost-plus contract Agreement with a supplier, in which goods and services are charged at cost plus an agreed percentage markup.

Cost-plus pricing Pricing method by which markup is added to the unit cost of production, thereby arriving at the retail or wholesale price.

Cost pool Agglomeration of costs from various sources, assigned to a cost center.

Cost-price squeeze Situation in which prices cannot be raised but the costs of production cannot be reduced.

Cost-push inflation Increase in the price of goods and services, caused by an increase in production costs, wages, and raw materials, as well as an increase in the money supply resulting in higher consumption.

Cost-volume-profit (CVP) Analysis method to highlight the relationships between costs, gross profits, and net profits; used to calculate which products and services are contributing most to a company's overall profits.

Cottage industry Business characterized by many small-scale units with low capitalization and few workers, widely dispersed over a region.

Counter purchasing Arrangement in international trade whereby trade in one direction is balanced by trade in the other direction.

Countertrade Payment for imports in a form other than hard currency, as, for example, in a barter.

Country risk Volatility associated with investment or conduct of business in a country where the political regime is unstable or unfriendly, or where the government may not honor international obligations.

Country club management Managerial style that is focused on public relations and the maintenance of Old-boy networks, rather than on profits.

Cournot competition Situation in which Oligopolies compete on the basis of quantity.

Coverdale, Ralph (1918–1975) British founder of the Coverdale Training Programs. He is the author of *Real Thinking* (1977).

Coverdale training Sensitivity training program based on group dynamics developed by writer Ralph Coverdale. This method emphasizes the performance of real group tasks rather than Role-playing and is designed to enhance social skills.

Covey, Stephen (1932–2012) Management consultant who offered a holistic approach to work based on Mormon principles; author of The *Seven Habits of Highly Effective People* (1989). He was a professor at the John M. Huntsman School of Utah State University.

CPA Certified public accountant.

CPA Customer profitability analysis

CPD Continuing professional development.

C2 principles Code devised by Thomas Dunfee and David Hess of the University of

Pennsylvania, on handling corrupt practices and the solicitation of improper payments.

CQ Cultural (intelligence) quotient.

Crash In finance, a disastrous fall in stock market prices, usually preliminary to a RECESSION.

Crash cost Additional cost involved in producing a desired outcome with a short lead time.

Creative accounting Euphemism for extralegal accounting practices to manipulate assets and mislead investors and auditors. It involves taking advantage of loopholes and ambiguities in accounting law, which enable smart accountants to suppress the truth without suggesting a falsehood. Creative accounting usually involves the separation of legal titles from risks, the linking of several transactions with a view to obscuring the financial impact of each, and the inclusion of options. Also known as OFF-BALANCE SHEET or WINDOW DRESSING.

Creative conflict Technique of conflict resolution associated with management thinker MARY PARKER FOLLETT, which encourages opposing views as a means of exploring new ideas and integrating them into a solution that is a synthesis.

Creative destruction Term devised by economist JOSEPH SCHUMPETER to describe the destabilizing effects of FREE MARKET capitalism, in which traditional markets

and companies are always overtaken by new ideas, products, technologies, and structures.

Creative financing Euphemism for any unorthodox arrangement for obtaining a loan from a commercial lending institution. It includes loans from the seller, balloon payment loans, wraparound mortgages, land contracts, and sale leaseback. It is usually employed where the interest rates are high or the buyer is not creditworthy.

Creativity Application of imagination to finding solutions to problems and decision making, including BRAINSTORMING and LATERAL THINKING. Creativity is managed like other facets of corporate culture, through means such as DECENTRALIZATION, providing resources for new initiatives, encouraging experimentation, accepting freedom to fail, reducing bureaucracy, rewarding excellence, and encouraging risk taking.

Creativity management Management technique that stimulates and enhances the level of creativity and innovation in an organization.

Credit 1. Reputation and/or financial standing, as established by past behavior. 2. Sum of money that is granted by a lender, to be repaid in stated amounts over time. 3. Entry on the right side of a double-entry bookkeeping system, showing a positive balance

Credit card Plastic card issued by a bank

or mercantile firm to approved customers, allowing them to pay back the amount borrowed over time. Card users receive a statement of money owed and either pay the full amount or make a minimum payment and pay interest on the outstanding balance.

Credit control Credit policy of a business in which clients are rated for creditworthiness on the basis of certain criteria and delinquents are dunned for repayment.

Credit crunch Period during which lenders are unwilling to lend money to borrowers with less than a sterling credit rating or during times when interest rates are rising rapidly.

Credit-default swap (CDS) Also, credit-derivative contract. It is a transfer of credit exposure and is generally considered an insurance against nonpayment by the purchaser. The seller of the swap guarantees the creditworthiness of the debt. CDS is unregulated. It is generally used against default of municipal bond, corporate debt, and mortgage-backed securities and are sold by banks, insurance companies, and hedge funds.

Credit enhancement Act of raising the credit rating of asset-backed securities, using various techniques; done by the issuer (internal enhancement) or a third party (external enhancement).

Credit guarantee Insurance of creditworthiness provided by the state or a commercial organization.

Credit line Extent of credit available to a borrower, as set down in the credit agreement.

Credit rating Assessment of creditworthiness by credit-reference agencies, based on information collected by them from banks, debt collectors, bankruptcy proceedings, credit card companies, and courts. This information, known as *credit reference*, provides a financial history, including delinquencies, mortgages, payment history, delayed payments, and debt-to-resource ratio.

Credit risk Possibility associated with chronic defaults or delayed payments, as an indication of a party's inability to meet its financial obligations on time.

Credit squeeze Reduction in economic activity by a government, brought about by restricting the money supply and reducing the amount of borrowing in an effort to reduce INFLATION.

Credit union Cooperative bank that enrolls people as members and makes loans to them. In the U.K., called *building society*.

Creditors' committee Group of creditors of an insolvent company or an individual representing all the creditors; oversees the actions of the ADMINISTRATIVE RECEIVER.

Creditors' voluntary liquidation The dissolution of an insolvent company by a special resolution of its members.

Creeping expropriation Gradual imposition of regulatory controls over private or foreign companies, which in effect makes it more difficult for them to survive.

Creeping inflation Steady and gradual INFLATION that, over a period of time, leads to a decline in purchasing power.

Creeping takeover Accumulation of a company's shares by purchasing them over a period of time, preliminary to a TAKEOVER BID.

Crisis management Form of management focused on isolating each crisis so as to address it separately, and not allowing crises to coalesce into bigger and more complex ones.

Critical event In CRITICAL-PATH ANALYSIS, an event such as the start or completion of an activity.

Critical-event technique Analytical method used to identify the factors that were critical to the success or failure of individuals or systems in a given setting in the past, so as to improve response to future problems. Also termed *critical incident technique*.

Critical management studies Radical approach to management, based on environmentalism, feminism, and poststructuralism, that seeks to discredit traditional organizational theories and assumptions.

Critical mass In business, the threshold number of customers or users needed to sustain the growth of a product or service.

Critical-path analysis Form of operational research in which a project is represented by a diagram containing a time schedule for each segment of the project, then a line is drawn showing the sequence of tasks and the cost and time factors involved.

Critical success factors Organizational strengths and weaknesses seen as affecting the success of an endeavor.

CRM CUSTOMER RELATIONSHIP MANAGEMENT

Crony capitalism Business activity that thrives on favoritism and nepotism and other undemocratic values.

Crosby, Philip (1926–2001) Management guru who promoted quality as the essential ingredient of business success. Author of *Quality Is Free* (1979), *Quality Without Tears* (1984), and *Completeness* (1994). Trained as a physician, Crosby became an engineer and worked in a number of companies, such as Crosley Corp, Bendix, Martin Marietta, and ITT. He then established the Crosby Quality College, in Winter Park, Florida, and became a consultant. He is associated with many quality-related concepts, such as ZERO DEFECT, quality management, MATURITY GRID, and cost of nonperformance.

Cross fertilization Use of successful ideas

from one department or agency in another, in the hope of gaining similar results.

Cross licensing Collaboration in research and development between two institutions or firms, resulting in synergistic innovation.

Crossing the chasm Attempt to close the gap between the use of technology by early users and its later reception by more experienced users.

Cross selling Practice of selling related products and services to an existing captive clientele. Cross selling reinforces customer loyalty and retention.

Crowdsourcing Delegation of a task, such as research or a problem solution, to the general public through the Internet.

Crown jewel option Form of a POISON PILL, in which a target company defending itself against a HOSTILE BID allows a friendly company to acquire its most profitable assets so as to make the takeover less attractive to the predator.

Cultural intelligence Ability and sensitivity to the cultural diversity of a globalized market and the ability to adapt to cultural differences and take advantage of them.

Cultural literacy Familiarity with the cultural values, norms, mores, and traditions of a country that is not native. It is the first step toward developing empathy for and

tolerance of diversity, and a means of avoiding prejudice and XENOPHOBIA.

Cultural noise Impediments to successful verbal and nonverbal communications across cultural barriers and verbal idiosyncrasies.

Culturalist One who upholds the theory that organizations are cultural microcosms, with their own symbols, norms, codes, and values.

Culture lag The difference between older, learned values and habits and a newer CORPORATE CULTURE.

Culture shock Feelings of disorientation that employees sent overseas experience when they arrive in another culture with different values and traditions. This adjustment involves learning the cultural alphabet of the new country and adapting to its different mores.

Cumulative timing Delays in the onset of an event that results in a proportionate delay in the duration of an event. It is used to ensure that the length of the entire event is close to its desired duration.

Currency future Financial futures contract in which a currency for forward delivery is bought or sold at a given exchange rate.

Currency option Contract to buy or sell a currency at a fixed exchange rate within a certain period. The agreed-upon price is called EXERCISE PRICE or STRIKE PRICE.

Currency swap Exchange of specified amounts of one currency for another, at an agreed-upon price. If both currencies bear interest at a fixed rate, it is an *ordinary swap*; if both currencies bear interest at a floating rate, it is a *basic swap*; if one currency has a floating rate and the other has a fixed rate, it is a *cross-currency interest-rate swap*.

Current assets Fluid business assets that may be cash or goods. Compare FIXED ASSETS.

Current-cost accounting Method of accounting in which assets are valued at their current cost, their replacement cost, or their net realizable value. This separates gains from operating profits, thereby preventing their distribution to shareholders. The method makes several adjustments to the historic cost-accounting profit-and-loss account, such as for depreciation and monetary working capital.

Current liability Amount owed by a business, due and payable within the fiscal year. Includes taxes, trade credits, bills of exchange, Social Security, dividends, accruals, deferred income, overdrafts, and bank loans.

Current ratio Relationship of CURRENT ASSETS to CURRENT LIABILITIES, used as a test of LIQUIDITY. Too low a ratio indicates poor liquidity and too high, poor management of working capital.

Curriculum vitae (c.v.) Document listing the educational and professional qualifications, achievements, and background of an individual, used to determine suitability for an open position.

Custom of the trade Practice or convention that is peculiar to a trade or business, as applied to legal disputes.

Customer database Information on individual customers or prospects, including geographic and demographic data and buying habits, preferences, and behavior.

Customer-delivered value Difference between total customer value and the total customer cost of a product.

Customer profitability analysis Examination of profits by customer rather than by product; helps to identify the relatively small number of customers who account for most of the profits.

Customer relationship management (CRM) Integrated and computerized database system that provides salespeople with available information on customers.

Customer satisfaction Degree to which customer expectations of a product or service are met or exceeded, so that customers return to the same products or services to meet their future needs.

Customer service Actions by a company oriented toward meeting the needs of its customers, including providing product information, making repairs and doing maintenance, offering guarantees, dealing with complaints, and providing after-sales follow-ups.

Cutthroat competition In a market where the supply exceeds demand, efforts by sellers to undercut the competition in order to get rid of their stock by any means.

CWO CASH WITH ORDER

Cycle In economics, a period of business activity characterized by a wavelike rise and fall, with growth and decline. Anticipating business cycles can help reduce the negative impact of these cycles and create a more stable, productive trajectory.

Cyclical time A period of time measured in a pattern of repeated events occurring at regular intervals, as in the seasonal work of a farmer or the repetitive work of assembly-line employees. Opposed to LINEAR TIME.

Cyclograph Method of studying work movements, developed by work-study experts FRANK and LILLIAN GILBRETH.

Cyert, Richard Michael (1921–1998) American economist and statistician and president of Carnegie-Mellon University. His books included *Models in a Behavioral Theory of the Firm* (1959), *Management Decision Making* (1971), and *Computational Organization Theory* (1994).

D

Daisy chain In finance, buying and selling the same commodity several times over as a way of inflating its trading activity on a stock exchange.

Danger pay Compensation offered to employees who work where prevailing unrest poses a great danger to their physical well-being.

Databank A collection of DATABASES.

Database An organized electronic collection of information according to a schema that is built into a database management system.

Database marketing Marketing based on extensive use of DATABASES to attract new customers and explore new markets.

Data capture Insertion of information into a computer system at the point of sale or other means.

Data dredging Process of drawing conclusions from data not warranted by the data alone.

Data file Computer file, divided into records and fields, that contains data as distinguished from a file that contains a program.

Data mining Process of extracting usable information from raw data through the use of algorithms and statistical models to form predictive models that can identify significant patterns of use.

Data protection Safeguards for personal data in a company's files to prevent potential misuse, especially without permission. The protections conform to the privacy rights and laws in force, in that data are obtained fairly and lawfully and used only for specified and legal purposes; personal information is not disclosed or used in a manner inconsistent with the purpose behind its collection; it is not exploited excessively; it is accurate and up-to-date; it is kept no longer than necessary; it is protected against unauthorized and unlawful processing and against accidental loss or destruction; and it is not transferred to a foreign jurisdiction. Data subjects have the right to find out what information is held about them and to rectify, block, erase, and destroy data that are inaccurate and irrelevant, so as to prevent their disclosure or sale to third parties, and to be compensated for infringement of privacy rights.

Data warehousing Assembly of data from multiple sources into one, single file for easier access.

Dawn raid Attempt by one company or investor to acquire significant holdings in the equity of another company by acquiring all available shares as soon as the stock exchange opens, before the target company suspects a TAKEOVER BID.

Day in the sun Time when a product or issue is most successful in the marketplace.

Daybook Book in which specific transactions are recorded for prime entries.

Dead-cat bounce Temporary, inexplicable rise after a fall in stock prices, which does not indicate an upward trend.

Dead time Unproductive time spent by workers waiting to begin work.

Deadline Time by which a contract must be completed or a sale must be concluded.

Death valley curve Movement on a graph that tracks the decrease in VENTURE CAPITAL invested in a company as that company meets its startup expenses and before its income reaches predicted levels. At this point, the company becomes less attractive to new investors.

Debenture Unsecured business loan re-

payable by a fixed date that pays a fixed rate of interest. Payment of interest on debentures takes precedence over payment of dividends. *Perpetual debentures* are not redeemable. *Secured debentures* have a fixed charge on the borrower's assets. Some debentures are convertible into ordinary shares at a specified price. The advantage to the debenture's issuer is that it carries a lower rate of interest than overdrafts and has a longer maturity date. Trustees may be appointed on behalf of debenture holders.

Debit In DOUBLE-ENTRY BOOKKEEPING, an entry on the left-hand side of an account, showing the amount owed to creditors.

Debit card Bank card issued to a customer enabling that person to pay for goods or services by directly debiting his or her bank account.

De Bono, Edward Charles Francis Publius (1933–) Maltese-born British physician and thinker. In his book *Six Thinking Hats,* he coined the term LATERAL THINKING. He founded the Cognitive Research Trust in 1969 and the Edward De Bono School of thinking in 1979. He is the author of 82 books including *Mechanism of the Mind* and *I am Right, You are Wrong.*

Debt-equity ratio Percentage of a company's equity in relation to its longer-term debt, including PREFERENCE SHARES. This ratio is an indication of the financial health of a company and is used by banks to determine that company's credit worthiness.

Debt-for-equity swap Transaction in which debt is swapped for equity during the reorganization of a troubled company.

Debt rating Level of creditworthiness of an institution, based on generally accepted criteria such as economic and political stability. The company's debt rating affects the interest rate when it borrows money.

Debt restructuring Adjustment of a debt through a rescheduling of payments and terms, either under court order or through negotiation, to give a company more time to meet its financial obligations.

Debt-service ratio In international trade, the proportion of annual export earnings needed to service a country's external debt obligations.

Debureaucratization Breakdown of the hierarchical structure of authority, with redefinition of managerial function and devolution of responsibility downward.

Decentering Process of relying on old principles and guidelines in a rapidly changing market, with new players, products, and needs.

Decentralization Delegation of decision-making authority to subordinates and subsidiary units to encourage greater local responsibility. The advantages of decentralization are greater relevance to the immediate environment, greater efficiency, and better motivation of associates. The disadvantages are wasteful competition, duplication of functions, and loss of central control.

Decision analysis Consideration of the key decisions in an organization, as opposed to holding unexamined assumptions. This is one of management guru PETER DRUCKER's three techniques for crafting the best organizational structure for a corporation.

Decision band method Job-evaluation technique developed by sociologist T. T. Paterson, in which all job levels in an organization are analyzed and graded according to six decision-making criteria, in descending order of importance: policymaking decisions, programming decisions, interpretive decisions, routine decisions, automatic decisions, and vegetative decisions.

Decision making Act of making rational choices among multiple options or courses of action, based on experience, tradition, available means, and CRITICAL-PATH ANALYSIS. Seat-of-the-pants decisions are based on gut feeling. Similarly, many decisions are made in the absence of complete information and without knowledge of the intended or unintended consequences. Uncertainty always increases the number of possible outcomes to a decision. DECISION TREES can sometimes clarify the problem by assigning probabilities to each possible outcome. Principled decision making, whereby problems are reduced to a manageable size, can be used to assist analytical decision making. DECISION SUPPORT SYSTEMS use available information to arrive at better decisions. Sharing of information can lead to collective intuition. Additionally, conflict may stimulate better decision making by fostering creative thinking and yielding better understanding of available options.

Decision-making unit Informal group in an organization vested with the task of making purchasing decisions based on price, need, and availability.

Decision model Simulation of elements or variables inherent in a business decision, based on consideration of negative and positive factors. Decision models include DECISION TABLES.

Decision science Application of accepted scientific principles and models to decision making and problem solving.

Decision support system (DSS) Computer information system that performs complex data analysis that helps users make informed decisions.

Decision table Way of graphically presenting the estimated probabilities of outcomes, each with its maximum and minimum benefits, to aid decision making.

Decision theory Theory in which various mathematical techniques, such as GAME THEORY, RISK ANALYSIS, and SENSITIVITY ANALYSIS, are used to forecast likely outcomes of different decision options.

Decision to participate Behavioral theory that people participate in an organization's activity so long as the benefits to them of doing so outweigh their expected contributions.

Decision tree In decision making, a diagram that illustrates the choices and possible outcomes of each possible course of action.

Deconglomeration Split-up of a conglomerate through the devolution of power to its constituent parts.

Decouple To separate two corporate units that were bound together.

Decruitment Placement of senior staff on reduced pay with lower responsibilities in the years immediately preceding their retirement.

Deed A written, validly executed, duly signed, witnessed, and delivered document.

Deep discount An interest rate higher than 15% of the redemption value of a loan stock.

Deep market Highly liquid market for a commodity, currency, or security with a large number of transactions in which the spread between bid and offer is narrow.

Deep throat Anonymous source of top-secret information; allusion to informer during the Nixon Watergate scandal.

Deep web Secure classified data in government and military websites. Also *invisible web*.

De facto Applied to a situation or thing that exists as a matter of reality, rather than as established by law, as in de facto discrimination.

Default 1. To fail to do something as required by law, especially to make a payment on time, comply with the terms of a contract, or observe the rules of legal procedure. 2. Predetermined setting in computer software to facilitate use.

Defender strategy Competitive tactics that protect a company's market share by concentrating on existing products, improving quality, and offering lower prices and superior customer service. Compare PROSPECTOR STRATEGY.

Defender takeover bid HOSTILE BID for takeover of a company that is opposed by the directors of the target company.

Defensive interval ratio Relationships between income and assets on the one hand and expeditures and liabilities on the other, which demonstrates the ability of a business to meet its current debt obligations by calculating the time for which it can operate on current liquid assets.

Defensive investment Strategy for investment with the primary goal of avoiding risk rather than maximizing return. Opposite of SPECULATION.

Deferred Delayed. In accounting, relating to payments that are payable only at a later date and not in the accounting period under review.

Deficit financing In government, spending that is financed through issuance of debt. This KEYNESIAN ECONOMIC concept, by which fiscal policy is used to promote economic growth through government spending, is based on the premise that the resulting growth in economic activity will bring in the funds needed to offset that debt.

Deflation State of economy in which there is a decline in prices, accompanied by falling levels of employment, output, and trade. Opposite of INFLATION.

Deflationary gap Difference between the theoretical level of spending necessary to maintain full employment and production and the actual spending by public and private sectors.

De Geus, Arie Dutch business consultant whose book *Living Company* (1997) described the characteristics of a long-lived company as one of financial conservatism, sensitivity to the natural and social environment, cohesiveness, and tolerance for unconventional thinking.

Deindustrialization A decline in the manufacturing sector resulting from a loss of competitiveness, loss of skilled labor, and flight of capital.

Delayed gratification Act of forgoing immediate gratification for the sake of greater or more genuine satisfaction in the future; often applied to market research.

Delayering Removal of some middle layers of management in an organization so as to create a more flexible and responsible hierarchy.

Del credere agent A selling agent who guarantees to pay for goods sold on behalf of a principal if the buyer fails to do so.

Delegation Process of giving decision-making authority to subordinate employees. The delegation of authority or responsibility must be accompanied by empowerment, selection, and planning. The manager needs to specify the performance standards of the assignment, and the authority and responsibility must be balanced.

Delegatus non potest delegare Legal principle that a delegate cannot further delegate—that is, that a representative or delegate with vested authority cannot grant that power, trust, or authority to a third party without authorization from the principal.

Deleveraging Sale of a company's assets and the RETRENCHMENT of its staff to reduce debt.

Delphi technique QUALITATIVE FORECASTING technique by which a panel of experts respond to questions from a forecaster or coordinator, who summarizes the responses and repeatedly resubmits them to the panel until the process yields an objective assessment.

Demand In marketing, the need for a product, translated into a potential purchase, which in turn determines the volume of its production and its price.

Demand curve Movement on a graph that illustrates the relationship of a product's price to its sales.

Demand elasticity Extent to which demand for a product influences its price. When demand is inelastic, price changes have no effect, and when demand is elastic, even small changes in price affect the volume of sales.

Demand inflation Economic condition in which prices increase because of increased demand that cannot be met.

Demand management Stimulation or reduction of demand to achieve a desired level of employment and economic stability.

Demand-pull inflation An increase in prices created by excess money for too few commodities.

Demand-pull innovation Development of new products triggered by unmet needs.

Demarketing Actions aimed at discouraging consumers from buying or consuming a particular product, such as cigarettes.

Demerger Split-up of a large company or conglomerate into a number of units or sold off in an effort at consolidation.

Deming, W. Edwards (1900–1993) American champion of TOTAL QUALITY MANAGEMENT, who formulated 14 points for quality control that revolutionized Japanese manufacturing. He was subsequently responsible for a quality revolution in the United States and many other industrialized countries. Edwards reminded management that most business problems are systemic and that management more than labor should be responsible for correcting them. His books include *Out of the Crisis* (1986), *The New Economics* (1993), and *Statistical Adjustment of Data* (1943). One of his best-known theories is the System of Profound Knowledge, which encompasses (1) appreciation of a system, (2) knowledge of variation, (3) theory of knowledge, and (4) knowledge of psychology. His theory of optimization states that the goal of an organization should be to maximize the entire system and not merely the constituent subsystems. His theory of variation states that companies should eliminate variation in quality by focusing on certainty and standards in production and design. He said that most variations are due to common structural and design inadequacies, but about 20% are due to assignable external causes. His theory of knowledge states that knowledge is not possible without theory and experience alone does not constitute a theory. And his theory of psychology delves into the forces that drive human interactions, which are based on psychology.

Deming then described what he termed "the seven deadly sins or diseases of management": (1) lack of constancy and purpose to plan, (2) emphasis on short-term profits, (3) performance appraisals and merit ratings that discourage the fearful, (4) job-hopping, (5) management based on quantitative results alone, (6) excessive medical costs, and (7) trial lawyers. He formulated 14 points to counter these seven deadly sins: (1) have consistency of purpose; (2) do not accept delays and mistakes and poor workmanship; (3) do not depend on inspection alone to ensure quality; (4) do not look to the price tag alone but value long-term relationships, loyalty, and quality; (5) continuously improve production and service; (6) train on the job; (7) have supervisors be coaches, not dictators; (8) create a fear-free environment; (9) break down internal barriers through better communication; (10) avoid slogans; (11) eliminate numerical goals, standards, and quotas; (12) foster pride in workmanship; (13) encourage self-improvement; and (14) engage the management in implementing these 14 points.

Deming prize Award established by the Union of Japanese Scientists and Engineers in honor of W. EDWARDS DEMING, father of TOTAL QUALITY MANAGEMENT. The prize is given to companies that have shown a strong commitment to quality control as an imperative in management.

Democratic leader Egalitarian leader who successfully delegates authority and promotes consensus decision making as a deliberate management policy. Organizations with democratic leaders tend to be more flexible, innovative, and motivated.

Democratic management Style of management that emphasizes consensus, persuasion, and consultation at all levels of decision making.

Demographic segmentation Division of markets into groups based on demographic variables such as age, gender, family size, life cycle, income, occupation, education, religion, race, and nationality.

Demography Study of growth, decline, and transitions in human populations, especially by race, gender, age, fertility, marriage patterns, and mortality.

Denationalization See PRIVATIZATION.

De novo (Latin, "begin again") In computer system design, new cost burdens brought on when attempting to eliminate inequalities.

Department Traditional unit of an organization, devoted to a particular segment of the business activity and led by a departmental head.

Department store Retail organization that sells a wide variety of products and services, often part of a chain of stores.

Departmentation Establishment of subunits charged with specific functions or oversight of specific territories, products, customers, or tasks.

Depreciation 1. Diminution in the value of a fixed asset owing to wear and wear and/or obsolescence. 2. Fall in the value of a currency with a floating exchange rate relative to other currencies.

Depressed area Region where economic performance is low and unemployment is high relative to the national average.

Depression Extended or serious RECESSION in business activity, characterized by falling production, falling prices and sales, stock market crash, high unemployment; sometimes accompanied by INFLATION.

Depth interviews In marketing, unstructured interviews as part of a market research project. The interviewer encourages the interviewees to offer their candid responses informally and then compiles their responses for a formal report.

Depth of product line Description of the number of items in a product line.

Deregulation Elimination of regulations and rules governing business activity in stipulated areas of activity. Deregulation is often a reflection of both political and economic developments. It may come about as a more conservative political base gains power; or it may be the result of growing globalization and increasing influence of multinationals, who are relatively immune to domestic pressures; or it may accompany a realization that certain regulations are contributing to inefficiencies in the marketplace. Technology also makes certain existing regulations obsolete. Lastly, producers and manufacturers have powerful lobbies that craft legislation privatizing industries that had been historically under state control.

Deregulation can have a profound impact on the marketplace by reducing barriers to entry, encouraging diversification, and enhancing competition. New firms bring cost-cutting technologies essential for survival, additional capacity, and more consumer-friendly, competitive practices. As new companies enter the marketplace, prices and profitability fall and there follows a period of consolidation marked by mergers and acquisitions, as well as the departure of many new entrants. For larger companies, UNBUNDLING as a result of deregulation gives customers greater ability to make product/service and price/performance tradeoffs. The post-deregulation reorganizations last characteristically about five years.

Corporate culture changes in the process of deregulation. Companies become more opportunistic, adopting a number of strategies: (1) Broad-based distribution integrating operations information gathering and marketing over a wide geographic area. (2) Cost-focused strategies to achieve economies of scale and segment-focused strategies that provide expensive or premium services at premium prices; segments include niche markets that are more profitable with fewer providers. (3) A striving for synergies by REBUNDLING products and using alternate delivery systems, sale of high value-added items or personalized or customized services, and exploitation of small community markets. (4) Sharing of utilities by offering services to smaller firms that, if done alone, would be unprofitable. In short, deregulation is both a challenge and an opportunity to restructure and gain new momentum. The initial turbulence may introduce some uncertainty for a few years, but appropriate strategies help companies survive and grow.

Derivative Financial instrument, devised in the 1990s, that links the price of a commodity or currency to its demand in the future. The main types of derivatives are FUTURES contracts, FORWARDS, CREDIT-DEFAULT SWAPS, and OPTIONS. They are traded on derivative markets or OVER THE COUNTER.

Derivative department Department spun off from a major department but still acting as its unit.

Descriptive research Market research that explores the potentials of a market, the attitudes and buying habits of its consumers, and the demographics of the group.

Descriptive statistics Branch of statistics that provides marketers with a summary of available data, including consumption levels and other variables.

Designed capacity Maximum theoretical output of an operating system in units, based on technical capability, setup times, maintenance, and schedules.

Desk audit Work audit.

Desk research Market research that uses available data in the company files rather than collecting new data from the field.

Deskilling Process by which an operational system is automated, thereby requiring minimal human intervention and characterized by simple and standardized procedures.

Devaluation Reduction in the value of a currency in relation to gold or the U.S. dollar. A bold move in monetary policy designed to offset a serious crisis brought about by high INFLATION, adverse continuing BALANCE OF TRADE, and decline in exports. Its goal is to promote exports and discourage imports, although in practice it can have the opposite effect. Devaluation is a drastic option available only to currencies with a fixed rate of exchange. For currencies with a floating exchange rate, devaluation and REVALUATION take place continuously and automatically.

Development stage Point in the development of a new product when the concept is transformed into a prototype and a marketing strategy is developed.

Deviation Departure from a quality standard and the extent of the departure.

Diagonal communication In management, the crosswise flow of information between departments and hierarchic levels.

Diagonal expansion Business growth resulting from the creation of new products with the same equipment currently in use.

Dialectics The attempt to solve a problem through dialogue involving differing points of view.

Diamond-water paradox ADAM SMITH's question as to why diamonds are in such high demand and water in such low demand when the former is a luxury and the latter is a necessity.

Diemer plan Wage incentive plan that calls for a 50% salary over and above wages

for each 1% of the production above the task, with a bonus of 10%.

Differential analysis Assessment of the impact on costs and revenues of specific management decisions that identifies *differential cash flows*—that is, cash flows that are impacted by a specific decision.

Differential pricing Method of pricing a product with different customer bases at different prices. The method is based on the principle that maximum market penetration is achieved when prices are customized to the particular market.

Differentiated marketing Marketing designed to meet the unique or peculiar needs of a niche audience, such as dieters. Each market segment has not only a product modified to meet its needs but also a customized strategy that highlights the distinctive features and benefits of the product.

Differentiation In ORGANIZATIONAL THEORY, the process an organization undertakes to cope with an increasingly complex environment by way of multiple specializations.

Diffusion of new products Process by which innovations and new technologies spread through society and become accepted, as well as commercially viable.

Diffusion of responsibility In social psychology, the way a call to action or a request for assistance is spread and generalized so that no one feels a responsibility to respond.

The term is stretched to apply to decision-making responsibility in business.

Digerati Experts in computer operations and cyberspace, as in *literati*.

Digital brand Brand identity or logo that is different from the company's traditional one. Also termed *online brand*.

Dilbert principle Associated with the cartoon character Dilbert, this states that corporations allow their employees to rise to their highest levels based on their incompetence rather than their competence. The implication is that the workhorses of a company are its middle-level employees and that the higher echelons are show horses. See also PARKINSON'S LAWS, PETER PRINCIPLE.

Dilutée Worker who has received shortened training and is therefore considered semi-skilled.

Dilution of equity Increase in the number of ordinary shares of a company without a corresponding increase in assets or profits, leading to a fall in the value of those shares and lower dividends.

Diminishing returns In economics, the point beyond which any additional input of resources will result in a proportionate increase in outcome. See also LAW OF DIMINISHING RETURNS.

Dink Affluent couple with no children, considered a prime marketing prospect.

From "double-income-no-kids."

Direct costs 1. Production costs that can be directly charged to the producing unit, such as labor and materials. 2. Production costs incurred by the cost center that can be allocated directly without being treated as overhead.

Direct marketing Sales and marketing of a product from producer to consumer, without an intermediary. Traditional direct marketing is through mail order; television, radio, and social media; telemarketing; websites; and related formats.

Directive interview See STRUCTURED INTERVIEW

Direct taxation Schedule of graduated taxation imposed on personal income, as distinct from indirect taxation such as a *sales tax* or VALUE-ADDED TAX.

Director Person legally entrusted with the conduct of a company, with legal responsibility for all its actions and assets and liabilities. Under the articles of association, the body known collectively as the BOARD OF DIRECTORS is the executive of a company. The day-to-day operations of a company may be vested in a person elected by the board of directors known as the MANAGING DIRECTOR. Directors are required to submit an annual report to the company's shareholders.

Director's report Annual report prepared by the DIRECTOR of a company, as required by law. It must provide information on the principal activities of the company; current position in relation to the industry; likely prospects and future developments; principal risks and uncertainties likely to affect future performance; sale, purchase, and valuation of assets, dividends, and transfers to reserves; employee statistics; and gifts to charity.

Disaster management In business, management of the aftermath of a large-scale natural or manmade disaster in an effort to contain the fallout and reduce its ill effects on human resources and corporate image.

Disciplinary takeover Direct control taken in response to a chronic problem or poor management, either by the board of directors itself or with its support.

Disclaimer Clause in a contract or advertisement that reduces a company's direct liability in the event of harm caused to the user or buyer.

Disclosure Obligation in legal proceedings to communicate all relevant facts and not suppress any information that might have the effect of distorting the resultant decision making.

Discontinuous innovation Product or service that represents a breakthrough in technology, or is likely to enhance consumer satisfaction and lifestyle, that calls for new forms of consumer behavior and responses. Introduction of the home computer in the 1980s is an example.

Discotectic state Confusion, uncertainty, and instability created when companies undergo rapid change with which they are ill equipped to cope.

Discount 1. Reduction or deduction in price in return for a specified benefit. 2. A method in capital budgeting to predict future streams of cash flow.

Discovery Period before a contract comes into force, during which either side may gather information to verify that the facts as represented are accurate.

Discretionary account Account placed with a stock broker, commodity broker, or securities house in which the agent is empowered to carry out transactions within certain parameters without referring back to the principal.

Discretionary costs Costs attributed to managerial decisions in certain areas, as research and advertising. Also termed *managed costs*.

Discriminating monopoly Form of monopoly in which products or services are sold to consumers at different prices, charging each segment the maximum price it will bear; for example, when a utility company charges different rates for its private customers and its industrial customers.

Discrimination Practice of favoring one group over another, based on race, gender, age, sexual orientation, religion, or disability; illegal with regard to consumers.

INDIRECT DISCRIMINATION results when the universal and objective application of a legal provision or practice puts one group at a disadvantage.

Discriminatory pricing Setting different prices for a product in two or more places or markets, reflecting the peculiarities of those markets and not additional costs.

Diseconomies of scale Proportional costs of gaining additional market share that offset the ECONOMIES OF SCALE.

Disempowerment Elimination of special privileges that had been previously accorded to certain consumer groups.

Disequilibrium State of instability, flux, and change, characteristic of markets subject to new forces or undergoing rapid change.

Disflation Reversal of inflationary pressures, brought about by appropriate monetary measures.

Disintermediation Elimination of middlemen, such as brokers and bankers, from financial transactions as a consequence of new technologies and globalization.

Dispatching rule Any of five rules used in deciding the priorities in fulfilling orders: (1) first come, first served; (2) by earliest due date; (3) by shortest processing time; (4) by longest processing time; and (5) by ratio of time until due date.

Disproportionate stratified sampling Method by which the size of the sample is not proportionate to the size of the stratum. For example, a group that accounts for 80% of sales may be 20% of the population, and therefore may not be appropriately represented in the stratum.

Dissatisfiers Term coined by theorist FREDERICK HERZBERG to describe events that create dissatisfaction in the workplace and that demotivate people. See HERZBERG'S TWO-FACTOR THEORY.

Disseminator Managerial role identified by business thinker HENRY MINTZBERG, whereby the manager acts not only as the gatekeeper of information but also the dispenser of information.

Distance selling Sale of goods indirectly through the mail, television, telephone, e-mail, or Internet, as distinguished from sales in a brick-and-mortar retail outlet. Many CONSUMER PROTECTION laws apply to distance selling.

Distancing Subcontracting to outside contractors work that was formerly done in-house.

Distribution Payment made to shareholders in a company or someone with an entitlement to the proceeds, profits, or reserves according to an agreed-upon formula.

Distribution management Management of the resources of and the planning for efficient transfer of goods, materials, and finished products, including warehousing, handling, inventory, and packaging.

Distributive bargaining Form of collective bargaining in which the subject's resources are limited and therefore one side's gain is the other side's loss, as in a ZERO-SUM GAME.

Distributive leadership Delegation of leadership functions or sharing of authority as a matter of policy.

Divergent thinking Creative and original thinking that, by definition, deviates from conventional thinking and produces multiple solutions to a problem. Distinguished from LATERAL THINKING and CONVERGENT THINKING.

Diversification Expansion of the scope of business activities into markets outside traditional interests, especially to avoid over-reliance on a narrow range of products. GROWTH and diversification are parallel developments. Diversification is driven by a search for SYNERGY and may be achieved through several strategies: (1) dominant business strategy, (2) diversification strategy, (3) conglomerate strategy, and (4) acquisition strategy. There are a number of risks associated with diversification, especially that of lack of integration capacity, lack of board follow-up, unrelatedness, incorrect market identification, clash of corporate cultures, lack of synergy, inadequate skills, and imposition of the wrong style of management. External diversification takes place through mergers and acquisitions. Diversification may be vertical or horizontal. *Horizontal diversification* involves integration of operations at the same stage of

production. *Vertical diversification* occurs when firms integrate operations at a different stage of production.

Diversity management In human resources, the concept of maintaining a harmonious workforce that is culturally disparate and heterogeneous in its composition, language, race, and religion, and in massaging those differences. The challenge is to make diversity an asset rather than a liability in a company's operations.

Divest and exit strategy Strategic option to sell an asset or close down a product line in order to exit an unprofitable market.

Divestment Business retrenchment strategy in which parts of the company are spun off to create a more homogeneous organization with more focused objectives and strategies. Generally, the parts sold are the less profitable ones.

Dividend Distribution of part of the earnings of a company to its shareholders.

Dividend reinvestment program (DRIP) Program for investors whereby dividends are used to buy additional shares instead of issued as cash income.

Divisionalization Creation of self-managing units within an organization, accompanied by devolution of authority to these units. In large corporations, the functional structure grows unwieldy and inefficient. In the 1980s and 1900s, superior information technology and trends toward DELAYERING extended the concept to small businesses. Earlier, the divisional form was important in the development of an international strategy; as industries moved from regional orientation to global, complex and multiple reporting relationships became common, and country executives reported to both area and product divisions.

Dog In business, an unpromising and unprofitable product that is a drag on a company's profits.

Dollarization Adoption of the U.S. dollar as a national currency, usually as a means of controlling INFLATION and INTEREST RATE volatility.

Domicile Place of residence or business or professional activity, irrespective of citizenship. The country might require work permits and business or resident is subject to local tax laws. Under COMMON LAW rules, a person's civil status is determined by domicile and not by citizenship.

Dominant business strategy Business operation in which 70% or more of the profits come from one key product or business, as in the case of oil companies such as Exxon. There are four types of dominant businesses: (1) dominant-vertical, involving selling a variety of end products, none of which contributes more than 85% of the sales; (2) dominant-constrained, or businesses that have diversified nonvertically by building on the original dominant activity; (3) dominant-linked, or businesses that have diversified nonvertically by building

on different strengths, resources, or skills; (4) dominant-unrelated, or businesses in which a preponderance of nonvertically diversified activities are unrelated to the dominant business.

Dominant-element job evaluation Technique in job evaluation, in which only the most important element in a job is considered relative to others.

Doomsday strike Strike at the end of a period covered by a wage agreement or on the eve of negotiations.

Double-dip recession Period of recession characterized by brief economic growth, followed by a slide back into recession.

Double-entry bookkeeping Method of recording transactions twice in account books, as a credit and as a liability. All books are required to balance.

Double-loop learning Organizational learning in which the emphasis is on learning how to learn. It involves critical examination of the assumptions underlying corporate responses in times of high uncertainty and unpredictability.

Double taxation Taxation of the same income in two different countries or contexts; for example, in both the country of domicile and the country of nationality, or taxation of corporate profits and shareholder income taxation. International double taxation is governed by treaties and agreements that provide relief to varying degrees.

Doughnut principle Formulated by business thinker CHARLES HANDY in his book *The Empty Raincoat* (1994), theory that presents organizations as doughnuts whose hole represents their core activities and values.

Dow Jones Industrial Average (DJI) Index of security prices issued by Dow Jones and Company, using New York Stock Exchange listed stocks. The DJI is a narrow index of only 30 constituent elements. It was begun with 11 companies, had 41 in 1932 when the market crashed, and tracked over 14,000 stocks in 2007.

Downsizing Reduction in the size and footprint of an organization to improve profitability, gain traction in the market, and improve focus and strategic leverage. It is distinct from REENGINEERING or CORPORATE RESTRUCTURING and may or may not be accompanied by staff reductions, departmental consolidations, and office closings. While companies implement downsizing plans to increase profitability and productivity, these steps do not always yield those benefits and may lead to loss of skilled workers, decline in customer service, and loss of morale. See RIGHTSIZING.

Downshifting Lifestyle change in which an employee exchanges the bustle of corporate culture for a temperate routine that affords more time with family and less stress.

Downstairs merger Merger in which the parent corporation become a subsidiary.

Downstream 1. Reference to a latter stage in the production process or the value chain. 2. Funds borrowed by a parent company for use by a subsidiary. Compare UP-STREAM PROGRESS.

Downstream progress Movement toward more realizable goals that involve going with the flow and riding a wave. Compare UPSTREAM PROGRESS.

Downtime Period of time when an operation is idle or suspended.

Downward communication Communication from senior management to lower levels of employees. Compare HORIZONTAL COMMUNICATION and UPWARD COMMUNICATION.

Doz, Yves French management expert whose book with Gary Hamel, *Alliance Advantage* (1998), tackled the complexities of globalization and focused on strategic partnering.

Dragon market Any of the emerging markets in the Pacific Rim, especially Indonesia, Malaysia, Thailand, and the Philippines.

Drawdown Depletion of funds from a line of credit or transfer from one account to another.

DRIP DIVIDEND REINVESTMENT PROGRAM

Drip-feed To fund a new company in stages rather than with an initial lump sum.

Drop lock Bond initially issued with a variable rate of interest, which converts to a fixed rate if the index or rate falls below a set amount at a particular date.

Drop shipment Goods shipped directly from the manufacturer to the consumer or retailer.

Drucker, Peter (1919–2005) American management guru who popularized the concept of MANAGEMENT BY OBJECTIVES and introduced the concepts of ACTIVITY ANALYSIS, DECISION ANALYSIS, and RELATIONS ANALYSIS.

Drum-buffer-rope Manufacturing process that factors in possible delays or problems.

Dry test Prior to large-scale manufacturing, a trial run during which consumers are asked to use a product and express whether they would be interested in purchasing it. If the test is negative, the product will be cancelled.

DSS DECISION SUPPORT SYSTEM

Due diligence 1. Inspection of a company's financial or other records prior to its sale or merger, as required in the LAW OF CONTRACTS 2. Level of care and judgment that a reasonable person is expected to exercise in a given situation to prevent mala fides.

Dumbsizing Reducing the size of a company so drastically that it becomes inefficient.

Dumping Sale of goods abroad, below their marginal cost, in order to gain a foothold in the market. Dumping is illegal under international trade agreements because it is against fair trade.

Dun and Bradstreet Largest mercantile agency in the United States, offering credit data and ratings.

Dunfee, Thomas W. (1942–2008) Professor of Legal Studies and Legal Ethics at Penn State University and President of the Society for Business Ethics. He was one of the foremost scholars in the field of business ethics. His path-blazing work, *Ties that Bind: A Social Contracts Approach to Business Ethics* (1999), is an influential text.

Dunning, John Harry (1927–2009) British economist who specialized in the economics of international direct investment In 1980 he published the eclectic paradigm or OLI-Model/Framework. His best-known works are *Globalization of Firms and Competitiveness of Nations* (1990), *Alliance Capitalism and Global Business* (1997), and *Making Globalization Good: The Moral Challenges of Global Capitalism* (2005).

Dunscore Index developed by DUN AND BRADSTREET to measure the position and ranking of industries over time.

Duopoly Market in which there are only two producers, thus reducing competition. See MONOPOLY.

Duopsony Market in which there are only two buyers.

Dupin, Charles (1784–1873) French engineer who pioneered industrial education in France. His *Discourse on the Condition of the Workers* (1873) introduced such concepts as *time study* and *balanced workloads*.

Dutch auction Auction sale that begins with a top price, which then is successively reduced until an acceptable buyer is found.

Dutch disease DEINDUSTRIALIZATION following the discovery of natural resources, such as oil and gas. Such a discovery leads to a boost in the economy and the value of the currency, making exports of manufactured products more expensive. This phenomenon occurred in the Netherlands following the 1959 discovery of North Sea gas.

Duty to bargain As stipulated in the Taft-Hartley Act, an obligation of employers and employees to bargain in good faith before a lockout or strike.

Dynamic administration Management theory that focuses on changing human relationships. It helped to develop such concepts as empowerment and visionary leadership.

Dynamic capabilities Resource-based business strategy that adapts to changing business environments quickly and nimbly to gain competitive advantage. The strategy combines innovation, boldness, sharper focus, consumer feedback, and reconfiguration of a company's structures, as well as its competencies.

Dynamic equilibrium Economic state in which all the factors of production and consumption are so matched that there is a stable rate of growth.

Dynamic pricing Method of pricing goods and services that changes in line with patterns of demand.

Dynamic theory of profit Developed by economist FRANK KNIGHT, a theory on the relation between assumption of risk by entrepreneurs and their rewards.

Dynamically continuous innovation Development of products through marginal improvements in shape or design, without altering function or use. For example, Apple issues and markets new versions of its iPad without significantly enhancing its basic design or product life cycle.

Dystopia Place where misery prevails; the opposite of *utopia*.

E Prefix for "electronic," as in E-BUSINESS, E-COMMERCE, e-banking, e-learning, e-mail. Takes hyphen, although wider use will bring elimination of the hyphen.

Early adopter Company that is quick to recognize the potential of innovative technologies and procedures.

Early retirement Cessation of work before reaching the mandatory retirement age, either voluntarily or as part of a company's DOWNSIZING.

Earnings per share Company's consolidated profits divided by the number of ordinary shares, used as a measure of performance.

Easterlin, Richard (1926–) Professor of Economics at the University of Southern California. He is known for his "Easterlin paradox," which states that happiness at the national level does not increase with wealth once basic needs are met. He is also known for the "Easterlin hypothesis," which states the positive relationship between income and fertility is dependent on income relative to aspirations.

Easterlin paradox Theory proposed by economics professor RICHARD EASTERLIN that increasing wealth does not produce corresponding growth in happiness.

EBIT Earnings before interest and taxes

EBITDA Earnings before interest, taxes, depreciation, and amortization

EBQ ECONOMIC BATCH QUANTITY

E-business Electronic direct marketing using the Internet. Also termed E-COMMERCE.

EC EUROPEAN COMMUNITY

ECB EUROPEAN CENTRAL BANK

Echo-chamber effect Limiting effect of junior staff parroting the ideas of senior management uncritically.

Eclectic paradigm Model developed by international business expert JOHN HARRY

DUNNING to explain variations in the scope of foreign direct investment.

Ecocentric management Ecologically aware management approach that treats environmental issues as a core concern rather than as a peripheral one.

E-commerce Electronic commerce or Web-based commercial transactions.

Econometrics Branch of economics specializing in studies of quantitative relationships between economic variables.

Economic appraisal Method of capital budgeting that uses discounted cash-flow techniques to identify preferred investments. In addition to cash flow, it factors in anticipated economic benefits and annual costs over the lifetime of a project.

Economic batch quantity (EBQ) Optimum size of a production batch to justify production costs.

Economic benefits Inventory of material and financial benefits accruing from a project as a measure of its rationale. For example, the construction of a new road may mean a reduction of driving time, fewer accidents, and lower insurance costs as its economic benefits.

Economic costs Inventory of material and financial costs to be offset by ECONOMIC BENEFITS. For example, the construction of a new road may mean budgetary deficits,

cost of subsidies, and costs of interruptions in services during construction.

Economic efficiency Theory that no one can be made better off without at the same time somebody's becoming proportionately worse off.

Economic growth Expansion of an economy in terms of output and income, usually measured as GROSS NATIONAL PRODUCT and GROSS DOMESTIC PRODUCT per capita.

Economic man In economic theory, a person who makes right, informed, and rational decisions in regard to individual economic activities and thus maximizes their ECONOMIC BENEFITS.

Economic and Monetary Union of the European Union Group consisting of the 17 members of Eurozone and 10 non-Euro states. These are states that have demonstrated successful economic convergence by maintaining limited deviation against the Euro.

Economic sanctions In international relations, a tactic by which a more powerful nation or group of nations imposes on a less powerful nation an embargo or restrictions on imports and exports, as well as financial transactions and travel; done as a means of applying pressure on the less powerful nation to either act or desist from acting in a certain manner.

Economic theory of the firm Belief that

the only external duty of a company is to its shareholders and its only function is to make profits.

Economic union Common market or trading bloc of neighboring countries or countries with strong affinities.

Economies of scale Reduction in the average cost of production and concomitant unit costs that accompany an increase in output. Economies of scale may lead to a cycle in which prices go down and sales go up, resulting in a gain in market share. For the economies of scale to be effective, costs must remain stationary. Economies of scale can be internal or external: *internal economies* may be plant related or organizational; *external economies* are benefits experienced through improved infrastructure and the location of ancillary industries. Economies of scale provide a competitive edge over new entrants, who must operate at a cost disadvantage.

Economies of scope Increase in costs incurred as a company diversifies its products and services to serve a broader market.

Edutainment Education + entertainment, a term used in the media industries.

EEO EQUAL EMPLOYMENT OPPORTUNITY

Efficiency 1. *Technical efficiency* is the ability of an organization to produce maximum output with minimum inputs. 2. *Eco-*nomic efficiency* or *productive efficiency* is the ability of an organization to produce and distribute at the lowest possible cost, regardless of its production costs. 3. *Allocative efficiency* derives from the rational, timely, and productive allocation of resources. 4. *X-efficiency* is the extent of market exploitation by the company; it has three main components: intraplant motivational efficiency, external motivational efficiency, and nonmarket input efficiency.

Efficient market hypothesis In management finance, a principle that market yield is conditioned by the availability of and access to the right information; formulated by economist EUGENE FAMA.

EFT Electronic funds transfer

EFTA European Free Trade Association, a former common market.

Egoistic need Individual needs for job satisfaction other than remuneration.

Eight-hundred-pound gorilla Crucial player in a situation whom everybody ignores for fear that he or she may create further complications or prove too difficult to manage.

Eighty-twenty split Developed by VILFREDO PARETO, the principle that only 20% of all business activities contribute to its profits and that 80% are dead weight. The principle also applies to personnel, advertising, and inventory. See also PARETO RULE.

Elasticity Sensitivity of one variable to another. The common use of elasticity is in regard to price, when an increase in costs leads to a decline in demand.

Electronic data interchange Electronic exchange of structured information, such as invoices, between different organizations using industry standards.

Eleemosynary Charitable, not-for-profit work engaged in by quasi-public corporations.

Elvis year Successful year for a product or company, when it reaches the peak of sales.

Embargo Interdiction of trade with certain countries, or in certain commodities, or in information in certain sectors, as a form of political punishment and ostracism.

Emergent change Approach to organizational change in a complex organization operating in a volatile, unstable, or uncertain environment. Its conceptual core are the interlinked ideas of KAIZEN, a Japanese term for continuous improvement, and a learning culture that encourages continuous relearning by managers.

Emerson efficiency plan Employment compensation plan in which workers are paid a minimum salary and given financial incentives to increase production.

Emory, Frederick Edmund (1925–1997) Australian psychologist who contributed to

the development of theories of INDUSTRIAL DEMOCRACY.

Emoticon Expressive symbols used in Internet communications, such as ☺ for a smile.

Emotional capital Shared experiences, values, and aspirations among employees, seen as a morale builder.

Emotional intelligence (EQ) Ability to control emotions and articulate them, and to respond appropriately; seen as a sign of maturity.

Emotional labor Work of managing one's emotions in the course of dealings with customers or employees.

Empire building Pursuit of power through dominance in a field of endeavor; in business, the acquisition of more corporations.

Employee Person who works under the direction of another in return for wages or salary. Employees have legal protections, unlike independent contractors.

Employee buyout Transaction by which employees buy up all or most of a company's outstanding shares.

Employee empowerment In human resources, motivational strategy to reengineer organization structures by channeling more responsibility to employees. Empowerment gives more personal satisfaction and fulfillment, and in some cases may lead to greater monetary rewards and enhanced prospects for promotion. It also helps to identify and develop hidden talents and abilities.

Employee evaluation Formal assessment of an employee's professional performance and conduct as measured by certain objective and fair criteria, with the goal of establishing eligibility for promotion.

Employee participation Right of an employee to buy shares in the company (employee stock option plan) and thus gain membership in the governing councils and boards, and be able to express opinions on matters pertaining to company policies and programs.

Employee wellness In human resources, management attempts to address employee problems like alcoholism, divorce, smoking, poor nutrition, lack of exercise, obesity, and stress, which affect performance and efficiency in the workplace.

Employment agency Private business engaged in introducing suitable candidates to employers in return for a fee (usually a percentage of the initial salary) or to provide temporary staff who work at hourly rates. Employment agencies that specialize in filling managerial and executive positions are known as HEADHUNTERS.

EMS European Monetary System.

Endogenous Relating to factors or influences within an organization; opposite is EXOGENOUS.

Engels, Friedrich (1820–1895) German-born associate of Karl Marx. He worked with Marx on his *Communist Manifesto* and supported him financially to write *Das Kapital*. His major works included *The Condition of the Working Class in England* (1844), *Socialism, Utopian and Scientific* (1880), and *The Origin of the Family, Private Property and State* (1884).

Engels's law Developed by economic theorist Friedrich Engels, the principle that the lower the household income, the greater the proportion of income spent on food.

English disease Supposed predilection of English labor unions to strike to gain their demands rather than to negotiate.

Engross To purchase a large quantity of a good so as to obtain a monopoly on its resale at prohibitive prices.

Enlightened marketing Five layers of efficient marketing, including consumer-oriented marketing, innovation marketing, value marketing, sense-of-mission marketing, and societal marketing.

Enterprise culture Economy that favors initiative, innovation, private enterprise, and personal responsibility.

Enterprise resource planning Strategic approach that integrates all the business activities and processes throughout an organization, including project management, supplier management, product data management, and scheduling in a seamless, real-time program to streamline operations, eliminate overlaps, and save money.

Enterprise zone Geographical area set aside by a government exclusively for private-sector activity and granted exemption from certain fees and taxes, as well as statutory controls.

Entitlement Right to stipulated benefits, as determined by prior laws and agreements and as earned over time. Often applied to social programs.

Entrapment In business, the resource limitations that inhibit growth and innovation.

Entrepot trade Trade that passes through a certain port or airport on its way to another destination, and that makes use of its warehouse and customs facilities or uses them for re-export. Some of the world's major entrepot trade centers are Rotterdam, Singapore, and Hong Kong.

Entreprenerd Blend of the words *entrepreneur* and *nerd*, slang for an Internet startup capitalist.

Entrepreneur Someone who starts his or her own business from scratch. Also, someone who invests capital in the development of a new company and assumes the accompanying risks in the hope of realizing profits. Entrepreneurs are the building blocks of capitalism.

Entrepreneurship Process of identifying opportunities and marshaling resources so as to create new products and services for which there is a felt need, in anticipation of subsequent profits.

Entropy In information theory, the degree of openness to change and the lack of rigidity in an organization and its structure.

Environment costs Expenses associated with compliance with environmental legislation, including appraisal costs, prevention costs, internal failure costs, and external failure costs.

Environmental audit Financial review of the impact of any development or activity on the immediate environment, both short and long term. Its purpose is to ensure that the development or activity is in full compliance with prevailing legal requirements and environmental laws. Areas covered by the audit include energy usage, wastage, recycling, conservation, and pollution. Also termed *green audit*. See also SOCIAL AUDIT.

Environmental ethics Application of principles of honor, dignity, conservation, and preservation of the natural world and its ecosystems, especially as they apply to pollution, resource depletion, animal exploitation, waste disposal, erosion, loss of species, and climate change. It replaces an anthropocentric ethic with a holistic one, in which all species are given equal weight.

Envy ratio Ratio of the number of shares

available to individuals to the number of shares available to institutions.

Ephemeralization From futurist writer Buckminister Fuller, the theory of increasing the rate of a product's obsolescence in order to increase the recycling of its constituent materials.

EPS EARNINGS PER SHARE

EQ EMOTIONAL INTELLIGENCE

Equal Employment Opportunity (EEO) Legislation that prohibits discrimination based on religion, gender, race, or color in hiring, promotion, and firing.

Equal pay Legislation that bars discrimination based on gender, race, religion, or color as it relates to compensation or salary; the legislation stipulates that equal pay must be guaranteed for work of equal value.

Equilibrium price Price that reflects a balance of SUPPLY AND DEMAND.

Equity 1. Beneficial interest in a property comprising its value less its liabilities. 2. System of law developed parallel to COMMON LAW in which the focus is on fair performance rather than on damages.

Equity Theory Theory that attempts to explain relative satisfaction in terms of perceptions of fairness or unfairness in the distribution of resources in society. It

was first developed by J. Stacey Adams, a psychologist. The structure of equity in the workplace is based on the ratio of inputs to outputs.

Equivalent mean investment period Period of time between the commencement of a project and its breakeven point.

Ergonomics Discipline that merges physiology, physiognomy, and psychology to design work environments for optimal efficiency and safety. Ergonomics has particular application to emerging technology by defining the workplace and the use of computers. It studies the physiological, psychological, and engineering design aspects of a job, especially as affecting fatigue and safety, and governs the placement of tools and instruments on the basis of ease-of-use, intuition, and posture.

ERG theory EXISTENCE, RELATEDNESS, AND GROWTH THEORY

Escalation of commitment Increasing commitment to a project that is falling apart. This stance is generally adopted to save face after a project has misfired, in an attempt to recover some of the lost investment or reputation. Often termed *throwing the helve after the hatchet* or *throwing good money after bad*. Also called *creeping commitment*.

Escalator clause Contract paragraph that permits adjustment of prices or wages in accordance with certain accepted indexes of productivity, increased cost of living, or greater material costs.

Escape clause Wording in a treaty or agreement that permits one or both parties to opt out of meeting an obligation or to suspend portions of the agreement if they become too onerous or impractical to enforce.

ESOP Employee share ownership plan.

E-tailer Retailer operating through Internet sales. See also E-BUSINESS.

Ethical behavior Application of moral and ethical imperatives to the conduct of business and adherence to principles of behavior and standards to judge outcomes. In its elementary form, it is the compliance of business to the laws governing business transactions, and in its societal form, it is the focus on public welfare underlying business decisions. A company's codes of ethics spell out the ethical imperatives of its operations and personnel.

Ethical investment Socially responsible investment in a company in terms of its goals and strategies as distinguished from investment driven solely by profit motive.

Ethnic marketing Marketing directed at an ethnic minority community and that focuses on culturally relevant products and services, often using the language of that community.

Etzioni, Amitai (born Werner Falk) (1929–) Israeli-American sociologist and intellectual. His principal contribution to sociology was his theory of communitarianism, which sought to create a common ground between liberalism and conservatism. He is the author of 24 books of which the most influential were *The Spirit of Community: The Reinvention of American Society* (1993) and *A Responsive Society* (1991).

Etzioni model Organizational theory developed by sociologist AMITAI ETZIONI, who classified organizations in terms of the kinds of power they wielded, such as coercive (prisons and army), utilitarian (business), normative (schools), and mixed.

EUREX Largest futures and options market in the world dealing primarily with European derivatives. It is run by Deutsche Borse AG and SWX Swiss Exchange.

Euro Currency used by the members and institutions of the European Union as the official currency of the Eurozone, which consists of the 17 members of the European Union: Austria, Belgium, Cyprus, Estonia, Finland, France, Germany, Greece, Ireland, Italy, Luxembourg, Malta, the Netherlands, Portugal, Slovakia, Slovenia, and Spain. It is the world's second largest reserve currency and the second most traded currency after the U.S. dollar.

European Central Bank (ECB) Central bank for the Euro System.

European Community (EC) See EURO-PEAN UNION.

European Monetary System (EMS) European Monetary System.

European Union Supranational community of 27 European nations with common economic, political, and social bonds; created in 1993, from the EUROPEAN COMMUNITY. The original 12 nations—Belgium, Denmark, France, Germany, Greece, Ireland, Italy, Luxembourg, the Netherlands, Portugal, Spain, and the United Kingdom—were joined by Austria, Sweden, and Finland in 1995; by Cyprus, Czech Republic, Estonia, Hungary, Latvia, Lithuania, Malta, Poland, Slovakia, and Slovenia in 2004; and by Bulgaria and Romania in 2007. The union has a constitutional framework with a parliament and an executive, known as the European Commission, as well as a judicial arm known as the European Court of Justice. Monetary cooperation is under the auspices of the EUROPEAN ECONOMIC AND MONETARY UNION, which oversees the European Monetary System and regulates and stabilizes the currency exchange rate.

Eurozone The 13 member countries of the European Union that have adopted the EURO as their national currency: Austria, Belgium, Finland, France, Germany, Greece, Ireland, Italy, Luxembourg, the Netherlands, Portugal, Slovenia, and Spain.

Eustress Positive impact of stress, as stimulation and excitement gained in meeting a tough challenge and enhanced performance; opposite of *distress*.

Evaluation of training Assessment of the effectiveness of a training program, as follows: (1) what the trainees think of the program; (2) what they learned from the program; (3) what new behavioral traits or skills have been imparted; and (4) what are the overall benefits from the program.

Evergreen fund Mutual fund that provides capital for new companies and acts as the midwife for new ventures.

Evolutionary economics Study of economics that incorporates biological dynamics and considers the corporation as a biological organism.

Evolutionary management Management style that adapts itself to change and incorporates new protocols in response to emerging needs and opportunities.

Ex ante (Latin, "before the event") Relating to a budget based on anticipated calculations that are later revised on the basis of actual figures.

Ex gratia (Latin, "by favor") Payment or favor made out of gratitude, moral obligation, or voluntary acknowledgment of a service, rather than because of legal right or liability.

Ex post facto (Latin, "after the event"). Label for financial data generated after payments have been made.

Exception principle Belief that managers should concentrate on problems that are the exceptions to the rules and let subordinates handle routine matters.

Exchange 1. Trade in goods, stocks, shares, commodities, currencies, or other financial instruments. 2. Place where such trade takes place.

Exchange control Restriction on the sale and purchase of foreign currencies or bonds.

Exclusive territory Geographical area assigned exclusively to a distributor or retailer.

Executive compensation Remuneration of principal company officers, including base salary, bonuses, long-term incentives, benefits, and perquisites.

Executive director Working director who is also a full-time employee of a company, generally in charge of a department.

Executive search Process of identifying suitable candidates for senior positions, done by recruiting agents or consultants known as HEADHUNTERS.

Exercise In law, the right to carry out a transaction based on previously agreed-upon terms.

Exercise price Price at which a specified security can be purchased in a call option or sold in a put option.

Existence, relatedness, and growth theory (ERG) Developed by American psychologist CLAYTON P. ALDERFER, a theory of workplace motivation involving a hierarchy of three motivational drivers: existence needs (physical and material), relatedness needs (relating with peers), and growth needs (desire to be creative and productive and for recognition). The theory is applicable to multiple environments, as in home, office, and society.

Existential culture In business, a corporate culture in which the organization exists to serve the individual rather than vice versa; coined by business guru CHARLES HANDY.

Exit interview In human resources, the interview conducted with employees before they leave the organization.

Exit strategy In finance, a plan by an investor to dispose of assets in an orderly fashion. Also termed *harvest strategy*.

Exogenous Relating to factors or influences that are external to the organization and therefore outside its control.

Expectancy theory In human resources, a theory of motivation that people perform better in accordance with the value they place on the outcome and their expectations of benefit or gain.

Expected monetary value In decision making, statistical term for the sum of outcomes in monetary terms multiplied by their respective possibilities.

Expected value In decision making, statistical term for the sum of possible quantitative outcomes in quantitative terms multiplied by their probabilities.

Expense account 1. Heading for each item of expenditure in an accounting system. 2. Amount paid to executives for out-of-pocket expenses when on business travel.

Experience curve Statistical curve that illustrates the inverse relationship between costs of production and employee experience. Costs go down as personnel gain more experience.

Expert system Tool of artificial intelligence that captures the expertise of knowledge workers and makes it accessible to nonexperts.

Explicit costs Direct cost outlays, such as for raw materials and labor.

Exploitative leadership Authoritarian leadership that looks upon employees as means for reaching their own ends.

Exploratory focus group In marketing, a group of representative users and customers who aid in pilot-testing a product by defining its problems, asking questions, generating hypotheses, and suggesting new ideas.

Exponential smoothing Statistical technique used in quantitative forecasting whereby more weight is assigned to the more recent data when charting trends.

Extended market mix In marketing, the 6 Ps: price, place, promotion, physical evidence, people, process.

External environment Institutions outside the business environment that have a strong influence on the conduct of business, such as government, nonprofits, trade unions, and political parties.

External growth Growth in the size of a business by means of merger, takeover, or joint ventures, rather than through internal growth. Typically, external growth accompanies can increase in market share through Horizontal integration or Vertical integration. The benefits of external growth are often offset by the clash of cultures when disparate companies are brought together and by the organizational changes and costs of implementing such mergers.

Externality Cost or benefit to a company that is not matched or compensated by proportionate financial reward. For example, a new housing development may increase the number of residences and purchasing power of the neighborhood, but it may result in overcrowding on roadways, increased pollution, and more demand for social services. Some other types of external costs are pollution on public waterways and the impact of built-up land on wildlife. EXTERNALITIES also impinge on individual rights and groups in public settings.

Also called *spillover costs*, external costs are borne not by the company initiating a project but by third parties and thus are subject to legal remedies. Also, they are sometimes self-correcting and sometimes carry benefits as well as damages. Beneficial EXTERNALITIES include the beautification of a neighborhood or an increase in property values following a new roadway.

Extinguish In business, to settle or terminate an obligation.

Extraordinary Relating to an exceptional event or account unrelated to the normal activities of a company, such as a meeting or resolution, or costs and expenditures.

Eyebrow management Communication by management whereby an idea is summarily dismissed by facial expression without giving a reason.

F

Fabless production Production subcontracted under strict supervision to outside firms.

Face-to-face skills Effective verbal communication skills, particularly in small groups.

Facilitator Person who helps groups to identify and solve problems by structuring the discussion and intervening to guide the participants to arrive at solutions.

Facility-sustaining activity Operations whose performance helps to sustain an organization as a whole, such as security, safety, and physical maintenance.

Factor 1. Business engaged in FACTORING. 2. Person who acts as an agent for a commission, or *factorage*.

Factor-comparison method Type of job and pay scales evaluation in which jobs are compared in terms of compensable job factors, such as skill, effort, decision making, working conditions, and responsibility.

Factoring Buying trade debts from a producer, thereby assuming the risk of debt collection and accepting the credit risk. In *service factoring*, the FACTOR assumes the risk and collects the debt, while in *service-plus-finance factoring*, the factor also finances up to 90% of the debt.

Factors of production Resources required to produce material goods, such as land and natural resources, labor, capital, raw materials, and managerial ability. For each factor there is an associated cost: for land and natural resources, there is rent; for labor, there are wages; for capital, there is interest; for raw materials, there is cost and inventory; and for managerial ability, there are human resources costs.

Failure mode and effect analysis (FMEA) Technique of analysis showing why systems fail and at what stage or point, as well as the consequences of failure. It also helps in establishing preventive maintenance and contingency or emergency plans.

Fair presentation In accounting, the requirement that accounts presented do not misrepresent the true situation of facts, suggest falsehoods, or suppress the truth.

Fair trade Exchange of products between developed and developing countries, based on guaranteed fair prices.

Fallen angel In finance, a security that has dropped below its original value.

False market Market in which buyers or sellers act on false information or on reports of a glut or scarcity, which distorts prices.

Fama, Eugene Francis (1939–) American economist known for his work on portfolio theory and asset pricing. He was Professor of Finance at the University of Chicago Booth School of Business. He coauthored the textbook, *The Theory of Finance.*

Family life cycle In marketing, the six stages of family life as they relate to sales of goods and services: (1) young and single; (2) young childless couples; (3) young couples with infants; (4) couples with older dependents; (5) older couples with no children at home; and (6) older singles including widows and widowers.

Fannie Mae Federal National Mortgage Association, founded during the New Deal era in 1938 to expand the secondary mortgage market by securitizing mortgages in the form of mortgage-backed securities. It is a government-backed enterprise, although it has been publicly traded since 1938. In 2011 it had total assets of $3.2 trillion.

FAQ 1. Frequently asked questions. 2. Fair average quality.

Fast track Career path for quick advancement, characterized by special training and rapid promotion, designed for people with management potential.

Fatigue In business, the point at which either workers or machines exhibit signs of stress, owing to wear and tear and overwork, either because of aging or poor environment.

Fault tree Analytical technique illustrating the ways in which components of a system are likely to respond or behave under stress.

Fayol, Henri (1841–1925) French pioneer of organizational theory and management, who established the structural principles of formal management. He introduced the concepts of CHAIN OF COMMAND, JOB DESCRIPTION, MANAGEMENT AUDIT, ORGANIZATIONAL CHART, and SPAN OF CONTROL. In his book *General and Industrial Management* (1916), he identified the major elements of management as planning, organization, command, coordination, and control. His principles of management included *esprit de corps* and SECURITY OF TENURE.

Fayol ladder The organizational chart or tree developed by Henri Fayol, with dotted-line paths to indicate channels of communication and hierarchic links.

FCPA FOREIGN CORRUPT PRACTICES ACT

FDIC FEDERAL DEPOSIT INSURANCE CORPORATION

Feasibility study Investigation into the viability of a project or undertaking based on its risks and benefits, including compliance with laws and regulations.

Featherbedding 1. Restrictive labor practice whereby more staff are employed than necessary as a conciliatory gesture to labor unions. 2. Lax legal regulatory climate in which companies make excessive profits.

Fed General reference to the FEDERAL RESERVE SYSTEM or FEDERAL RESERVE BANK.

Federal Deposit Insurance Corporation (FDIC) U.S. government corporation operating as an independent agency created by the GLASS-STEAGALL ACT OF 1933.

Federal funds Non-interest-bearing deposits held at the FEDERAL RESERVE BANK, which are traded between member banks.

Federal fund rate Overnight interest rate paid on federal funds by member banks of the FEDERAL RESERVE SYSTEM. It is a highly volatile money-market interest rate that affects every other financial transaction.

Federal Open Market Committee Policy committee of the FEDERAL RESERVE SYSTEM, which controls the level of money and credit in the U.S. banking system and regulates the money supply. Its members are the governors of the FEDERAL RESERVE BOARD and the presidents of the 12 FEDERAL RESERVE BANKS; they meet at least four times a year.

Federal organization Organizational structure in which departments and subsidiaries have considerable autonomy and are permitted to initiate projects, with overall authority resting in the central corporation. Many multinational companies have a federal organization demanded by their widespread operations.

Federal Reserve Bank Any of the 12 banks that constitute the FEDERAL RESERVE SYSTEM. They are located in Boston, New York, Philadelphia, Cleveland, Richmond, Atlanta, Chicago, St. Louis, Minneapolis, Kansas City, Dallas, and San Francisco.

Federal Reserve Board Main governing body of the FEDERAL RESERVE SYSTEM charged with overseeing the 12 FEDERAL RESERVE BANKS and with helping shape national monetary policy. Governors are appointed by the President of the United States and confirmed by the U.S. Senate for staggered 14-year terms. The board operates independently of the administration but is required to report annually to the House of Representatives.

Federal Reserve System Central bank of the United States, created by the Federal Reserve Act of 1913. It sets monetary policy, regulates the cost of money, and monitors the money supply. The system is run by the FEDERAL RESERVE BOARD.

Feedback Information or opinions about the quality of products and the performance of employees, obtained from clients and customers or associates and considered essential for evaluation, quality management, and continuous improvement. Feedback can be upward or downward.

Feedback control Management of the performance of an operating system, achieved by monitoring outputs and comparing them with the system's design parameters, then making adjustments for more efficient operation.

Feedforward control Management of the performance of an operating system, achieved by forecasting future problems and glitches and taking steps to avoid them.

Feigenbaum, Armand Vallin (1922–) American quality control expert who devised the concept of total quality control, later known as TOTAL QUALITY MANAGEMENT. He is the author of *Quality Control: Principles, Practice and Administration* (1945), *Total Quality Control* (1951), *The Power of Management Capital* (2003), and *The Power of Management Innovation* (2009).

Fiedler, Fred (1922–) One of the leading researchers in industrial and organizational psychology. He was a professor at the University of Washington. He is the author of the Fiedler Contingency Model, which is used to assess the traits and personal characteristics of leaders.

Fiedler Contingency Model Leadership theory of organizational psychology developed by FRED FIEDLER. According to Fiedler, there is no ideal leader. Both task-oriented and relationship-oriented leaders can be effective if their leadership fits the situation. The Contingency Theory can predict the characteristics of the appropriate situation for effectiveness. A favorable situation is when there is a good leader-member relation, a highly structured task, or a high leader position power.

Field In marketing, a district or region where research is conducted by a sales team or manager.

FIFO FIRST-IN, FIRST-OUT cost

Fifth discipline One of the characteristics of a LEARNING ORGANIZATION, which includes (1) systems thinking; (2) personal mastery; (3) mental models; (4) shared vision; and (5) team learning. The concept was formulated by MIT scientist PETER SENGE.

Finance 1. Management and manipulation of money. 2. Capital as a factor in the conduct of a business or in a business transaction. 3. Branch of economics dealing with money and its management.

Financial appraisal Evaluation to decide among a range of alternatives by which money can be obtained or spent. The appraisal usually includes CASH FLOW techniques, RATIO ANALYSIS, PROFITABILITY INDEX, and RISK ANALYSIS.

Financial crisis Collapse of the financial market and its lending institutions, leading to a RECESSION, as in the Wall Street meltdown of 2008.

Financial distress Situation in which a failing business enterprise contemplates insolvency and bankruptcy, leading to a restructuring and a search for working capital.

Financial futures Tradable contract for future purchase of currency, interest rate, or other financial asset. Financial futures enable traders to manage risks more effectively and to gain additional profits, but they are subject to great volatility.

Financial institution Establishment that provides financial services or trades in financial products; for example, banks and savings and loan associations.

Financial instrument Contract involving a financial obligation, such as a stock, bond, loan, and derivative.

Financial modeling Construction and use of planning and decision models based on financial data to simulate actual conditions. The models include discounted CASH FLOW, DECISION TREE, LEARNING CURVE, and BUDGETARY CONTROL.

Financial statement Annual review and report of a business's financial health, including profit-and-loss accounting, a balance sheet, a statement of gains and losses, and a cash-flow statement.

Financial year Year accepted by a business as constituting the accounting period for which its budgets are established. Also FISCAL YEAR.

Fire fighting Reactive management style that expends considerable effort in dealing with petty crises rather than taking broader actions to prevent them.

Firewall In a conglomerate, a barrier between the funding or ownership of one entity and other entities in the group so as to avoid spreading problems across the corporation. Also, in computers, a protective wall against viruses and worms.

Firm Business organization or partnership as a discrete entity.

Firm commitment In finance, an agreement by which the underwriter of an issue agrees to buy all unsold securities at the offering price.

First-in, first-out (FIFO) Accounting system in which costs for raw materials of each finished batch are determined as their earliest invoiced value.

First-mover advantage Head start gained by the company that is the first in the market with a new product or product line, including an enhanced reputation for being innovative and the ability to set industry standards. First-movers may exploit their head start to provide superior service at lower cost, pre-empt the competition, and displace traditional leaders, and thereby achieve customer loyalty There are also disadvantages to being first, such as investment in perfecting the technology.

First-tier market Main market in which the equity of a large company is traded. Compare SECOND-TIER MARKET.

Fiscal agent 1. Representative for a national financial institution. 2. Individual empowered to collect revenues on behalf of the U.S. Treasury.

Fiscal drag Deflationary impact of an increase in tax revenues under a progressive tax regimen.

Fiscal policy Use of government spending and taxation to influence MACROECONOMIC conditions.

Fiscal year Accounting period, also known as a *tax year* or *assessment year*.

Fishbone chart Diagram that identifies problems at each step in a problem-solving effort.

Fishbone technique Problem-solving method employed in TOTAL QUALITY MANAGEMENT.

Five forces model Formulated by theorist MICHAEL PORTER, a model that describes the five main forces of competition: (1) purchasing power of suppliers; (2) purchasing power of buyers; (3) threat of a potential new entry from outside; (4) threat posed by industries producing substitute goods and services; and (5) competition from rivals within the industry. In this model, suppliers can influence profits by raising prices, reducing quality, and reducing output. A supplier's influence may be strong if there are no available substitutes for the products offered, if there are switching costs, if the supplier has a dominant position, and if the product is unique. Buyers can threaten profitability by forcing prices down and demanding higher quality or more service. They are classified as commercial buyers or end consumers. Buyers have an advantage when the market entertains many sellers, when the products are undifferentiated, when there are available substitutes, and when the purchase represents a significant portion of the buyer's cost, turnover, or income.

The more powerful the buyer, the greater the leverage. New entrants dilute profitability by forcing a reconfiguration of the cost structures and development of new competitive strategies. The threat of substitute products is an ever-present danger that destabilizes the market. Intense rivalry may result from the existence of a large number of competitors with comparable resources, making it difficult for a winner to emerge and dominate the market. Slow industry growth may also encourage rivalry for market shares, as do lack of product differentiation, high fixed costs creating a temptation to reduce prices, and increased capacity utilization and high exit barriers.

Five Nines In marketing, implication that a product is almost perfect, as in 99.999%.

FiveS Methodology A workplace organization method that uses five Japanese words— *seiri, seiton, seiso, seiketsu,* and *shitsuke*—to describe organization of a work space for efficiency and effectiveness by identifying the items used and maintaining the work space. It has five primary phases: sorting, straightening, systematic cleaning, standardizing, and sustaining. Devised by Japanese business consultant Horoyuki Hirano.

Fixed asset Valued resource or investment, whether intangible or tangible. *Tangible assets* include real estate, plants, and machinery, and they must be written off through depreciation to the profit-and-loss account over their useful economic life. INTANGIBLE ASSETS include goodwill, patents, and trademarks, and they are amortized. Also *capital asset, durable asset.*

Fixed capital Amount of money tied up in FIXED ASSETS.

Fixed cost Expenses incurred in producing goods and services that are independent of the volume of production, such as rent.

Fixed-interest security Type of security that gives a fixed rate of interest, including GILT-EDGED SECURITIES, bonds, preferred shares, and debentures. They offer less scope for capital appreciation and their prices move inversely with the general level of interest rates.

Fixed pie Assumption that the market for a product is finite and that an increase in one segment will be at the expense of another.

Flag of convenience National flag of certain small countries, such as Panama or Liberia, flown by a ship owned by nationals of another country. Flag is flown to avoid paying high taxes, incurring high labor costs, and meeting stringent safety and environmental regulations.

Flagship Headquarters of a large retail chain that also serves as its largest and most prestigious store.

Flat organization Company with relatively few levels in its hierarchical structure. Compare TALL ORGANIZATION.

Flat tax Tax system with a single tax rate for all payers, with no exemptions except for standard personal allowance. Its advantages are simplicity, reduction of administrative costs, and elimination of loopholes; it also has a high income threshold at which taxes become payable. Its disadvantages are that it militates against the ability-to-pay principle and shifts the tax burden from the wealthiest to lower and middle classes.

Flexible firm Company that follows a flexible model in its division of employees (into core and noncore), number of employees, and pay and fringe benefits.

Flexible manning Work arrangement that allows variations in regard to hours worked, payments scheduled, and number of workers employed.

Flexible manufacturing system Automated and computerized production line that can be easily reprogrammed to manufacture any product in response to consumer demand. It consists of a group of numerically controlled interconnected machine tools, run by a central control system. Its benefits include less waste, fewer work stations, quicker changes of tools, reduced downtime, better quality control, reduced labor, more efficient use of machinery, and less turnaround time. It is best suited for high-volume production of many parts.

Flexible working hours (FWT) Work schedule without fixed starting and closing times. The workday is divided into a core period and several flexible periods from which an employee may choose the most convenient to complete the total number of hours per week or month. The period between the earliest permitted starting time and latest closing time is known as the BANDWIDTH. Additionally, an employee may carry forward a credit or debit of hours to the next work week. In French, this system is known as *Horaire Dynamique* and in German as *Gleitzeit*, or *gliding time*.

Flexibility Ability to adapt to change, maneuver in troubled waters, and take advantage of new opportunities quickly.

Flextime See FLEXIBLE WORKING HOURS.

Flight of capital Movement of money out of a country in response to political or economic instability.

Flight risk In business, an employee who is likely or planning to leave an organization.

Flight to quality Movement of investments to safer assets, such as gold, in times of economic volatility and uncertainty.

Float In business, to launch a new company.

Floating Denoting a debt, exchange rate, interest rate, or warranty not tied to a fixed correlate but, rather, is allowed to move up and down in unison with other indicators.

Floating labor Migrant labor that has no fixed company affiliation and shifts between places of employment, taking on whatever work is available.

Floor 1. Minimum price or rate at which a transaction can take place. 2. Area in a stock exchange set aside for face-to-face transactions.

Flow chart Diagram that shows the flow of materials, people, or information through a system and the hierarchic importance of each level.

Flow production Continuous manufacturing during which raw materials are fed at one end of the process and finished products emerge at the other end, as in petrochemicals, sugar, and steel.

Flow theory In human resources, the description of how people interact under stress or when faced with imminent change, and how they try to synchronize their actions with those of the external environment.

Flurry In finance, a burst of speculative activity in a market.

Flyback timing Work measurement noting each element of a job separately, as opposed to CUMULATIVE TIMING.

Flying-geese model View of economic development in which the developmental status of one nation has an impact on the economy of its neighbors.

FMEA FAILURE MODE AND EFFECT ANALYSIS

Focus group Exploratory research group of 8 to 12 paid participants headed by a moderator, who meet for in-depth discussions of problems and ideas in which they have an interest. In marketing, usually they meet during the conceptual stages of new product development.

Focused improvement Betterment of total performance, resulting from a study of constraints and bottlenecks, and with deliberate efforts made to eliminate them, one by one.

Focused strategy Business tactic by which firms divest themselves of their noncore activities and investments in an effort to maximize performance of the core competencies. Opposite of DIVERSIFICATION.

Follett, Mary Parker (1868–1933) British management writer and an adherent of the CLASSICAL SCHOOL OF MANAGEMENT. Follett was particularly interested in how conflicts are resolved, and she coined the term LAW OF THE SITUATION to describe the depersonalization of conflicts. Her book *Creative Experience* (1924) advocated integration as a means of reducing conflict without compromise or domination.

Followership In human resources, the study of followers and their psychology and motivations.

Follow-the-leader strategy Pricing strategy in which the bellwether or the market leader sets the price increase or reduction, and the others follow suit. This is common in industries with a weak competitive base.

Football-bell Shape of ideal business organization, recommended by management analysts HAROLD LEAVITT and Thomas L. Whisler in 1980; the model has more innovators in the top layer and fewer middle- and lower-level managers.

Footprint Physical space or premises occupied by a commercial unit.

Force majeure (French, "superior force") In a contract, an event occurring outside the control of either party, such as a riot, war, or revolution, that may excuse either party from its liabilities or from fulfilling the contractual obligations.

Forced choice In performance appraisal, a method of rating staff by providing descriptive phrases to be selected by the respondent as the most applicable.

Force-field analysis Analytical technique identifying negative and positive factors, and presenting them as a chart.

Ford, Henry (1863–1947) Founder of the Ford Motor Company and the 1913 inventor of the assembly-line model of production.

Fordism Management philosophy of assembly-line mass production, first initiated by Henry Ford.

Forecasting Art of predicting future trends and creating alternate scenarios, based on extrapolation of current trends or a study of past behavior under similar circumstances. Forecasts are based on methods such as the DELPHI TECHNIQUE or market research or polling.

Foreign Corrupt Practices Act (FCPA) 1997 Act of U.S. Congress prohibiting the use of bribes to facilitate the conduct of business in foreign countries.

Foreign exchange market Institutions where traders buy and sell currencies electronically. The principal foreign exchange markets are in New York, London, Tokyo, Singapore, Switzerland, Hong Kong, and Berlin. Nearly 85% of all foreign exchange transactions are in dollar, which is the *numeraire*.

Forensic accounting 1. Accounting undertaken in relation to a case pending in a court of law. 2. Accounting with the aim of uncovering fraud in past business transactions, initiated on the basis of partial or whistleblower information.

Form 10K Annual report mandated by law to the U.S. Securities and Exchange Commission by companies listed on any of the national stock exchanges. Form 10K is abbreviated quarterly return.

Forrester, Jay Wright (1918–) Pioneer American computer engineer and professor at MIT Sloan School of Management He is the founder of SYSTEMS DYNAMICS, which deals with the simulation of interactions between objects in dynamic systems. He developed ideas and theories that later became the foundation of SUPPLY CHAIN MANAGEMENT.

Forward price Predetermined delivery price of a commodity or currency or asset to be paid at a predetermined date regardless of market conditions.

Forward contract Contract related to the futures contract but is not traded in an exchange.

Forward integration Extension of a company's business operations further down the chain of production and retailing.

Forward market Exchange for dealing in FORWARDS contracts.

Forwards Contracts for commodities or securities for delivery at a future date, at a price agreed upon beforehand, called the *forward price*. These differ from FUTURES contracts in that they cannot be closed out by matching transactions.

Four-firm concentration ratio Measure of the combined market share of the four largest firms in a particular industry. A concentration of 40% indicates an OLIGOPOLY and a concentration of 80% is a MONOPOLY.

Four Ps Four fundamental principles of marketing—namely, product, price, place (or channel of distribution), and promotion.

Fourth level of service A company's highest level of service provided to its consumers.

Fourth market Exchange in unlisted securities, with trading conducted directly between investors.

Fourth World Least developed and poorest countries of the world. Term modeled on the Third World, or the nonindustrialized world and the First World or the industrialized world.

FRAC FREQUENCY, RECENCY, AMOUNT, AND CATEGORY

Fractional unemployment Temporary unemployment even in conditions of full employment, occurring when transitioning from one job to another.

Franchise License granted to a manufacturer, dealer, or trader to use a brand name in a particular area for a stated period, in return for royalties or fees. The licensee may also receive from the licensor technical expertise, financing, and inventory.

Frankfurt Stock Exchange Oldest and largest of the eight regional German stock exchanges, founded in 1820. It accounts for 75% of equity trading in Germany and has four markets, of which one is for bonds and one for small companies.

Freddie Mac Colloquial name for the Federal Home Loan Mortgage Corporation (FHLMC).

Free cash flow Measure of positive cash flow that is generated or consumed by a company, often defined as after-tax operating profit less net capital expenditure. It can be used to pay dividends, acquire other companies, invest in new opportunities, and reduce debt.

Free enterprise Economic system associated with CAPITALISM in which private business operates with minimum state intervention. Free enterprise is self-regulating and autonomous in terms of the control and ownership of businesses.

Free lunch Allusion to a free benefit, which in the negative ("no free lunch") carries a hidden price tag. The expression comes from the British pub tradition of offering free lunch so long as the consumer buys drinks at a hefty price.

Free market System of commerce that operates free from government interference, characterized by prices governed by supply and demand. Companies in a free market succeed or fail based on their ability to compete.

Free ride In finance, a situation in which traders or investors benefit from developments to which they do not contribute anything.

Free trade Unrestricted trade across national borders, including absence of tariffs and quotas. Free trade is guaranteed under GATT agreements, as well as regional trade agreements such as NAFTA and EFTA. The most important component of a free trade agreement is the MOST-FAVORED-NATION CLAUSE.

Freedom of contract Eligibility and right to enter into a legal contract. In the U.S. Constitution, it is called the *obligation of contracts*.

Freeze-out Attempt to pressure minority shareholders of a company that has been taken over to sell their stock to the new owners.

Freight absorption Pricing applied to all or part of the shipping costs as a service or bonus to customers.

Frequency marketing Strategies for marketing designed to encourage customers to make more frequent purchases, such as offering frequent-flyer miles.

Frequency, recency, amount, and category (FRAC) Four characteristics used to calibrate consumer behavior. *Frequency* is the time elapsed between purchases, *recency* is the date of the last purchase, *amount* is the average value of the customer's purchase, and *category* refers to the product in which the customer is most interested.

Friction-free capitalism Term coined by Microsoft founder BILL GATES to denote market efficiencies introduced by innovations like the Internet, which has abolished the physical distance between seller and buyer and has provided easy access to product information.

Friedman, Milton (1912–2006) American economist, Professor of Economics at the University of Chicago, and winner of the Nobel Prize in Economic Sciences. He is best known as a conservative thinker and the father of SUPPLY-SIDE ECONOMICS. His research into consumption analysis, monetary history and theory, and stabilization policy forms the basis of supply-side economics. He was opposed to all forms of Keynesianism and promoted an alternative macroeconomic policy known as Monetarism. His most influential book was *Capitalism and Freedom* (1962).

Friedmanite Follower of economist MILTON FRIEDMAN, the high priest of SUPPLY-SIDE ECONOMICS, representing the conservative wing of academic economists and promoting monetary theories that emphasize manipulation of the money supply as a driver of economic activity.

Fringe benefits Additional compensation for employment beyond salary, such as health insurance; fringe benefits are not viewed as taxable income.

Front office, back office Traditional division between the parts of an organization, with front office being open to scrutiny by the public and back office being off-limits. There is more concentration of authority in the back office.

Frozen assets Assets of a government, corporation, or person seized by a government as a hostile act pending the resolution of a dispute.

FTSE 100 Index of the 100 leading shares on the London Stock Exchange, compiled by the *Financial Times*.

Full employment Complete labor utilization in a country in which all able-bodied persons have gainful employment.

Full-line strategy Tactic by which companies saturate the market with all kinds of variations of a particular brand so as to preempt competition. Also termed *deep-line strategy*.

Function Discrete activity to which a department in a company is devoted, such as advertising or legal services. Budgets are prepared by departments oriented toward functions.

Functional departmentation Policy of segregating organizational work and allo-

cating tasks according to function. Those performing the same or similar kinds of work are grouped together based on their aptitudes and skills and placed under a common manager. Other kinds of departmentation are by numbers, time of duty, product, process or equipment, customer, or location.

Functional leader Member of a group who emerges to take on a leadership role and is accepted as such by other members.

Functional organization Form of organizational structure in which specialists carry out their functions without authority over the people outside their jurisdiction. The natural arrangement is by specialized FUNCTIONS, including a general manager, research and development, production, human resources, marketing, and finance and accounting. As firms grow, the functions become more fully developed. Finance and accounting are separated, as are sales and marketing; exports become an independent division. When multisite operations commence, they are placed under regional managers. A number of variants are introduced, such as product divisions.

Functional strategy Approach utilizing FUNCTIONS to achieve organizational goals, as a means of maximizing SYNERGY.

Fund Money managed on behalf of a client by a financial institution or to support a designated activity.

Fundamental analysis Evaluation of a

security by examining all macroeconomic factors (such as the overall economic conditions) and company-specific factors (such as the financial condition and management). The most important tool of fundamental analysis is the financial statement. It uses top-down or bottom-up methods. The former will include a study of the entire market, the specific technology sector, the industry as a whole and the performance of the stock, competition, and price movements. Opposite of technical analysis.

Fundamental term Key word or phrase in a contract that defines the essential contractual obligations.

Fungible Good or product that can be replaced by another without loss of value.

Fusion In business, the melding of employee outlook with that of management, as a result of indoctrination.

Future shock Term introduced by futurist ALVIN TOFFLER to describe the disorientation caused by too rapid change, not giving people time to adapt or assimilate.

Futures contract Contract between two parties to buy or sell a specified asset for a price (known as the futures price or the strike price) with delivery and payment at a future date (the delivery date). These contracts are exchanged at a futures exchange. The buyer is known as the "long" and the seller as the "short," reflecting their respective expectations. The assets being transacted may be commodities, bonds, stocks, or currencies as well as intangible assets such as stock indexes and interest rates.

Futures research Identification and study of alternative future scenarios to help in anticipating and planning for future developments.

G

GAAP GENERALLY ACCEPTED
ACCOUNTING PRINCIPLES

GAAS GENERALLY ACCEPTED
AUDITING STANDARDS

Gain sharing Form of output-based incentive that links rewards with the measure
of value added. VALUE ADDED is derived
from the total profits minus the value of
labor, raw materials, energy, and overhead
and is considered a reliable index of performance.

Galloping inflation Rapid, out-of-con-
trol INFLATION that augurs an economic
recession.

Game theory Mathematical approach to
predicting the outcome in situations where
participants have incomplete information
about each other's intentions. Introduced
by JOHN VON NEUMANN and OSKAR MOR-
GENSTERN, and developed by JOHN NASH,
JOHN HARSANYI, and RICHARD SELTEN.

Gaming In business, the application of
computer-based simulation and decision-
making techniques to a business problem
or transaction.

Gantt, Henry (1861–1919) American engineer and colleague of F. W. TAYLOR. Gantt
was a pioneer in management consultancy
and developed the GANTT CHART. He emphasized the human element in management and the role of motivation in increasing productivity.

Gantt chart Graph devised by HENRY
GANTT to measure work progress along a
time scale. The planned activity is shown
on a horizontal line and the completion
date is shown on a vertical line.

Gap In finance, the difference between interest rates on loans and interest rates on
deposits. This is a measure of risk used in
banking.

Gap analysis 1. In marketing, a tabulation
of all known types of consumer desire for
a category of goods, cross-listed with complementary features in existing products.
The analysis reveals the gap between consumer expectations and their fulfillment.

2. In management, the difference between mission and realized performance, and between aspirations and quantified objectives, with the goal of bringing performance up to the level of the goals.

Garage In finance, to transfer assets and liabilities from one nation to another, with the goal of achieving lower tax liabilities.

Garbage in, garbage out (GIGO) Slang expression capturing the belief that the quality of the output will match the quality of the input.

Garden leave clause Wording in an employment contract that provides for an extended period of notice on leaving employment, during which the employee is on full salary but is not required to report to duty. This clause is invoked when an employer wants to prevent an employee from joining a rival firm or divulging trade secrets.

Gatekeeper Manager who determines what information should be disseminated and what should be kept secret or suppressed.

Gates, Bill (1955–) Cofounder of Microsoft, the world's largest personal computer software company and the world's richest man.

GATT General Agreement on Tariffs and Trade

Gazelle In business, a fast-growing com-

pany that creates opportunities and grows by more than 20% annually.

Gazump To raise the price of or accept a higher bid in a situation where a lower sale price had been orally agreed to before a contract had been signed.

Gazunder To accept or offer a lower price before a contract is signed.

GDP Gross domestic product

GE matrix Tool for analyzing the relative strengths of brands within a large diversified corporation. Two measures are used to score the items: (1) attractiveness of the industry or service and (2) strength of the product. Individual products are shown as pie charts of various sizes, where the diameter of the pie indicates the size of the market and the size of the slice indicates the market share. Also known as *McKinsey matrix*.

Gearing For a company, the ratio of funds available from ordinary shares to debentures and preference shares. A company has *high gearing* when the majority of its funding is derived from fixed-rate interest charges and it has *low gearing* when its capital is predominantly in ordinary shares. If the company does well, the ordinary shareholders share in the windfall.

Genba shugi (Japanese, "respectable shop floor") Name for a career path in Japan, where top managers start their careers as shop-floor workers.

Gender segmentation Division of a market and its target population on the basis of gender.

General Agreement on Tariffs and Trade (GATT) Trade treaty supported by 95 world nations, with an additional 28 nations accepting its jurisdiction. Its goal is to expand world trade and provide a forum for the resolution of disputes. GATT is periodically revised in discussions called *rounds*.

General needs description Statement sent to vendors inviting them to submit bids to supply products a company intends to purchase, with specifications and prices.

Generalist Person with no special skills but who is proficient in all fields and can therefore function in a variety of roles. Opposite of a specialist.

Generally accepted accounting principles (GAAP) Standards and concepts of accounting that are applicable to all companies in a particular country.

Generally accepted auditing standards (GAAS) Rules and guidelines set down by the Auditing Standards Board of the American Institute of Certified Public Accountants.

Generation X Men and women born between 1963 and 1981, as constituting a particular cohort in terms of expectations and motivations. They are said to be looking for new but undefined challenges and a work-life balance in which new opportunities for learning are encouraged. See also BABY BOOMER.

Generic advertising Advertisements for a broad industry or a class of products, such as autos or wool, rather than a brand.

Generic strategy Approach to marketing products or services, using three basic elements: cost reduction, product differentiation, and focus. Introduced by MICHAEL PORTER, this approach is aimed at securing a long-term, sustainable advantage for new or existing products in new or existing markets. (1) Cost reduction should be continuous, so that the cost differential over competitors is maintained and reflects all stages of the value chain. That is, the greater the market share, the greater the cost reduction. It is a strategy that works best in stable environments. (2) Product differentiation is achieved either through marketing or through innovation. Differentiation should involve all parts of the value chain, and the markets should be able to be subdivided. This strategy is more appropriate to dynamic industry environments. (3) Focus exploits the differences in cost behavior in some segments and the special needs of buyers in those segments. Porter suggests that all three strategies should be pursued together, but they should not at the cost of the firm's primary mission; otherwise, the company will be "stuck in the middle," without any choices.

Gentleman's agreement Verbal contract that depends on the honor of those involved for its implementation.

Geodemographic segmentation Market segmentation that groups consumers according to demographic variables, such as age, gender, or age, and identifies them by postal code. The goal is to highlight affluent neighborhoods where people are likely to have solid buying habits.

Geographical departmentation Allocation of tasks and organization of work according to location. See Functional departmentation.

Gesellschaft mit beschrankter hafting **(GM BH)** In Germany, a company with limited liability.

Ghoshal, Sumantra (1948–2004) Management guru who formulated the Three P's—purpose, process, and people—to replace the Three Ss (strategy, structure, and systems) as a new model for transnational enterprise.

Giffen, Robert (1837–1910) Scottish statistician and economist. He gained a reputation as a financial journalist and later became controller-general of the Board of Trade. His principal publications include *American Railways as Investments* (1873), *Essays on Finance* (1884), *The Progress of the Working Classes* (1884), and *The Growth of Capital* (1890).

Giffen paradox Observation of Sir Robert Giffen that consumers buy fewer goods when prices fall and more goods when prices rise.

GIGO Garbage in, garbage out

Gilbreth, Frank (1868–1924) American management scientist who pioneered the time-and-motion study. Along with his wife, Lillian Gilbreth, he invented the Simo chart and Therblig.

Gilbreth, Lillian (1878–1972) Wife of Frank Gilbreth and his partner in many of his studies. Her book *Psychology of Management* (1914) was one of the earliest dealing with industrial psychology. As Professor of Management at Purdue University, she wrote about worker fatigue, scientific management as applied to home economics, and disabled workers.

Gilt-edged bond (g-bond) Bond that is attractive to investors because of the prestige of the issuing company.

Gilt-edged security High-grade bonds issued by a government or a corporation. They are highly rated investments with very low risk.

Ginnie Mae Colloquial name for the Government National Mortgage Association, which is the principal government-backed mortgage provider and guarantor in the United States.

Giro Method of money transfer in Europe, used for clearing and settling small payments.

Give-back Agreement by which employers persuade workers and unions to take a cut in wages and benefits in times of economic downturn.

Glacier studies Research conducted at the Glacier Metal Company, in London, by management thinkers ELLIOTT JAQUES and FREDERICK EMORY from 1948 to 1965. Their goal was to investigate the development of group relations and changes in employee roles and responsibilities. Out of the study came a methodology called *working through*, which examined social and personal factors in disputes. It also was discussed in Jaques's book *The Changing Culture of a Factory* (1951), where he introduced the concept of TIME SPAN OF DISCRETION, which stated that all jobs have some level of responsibility that requires discretion and judgment.

Glass ceiling General term for the invisible barriers that hinder career advancement for women.

Glass-Steagall Act 1933 legislation that separated commercial banking from investment banking in the United States and that established the FEDERAL DEPOSIT INSURANCE CORPORATION. The legislation was introduced as part of the New Deal to curb the speculation that led to the Great Depression. The act was repealed in 1999.

Global branding Globalization of trademarks and trade names so as to be sensitive to regional differences and national pride. Generally, neutral names are preferred to those with cultural ties to particular ethnicities.

Global brands Consumer products that have established a near-universal presence, like Coca-Cola, Nike, McDonald's, and Levi's. The nomenclature and logos of these global brands must have universal applicability.

Global bond Bond that is issued and traded in a country other than the one in which it is issued.

Global custody Safekeeping of securities by banks on behalf of clients.

Global firm Multinational company that operates in several countries, with its headquarters in one country.

Global information system Database that captures, stores, updates, manipulates, analyzes, and displays a whole range of information on a particular field of activity.

Global localization Strategy adopted by global corporations to have a global reach but also be sensitive to local needs. Also termed *glocalization*.

Global village Term coined by communications thinker HERBERT MARSHALL MCLUHAN to describe the worldwide cultural convergence, propelled by a borderless world communications system.

Globalization 1. Removal or breakdown of national barriers to trade, commerce, and industry, with business activities of all kinds flowing from new technologies, instant communications, deregulation, transnational investments, and better modes of travel and transportation. 2. Internationalization of consumer products, tastes, and skills as a result of broadened educational systems and the growth of English as lingua franca.

Globalization has rendered businesses less reliant on national markets and has given them considerable leeway in choosing industrial sites as well as greater access to cheap labor markets. They are able to offset losses in one country with profits in another country, while also avoiding punitive taxes. On the plus side, globalization has introduced ethnic diversity into management and staffing, and has encouraged devolution of power to local units outside the home country. Globalization follows six patterns: (1) licensing; (2) operation as a domestic corporation with exports through agents or distributors; (3) adoption of a multicountry strategy; (4) become a low-cost supplier to buyers around the world; (5) adoption of a global differentiation strategy to create products under a single brand; and (6) establishment of a strategic niche in important countries or regions. A result of globalization is the increasing homogenization of demand and supply, which can be exploited through radical economies of scale. Trading blocs such as the EUROPEAN UNION and NAFTA also promote incremental globalization.

GMAT GRADUATE MANAGEMENT ADMISSION TEST

GmbH *Gesellschaft mit beschrankter Haftung*, the abbreviation in Germany for a limited company.

Gnomes of Zurich Term coined by British politician Gordon Brown to characterize Swiss bankers, who have considerable financial clout and who use their laws to protect the identities of depositors who keep vast amounts of illegal money in Swiss bank accounts.

GNP GROSS NATIONAL PRODUCT

Go private Decision of a company to remove itself from a stock exchange and buy back all outstanding shares.

Go public Decision of a company to sell shares to the public, as listed on a stock exchange.

Gordon, W. J. See SYNECTICS.

Go slow Form of industrial action, often considered illegal, in which workers deliberately reduce their output by alternating periods of physical inactivity.

Goal convergence State of harmony in a business organization, achieved when top executives are in agreement on the goal and direction of the company and there is little or no power struggle, internal strife, or other friction.

Goal divergence State of disharmony in a business organization that occurs when there is open disagreement among executives on the fundamentals, such as the goal and direction of the company, and progress is hampered by power struggles, internal strife, and other friction.

Goal-setting Determining individual or collective performance targets for employees, based on four criteria: (1) challenging but realistic; (2) specific, not vague; (3) measurable; and (4) inclusive of employees. The three most common goal-setting procedures are top-down, bottom-up, and interactive.

Godfather offer Tender offer from a takeover firm that is so high that the management of the target company is compelled to recommend its acceptance.

Goffee, Robert Emeritus Professor of Organizational Behavior at the London Business School. Author of *Why Should Anyone be Led by You?*

Gogo fund Slang term for a mutual fund aimed at high returns at high risk.

Going concern In accounting, description of a sound enterprise that will continue to operate for the foreseeable future and therefore all assets are shown at cost and not at their breakup value.

Going-rate pricing Method of pricing goods that is based on prices of competing products rather than on SUPPLY AND DEMAND.

Gold standard 1. Monetary system or currency based on the price of gold held in reserve by a country. Almost all countries of the world are now off the gold standard. 2. Ultimate standard of excellence.

Golden handcuffs Financial incentives offered to key executives to persuade them to remain with the firm. Also GOLDEN PARACHUTE.

Golden handshake Compensation for loss of office, including severance pay, made to an executive, especially one who is forced to retire before the expiry of a service contract.

Golden hello Payment made to induce a person to accept employment and sever connections with a prior firm.

Golden parachute Financial benefits promised to executives in the event their employment is terminated, usually as a result of a merger.

Goldilocks economy Ideal economic state, with low inflation, steady growth, and high employment. Term is allusion to the children's story *Goldilocks and the Three Bears*, in which the porridge is not too hot nor too cold, but just right.

Goldratt, Eliyahu Israeli management guru who formulated his THEORY OF CONSTRAINTS.

Goodhart's law Principle developed by economist Charles Goodhart that the validity of an economic law is in inverse relationship to its general acceptance. Thus, the value of a specific variable as an indicator of economic activity decreases when it becomes a target of study. Formerly applied to when the money supply is used as a measure of economic growth.

Goodwill Intangible asset built up by a business over the years, reflecting customers' trust and confidence in the products and the company's reputation for fair dealings.

Gopertz curve Name for the curved line on a graph tracing the actual or potential sales of a new product over time, showing discrete stages of growth, plateau, and decline.

Gozinto chart Graphic illustration of how complete assemblies are built and the sequence of the assembly.

Grade creep Tendency in a corporate hierarchy with grades distinguishing levels of positions and functions to move those classifications upward to allow for increases in pay.

Graduate Management Admission Test (GMAT) Standardized test used by business schools to determine admission to graduate business programs.

Gramm-Leach-Billey Act 1999 Financial Services Modernization Act, which removed restrictions on banks entering the securities and investment markets that had been imposed by the GLASS-STEAGALL ACT of 1933. This act empowered the banks to set up holding companies to supply banking, insurance, and investment services.

Grandfathered in Transactions or activities permissible to those already engaged, or completed in the past, that are now prohibited to newcomers.

Grapevine Word-of-mouth form of communication, often characterized by rumor and unconfirmed reports.

Graphology Study of handwriting as an indicator of character, personality, work habits, and performance.

Graveyard market An extreme form of bear market ruled by fear on the part of both buyers and sellers.

Graveyard shift Nighttime work shift, usually from midnight to dawn.

Great man theory In business, the belief that every corporation owes its existence or preeminence to a single leader, who was instrumental in its success.

Green currencies Currencies of members of the EUROPEAN UNION using artificial rates of exchange for the purpose of a common agricultural policy, which serves as insurance against wide variations in rates.

Green marketing Sales of ecologically safe, recyclable, and biodegradable products, known as *green products*, targeting environmentally friendly consumers.

Greenmailing Purchase of a large bloc of shares in a company to be sold back to the company at a premium over the market value in return for a promise not to launch a takeover bid.

Greenshoe Option given by an issuer of

securities to an underwriter, guaranteeing the latter's right to buy and sell extra shares if there is a high initial demand.

Greenwash In public relations, accentuating the pro-environment policies and programs of a company to gain the accolade of an environmentally concerned community.

Gray-collar Worker who is neither BLUE COLLAR nor WHITE COLLAR.

Gray economy Informal economy comprising unpaid workers whose profits are not reflected in the national accounts. Most home-care workers are in the gray economy.

Gray knight In takeover battles, this is a bidder whose intentions are undeclared, unlike the WHITE KNIGHT, whose advances are welcomed and the BLACK KNIGHT, who is considered hostile.

Gray market 1. Legal market for goods in short supply. 2. Market for goods and services for senior citizens.

Gray wave Company with good long-term prospects but unlikely to be profitable in the near future.

Green card In the United States, a card issued to resident aliens granting them permanent resident status, thereby eligible to work and to apply for citizenship.

Gresham's law Principle that bad money drives out the good, developed by Sir Thomas Gresham, a financier.

Gross domestic product (GDP) Leading economic indicator, showing the total value of business activity—production, investment, services, and property—within a nation.

Gross national disproduct (GND) Total of all social costs and reductions in existing benefits incurred in producing the GROSS NATIONAL PRODUCT, such as pollution.

Gross national product (GNP) Leading economic indicator that adds the GROSS DOMESTIC PRODUCT to the total value of national income emanating from outside the nation.

Group In business, two or more companies in which one company (the parent) holds more than 50% of the shares of the other (the SUBSIDIARY).

Group decision making Participatory process in which several individuals act collectively to arrive at decisions, evaluate options, and select the appropriate course of action.

Group discussion In marketing, a meeting of between six and eight respondents who discuss a marketing problem under the guidance of an interviewer.

Group dynamics Study of organizational behavior within groups and the interactions of individuals within groups, especially as it applies to corporate functioning. It studies how groups form based on common interests, as well as the types of groups—such as task groups, status groups, age groups, gender groups, cultural and ethnic groups—and group cohesiveness.

Group norm Behavior expected of members of a group working as a team, especially in terms of productivity.

Group role Set of behavior patterns expected by members of a professional corps, partly in response to the expectations of others.

Group technology Arrangement of machines in batch production in which all machines that make a particular product are grouped together.

Group of 20 Major economies of the world represented by the EUROPEAN UNION, China, India, Brazil, Mexico, Australia, the United States, Canada, and others. They account for 80% of the GGP (gross global product) 80% of the world trade, and two-thirds of the global population. They meet annually.

Groupism Japanese business philosophy that puts the interests of the group above those of the individuals who constitute the group.

Groupo In Mexico, a family-owned conglomerate.

Groupthink Tendency of members in a group to adopt homogeneous views and opinions, partly in deference to peer pressure and partly in an effort to get along with others.

Growth In business, relating to or contributing to an increase or expansion, as in growth curve, growth rate, and growth stocks.

Guanxi In China, a relationship in a business and professional context, and a network that develops through such relationships.

Guaranteed annual wage Plan whereby an employer agrees to provide the employees a specified minimum amount of employment or income yearly.

Guerrilla marketing Surreptitious marketing designed to ruin a competitor and reduce its market share.

Guest worker Foreigner allowed into a country on a temporary visa, permitted to join the workforce as a way of meeting labor shortages.

GUI Government-university-industry partnership.

Gun jumping Insider trading.

Guru Expert in some particular area, consulted as a problem solver; similar to a *pundit*.

Habitual buying behavior Pattern of consumer purchases done out of habit or inertia, and not as deliberate choices or after study of product information.

Hackman-Oldham job-enrichment model Assessment of employee relations, guided by certain job characteristics that enhance personal satisfaction and work outcomes.

Halal Acceptable under Islamic law, especially in regard to injunctions against usury and applied to banking.

Halo effect In social psychology, the result of one dominant characteristic creating a favorable impression among associates. Compare HORN EFFECT.

Halsey, Frederick A. (1856–1935) Engineer and economist, father of the HALSEY-WEIR INCENTIVE SCHEME, by which incentives are introduced based on past production records. This was a revolutionary idea at the time, and was supported by the American Society of Mechanical Engineers.

Halsey-Weir incentive scheme Program whereby incentive bonuses are paid when production targets are exceeded, but not necessarily in proportion to the increase in production.

Hamel, Gary Management expert who introduced the concept of core competencies, and who stressed the need for strategizing as an ongoing, radical, and inclusive process for shattering assumptions about corporate governance.

Hammer, Michael Management consultant, co-author with James Champy of the book *Reengineering the Corporation* (1993).

Handy, Charles Management consultant known for his work on management structures and the future of work. Among the concepts that he has introduced are SHAMROCK ORGANIZATION, FEDERAL ORGANIZATION, DOUGHNUT PRINCIPLE, and *portfolio working*. Author of the book *Understanding Organizations* (1976).

Hang Seng index Arithmetically weighted index based on the capital value of selected stocks on the Hong Kong Stock Exchange.

Haram Forbidden under Islamic law, especially as relating to banking and the charging of interest on loans.

Hard-core unemployed Segment of the labor-age population that is willing to work but cannot find jobs.

Hard currency Money that is easily convertible into other currencies, such as the U.S. dollar and the pound sterling.

Hard landing Sustained period of economic growth that ends with the economy nosediving into a RECESSION.

Harrad Domar model Standard developmental model for economic growth, developed by Sir Roy Harrod in 1939 and Evsey Domar in 1946.

Harriman Forbidden under Islamic law, especially as relating to banking and the charging of interest on loans.

Harrington, H. James Author and consultant in the field of process improvement. His books include *The Improvement Process* (1997) and *High Performance Benchmarking* (1996).

Harsanyi, John Hungarian-Australian-American economist and winner of the Nobel Prize in Economics in 1994. He is best known for his contributions to the study of GAME THEORY and its application to economics, especially for his developing the highly innovative Bayesian Games, which are based on incomplete information. He

also contributed to the study of equilibrium selection.

Harvard case method Teaching technique developed at Harvard Business School, in which students learn business operations by examining case studies.

Harvesting strategy Technique for making a short-term profit from a product before reducing the marketing support, such as advertising, and withdrawing it from the market.

Harvey, Jerry B. Professor Emeritus of Management at George Washington University. His research dealt with the ethical and moral issues of organization. He published two books: *The Abilene Paradox and Other Meditations on Management* and *How Come Every Time I Get Stabbed in the Back, My Fingerprints Are on the Knife?*

Hawthorne effect Improvement in worker performance as a result of supervision and observation, more than from external or environmental factors. This was a conclusion of the HAWTHORNE STUDY.

Hawthorne study Research conducted at the Western Electric Company's Hawthorne plant in Chicago in the 1920s and 1930s, which formed the basis for modern industrial human relations. Its principal conclusion is known as the HAWTHORNE EFFECT. The study explored the effects and benefits of the physical environment on productivity, and discovered that workers' positive perceptions of a company's labor-friendly attitudes were more consequential in raising productivity than were actual reforms in the manufacturing process.

Hay method Job evaluation system based on three core factors: know-how, problem solving, and accountability, developed by the Philadelphia-based Hay Group.

Hayek, Friedrich August von (1899–1992) Austrian-British economist best known as a defender of classical liberalism. He is one of the major political philosophers of the 20th century. In 1974 he shared the Nobel Prize in Economic Sciences with Gunnar Myrdal for his "pioneering work in the theory of money and economic fluctuations and penetrating analysis of the interdependence of economic, social, and institutional phenomena." His classic work was *The Road to Serfdom*.

Hayes, Robert H. (1936–) Professor at Harvard Business School. Author *of Restoring our Competitive Edge: Competing Through Manufacturing* (1984).

Headcount In business, the number of employees in an organization.

Headhunter An employment agency or its representative that specializes in recruiting executives.

Heavy-half theory In marketing, the idea that half the customer base for a product is responsible for 80% of its purchases.

Hedge Financial transaction designed to mitigate the risk of other, related transactions. For example, the purchase of a large quantity of securities or raw materials can be hedged by insuring against the risk of their failure through purchase of a FUTURES contract.

Hedge fund Speculative, largely unregulated fund that provides very high returns. Typically these are mutual funds or partnerships that exploit market anomalies to make substantial gains. They accept only investors with large portfolios and many are domiciled in offshore tax havens.

Helgeson, Sally Business consultant and author whose book *The Female Advantage* (1990) studied female management styles and examined the effects of changing technology, demographics, and the knowledge economy on leadership patterns.

Helicopter factor Influence of leadership that views a whole field in a panoptic or stereoscopic fashion, rather than in narrow segments, and thus gains a broad perspective on an operation.

Henderson, Bruce Australian-born founder of the Boston Consulting Group, responsible for introducing the terms BOSTON MATRIX (*Boston box*) and EXPERIENCE CURVE.

Herding cats Description of managing a disparate group of people with conflicting interests and values.

Herfindahl index In marketing, a tool to measure the degree of competition in a particular industry, examining the proportion of market shares of all known players. The index reflects the distribution of those market shares, giving weight to the largest players, and is thus a better measure than CONCENTRATION RATIOS.

Herstatt risk Potential that a transaction may not be settled as expected and that the party may renege on its obligations. Named after the Herstatt Bank failure in 1974. Also termed *counter-party risk*.

Herzberg, Frederick Irving (1923–2000) American psychologist, noted for introducing the concept of job enrichment and the motivator-hygiene theory, also known as the two-factor theory. His 1968 article "One More Time: How do you Motivate Employees? in *Harvard Business Review* sold millions of reprints.

Herzberg's two-factor theory Explanation of employee motivation, introduced by early work theorist FREDERICK HERZBERG and covering the quality of supervision, job security, remuneration, and physical working conditions, whose absence may cause dissatisfaction but whose presence may not create satisfaction. Herzberg divided motivational factors into two classes: motivators (or satisfiers) and dissatisfiers (or hygiene factors). The latter, though not motivators in themselves, cause dissatisfaction if absent.

Hesiflation State of reduced growth in the economy, combined with strong inflationary pressures; term coined by Henry Fowler, Secretary of the Treasury during the Eisenhower administration.

Heuristics Problem-solving techniques that help managers arrive at solutions through experimentation, trial and error, and evaluation.

Hidden unemployed People who, though unemployed, do not appear in government statistics. This group includes workers who are chronically unemployed, those who have stopped looking for work and no longer qualify for unemployment benefits, and the long-term unemployed who have opted out of the labor market.

Hidden persuader Motivational and manipulative technique used in advertising; term popularized by popular writer VANCE PACKARD.

Hierarchy of effects In marketing, measurement of the impact of advertising and promotion on a target audience, progressing from awareness to action.

Hierarchy of needs See MASLOW'S MOTIVATIONAL HIERARCHY.

Hierarchy of objectives Taxonomy of corporate objectives, proceeding from short term through intermediate to long term.

High-contact culture In international business, a society in which it is acceptable to have physical contact, such as hugging, in public.

High-context culture In international business, a society in which feelings or emotions are not openly expressed. Verbal communication can be understood only within the cultural context and their meaning is tied to its cultural nuances.

High-involvement management Approach to management that encourages employee participation in decision making, training, incentives, and sharing of information as a means of cementing loyalty to the company.

High-involvement product Consumer product that is not purchased lightly or offhand, but only after considerable deliberation and comparative shopping, and thus the purchase represents an informed and deliberate choice.

Hirano, Horoyuki *See* FiveS Method-ology.

Hired gun In business, an outside consultant or adviser who proffers advice during crises.

Histogram Graphical display of data using bars of different heights.

Historical cost In finance, the value of a unit of stock or other asset calculated on the basis of its original cost, rather than in terms of current dollars after Inflation.

Historical cost accounting Bookkeeping system in which assets are valued at their original cost rather than in current dollars after Inflation. Inflation often makes this type of accounting misleading, but it is fairly objective and difficult to manipulate or inflate.

Hockey-stick growth Very rapid, expo-nential growth of a company, in which the trajectory resembles a hockey stick.

Hofstadter, Douglas Richard (1945–) American expert in cognitive sciences whose book, *Godel, Escher, Bach: An Eternal Golden Braid*, won the Pulitzer Prize in non-fiction in 1979.

Hofstadter's law Formulated by cognitive scientist Douglas Hofstadter, the observation that everything takes longer than planned, and that planning must always take into account delays and roadblocks that will lengthen the time for completion.

Hofstede, Geert Dutch business executive and consultant who investigated the interaction between culture and business in transnational settings.

Holding company Parent company that holds shares in other companies without necessarily managing them. Holding companies have a distinctive management structure, made up of the CEOs of the subsidiaries. In some cases, subsidiaries of holding companies have considerable autonomy, although their operations are subject to tight financial control. Traditionally, holding companies are unstable because the companies acquired through diversification often have dissimilar corporate cultures and different operating procedures. Often, there is little strategic fit between the acquirer and the acquired. But as the two are integrated, new priorities emerge, as do new structures. Holding companies often exist for legal and fiscal reasons, as well as to cushion the tax burden.

Holding pattern Undesirable human relations situation where an employee is in limbo after return from an overseas assignment.

Holdout In finance, a creditor who refuses to renegotiate with a firm in financial distress, holding out in the hope of getting better terms.

Holism Philosophy that the whole is greater than the sum of its parts and that therefore an organism needs to be judged in totality. In business, a *holistic brand* is one that is seen to be emblematic of an entire company or corporation.

Holistic evaluation Assessment of a plan or project not simply on its economic merits but also on its impact upon all human and environmental elements.

Home run In business, an excellent or memorable performance.

Homoffice Blended term for *home office*.

Hooper rating Percentage of people listening to a radio program or station; similar to Nielsen ratings.

Horizontal communication Communication between employees at the same hierarchic level. Distinguished from UPWARD COMMUNICATION and DOWNWARD COMMUNICATION.

Horizontal integration Meshing of marketing or production departments handling products or services with comparable consumer bases.

Horizontal structure Organizational operation primarily formed around a small number of core processes or work flows linking the activities of employees to the needs of suppliers and customers. The work is performed by teams rather than individuals, and while still hierarchical, it is flatter than a traditional organization. In a horizontal structure, the focus of decisions and resource allocation is on continuous performance improvement. Information and training occur on a JUST-IN-TIME basis rather than on need to know, and career progression is within the process rather than by function, making the individuals generalists rather than specialists. Compensation is based on team performance.

The four key quantitative performance indicators are based on customer need and are tied to work flow. These indicators are order generation and fulfillment, new product development, integrated logistics, and branch management. Cross-functional teams are created based on work flow and not individual tasks, and these are connected both upstream and downstream. A team leader is appointed, and everyone involved receives an assignment, with measurement systems set up. Leadership is important but so are teams that own the processes. Hierarchy is also important, but the teams constitute the rungs of the ladder. Work teams are self-managed and empowered; as problems develop, decisions are made quickly and action is taken in real time, without interrupting work flow. DELAYERING is used to combine related but formerly fragmented tasks, eliminating activities that do not add value or contribute to corporate goals. The work is driven by a desire to achieve customer value and product improvement, rather than shareholder value.

Horn effect Carryover results of a negative first impression of a person, especially a candidate for employment, affecting later judgment during an interview. See also HALO EFFECT.

Hoshin planning (Japanese for "compass needle") Japanese management strategy by which organizational goals are deployed throughout an organization and consist of five elements: vision, targets, planning, execution, and audits.

Hostile bid Takeover bid for control of a company, made against the wishes of the board of directors or its shareholders.

Hot desking Working without ˍˍe's own desk in an office; instead, using the desks of other employees who are away on assignments. As a result of increased technology and greater mobility of personnel, the definition of an office as a desk and a chair is being displaced by that of a peripatetic situation, or wherever the employee is working at the time. Support services can be transferred easily, and all communication devices can be mobile. Formerly, the corner office was looked upon as a status symbol, but status now goes wherever the employee goes.

Hot money In finance, money that moves at short notice from one financial instrument to another, in the hope of gaining more interest or avoiding political instability.

Hot stove In human resources, disciplinary action that is immediate, consistent, impersonal, and swift—similar to the effects of a person touching a hot stove.

Hotelling, Harold (1895–1973) American mathematician and economic theorist. He served as Professor of Mathematical Statistics at the University of North Carolina at Chapel Hill. He played a prominent role in the development of mathematical economics. A number of theories and principles in this field bear his name: Hotelling's T-Square Distribution, Hotelling's Law, Hotelling's Lemma, and HOTELLING'S RULE. He made pioneering studies in nonconvexity in economics associated with market failures.

Hotelling's rule In environmental economics, the principle that the satisfactory rate of depletion of nonrenewable resources is achieved when the extraction costs rise at ˍˍ same rate as the interest rate. Developed ˍˍ ˍnomist HAROLD HOTELLING in his 19ˍˍ paper on the subject.

House of quality Planning tool that brings engineers and customers together in the design process and that integrates customer needs into the design and development cycle.

Howard Sheth model Category of consumer behavior that illustrates the influence of advertising and promotion, developed by market research experts John A. Howard and Jagdish N. Sheth.

HRM HUMAN RESOURCE
MANAGEMENT

Hub and spoke Organizational model resembling the hub and spoke of a wheel, in which the subordinates form the spokes and the supervisor or manager is at the center.

Human asset accounting Measurement of the value of a company's personnel and their expertise, applied to accounting as are other physical assets.

Human capital Coined by economist and sociologist GARY BECKER, a term that denotes the general or specific skills acquired by a worker in the course of training or on the job. It characterizes wages as a return on human capital invested in work.

Human engineering See ERGONOMICS.

Human information processing Cognitive action in which thought, memory, interpretation, and decision making convert information into usable ideas.

Human relations school School of industrial sociology associated with Australian psychologist and sociologist ELTON MAYO, which sees better relationships between management and workers as the key to greater productivity. The role of management is, therefore, supportive and not directive.

Human relations theory Management philosophy that studies the role of non-work-related factors in motivating employees, such as professional pride, self-actualization, sense of belonging, and quest for achievement. Leadership styles, attitudes, and relationships can influence these factors.

Human resource accounting Theoretical approach to quantifying the contribution of HUMAN CAPITAL, showing it on the assets side of the balance sheet.

Human resource management Direction of the activities of employees with a view to maximizing their potential and professional participation in achieving corporate goals and targets. Also termed PERSONNEL MANAGEMENT.

Hurdle rate Minimum acceptable return on a project or development.

Hygiene factor See HERTZBERG'S TWO-FACTOR THEORY.

Hyperinflation Condition of economic RECESSION during which money loses so much value as to become useless and the monetary system breaks down to be replaced by barter, as occurred in the Weimar Republic in the 1920s.

Hypothecation 1. Authority given to a banker to sell goods pledged as security for a loan. 2. Dedication of a tax to meet a specific need or obligation, as in taxes on cigarette sales that are channeled into healthcare.

IAS INTERNATIONAL ACCOUNTING STANDARDS

Icarus factor Tendency of leaders to embark upon grandiose projects to stoke their own ego, only to fail; after the story of Icarus in Greek mythology.

ICE Involuntary career event, a euphemism for dismissal.

Idea hamster Person with a seemingly endless supply of new ideas.

Idea generation Systematic search for new product ideas in the marketplace.

Idea screening Systematic review of new products to determine their viability and market potential.

Identity management Creation and promotion of a corporate or brand identity so as to present a positive image to consumers and hide negative features or developments.

Identity theft Crime of stealing another person's identity and financial information for personal gain.

Ideogram Graphic symbol that represents an idea or concept. Thus, ideographic.

IFRS International financial reporting standard.

Illegal contract Agreement prohibited by law, especially when it promotes an illegal or tainted activity or is drawn up for illegal purposes. It is considered void and its terms are not actionable.

Illth From 19th-century British critic John Ruskin, the opposite of wealth in terms of well-being. Today, products or things that are harmful.

Imaginization Blend of the words *imagination* and *organization,* the generation of new perspectives and ways of understanding complex situations, and the interaction between capability and reality. Also, *imaginer,* a person who integrates creative ideas with the practical and possible.

IMF INTERNATIONAL MONETARY FUND

Immediate holding company Company with a controlling interest in another company, although it itself is controlled by a third company.

Impact In marketing, the total measurable effect of an action or product on a market, group, or person.

Imperfect competition Situation in which buyers or sellers have the right to alter prices, and where prices and supply are not subject to normal market forces.

Imperfect market Situation in which there are constraints on market freedom, such as barriers to entry or a paucity of sellers or buyers.

Impersonality Style of management that is mechanical and devoid of human interest.

Implied term Provision of a contract not spelled out explicitly but regarded as crucial by statute, and therefore implied.

Import substitution Manufacturing that produces products currently being imported. The action is designed to make a country self-sufficient.

Impression management Control of how a person makes an impression on others, especially to advance personal interests.

Improshare Productivity payment system developed by Mitchell Fein, in which employees are paid a cash bonus based on a percentage of their pay.

Improvement curve Graph showing the rate at which the quality of a product or activity improves in response to changes and innovations. Also Experience curve.

Impulse buy Purchase of a product without serious forethought and as a result of the product's emotional appeal and apparent need-fulfillment.

Imputed cost Expense not actually incurred, but introduced at the accounting stage to make pricing comparable with similar products.

In the black State of being profitable; from the black color used on the positive side of a bookkeeping ledger; opposite of In the red.

In the red State of being unprofitable; from the red color used on the negative side of a bookkeeping ledger; opposite of In the black.

In-basket training Method of training by which employees are given routine business correspondence and papers and are asked to handle them.

Incentive Inducement or reward that motivates a person to do something. Rewards may be in the form of bonuses, share options, health benefits, gym memberships, tickets to sports events, and awards or other forms of public recognition.

Incentive-compatible contract Agreement designed to ensure mutually beneficial behavior by both parties.

Incestuous In business, descriptive of transactions between related companies designed to evade regulations.

Inchoate instrument Negotiable instrument in which certain clauses and particulars are omitted.

Incidence of taxation Impact of a tax on those who ultimately share the burden, rather than on those who are nominally the taxee.

Incident process Case study in which participants collect further information at given stages and refine their responses based on the new information.

Income 1. Flow of money to an individual, group, or corporation over a course of time. 2. Sum of money earned by a person or organization as a salary or as profit, rent, or interest.

Income distribution Division of earned money across segments of a population.

Income effect Result in amount of purchasing power caused by changes in personal income.

Income redistribution Use of taxation as a means of adjusting the distribution of wealth across segments of a population. When redistribution is downward, it is generally viewed as a corrective social policy and sometimes includes a PROGRESSIVE TAX and various forms of income subsidies. When redistribution is upward, it is termed

TRICKLE-DOWN ECONOMICS and thought to yield economic growth.

Income smoothing Manipulation and creative corporate accounting involving certain items in financial statements to hide large movements in profits by spreading them over a number of years.

Income tax Direct tax on individual income. It has an exemption threshold, after which the rate often rises progressively in relation to the size of the income and the number of exemptions.

Income velocity of money Average number of times a currency, such as the dollar, is spent in purchasing goods and services.

Incomes policy State policy aimed at controlling inflation and maintaining full employment by holding down wages, prices, and income and by adjusting interest rates.

Increasing returns Situation in which greater input of resources leads directly to a proportionately larger increase in output.

Incremental cost of capital Overall cost of raising money. It reflects the combined costs of borrowing, market expectations, and related risks.

Incremental innovation Process of making continuous but small improvements to a product or service, as in the Japanese system of KAIZEN.

Incremental learning Education that takes

place in orderly steps, rather than through sudden revelation; opposite of INSIGHT LEARNING.

Incremental pricing Two-tier pricing system, one tier covering the full cost of producing a product and the other including the marginal cost of further production.

Incrementalism Management approach of considering a number of alternatives and then testing them by implementing them one at a time.

Incubation Period of time for fledgling industries and start-up companies during which they test their viability and create and test new products.

Indemnity Sum to be paid by one party of a contract to make good on losses suffered by the other party as a result of actions or a failure to act or from negligence, loss, damage, or intentional deception.

Independent demand Situation in which market demand is independent of the production schedule and can be affected by variables over which the manufacturer has no control.

Index Forecasting technique that links the amount of change to the pace of change, with a certain base period as the norm, thus showing trends over time.

Index fund Passive fund management such as the S&P 500. It is a mutual fund with a portfolio constructed to match a standard market index. It provides broad market exposure, low operating expenses, and low portfolio turnover.

Indexation Act of linking such economic variables as wages, taxes, annuities, and pensions to the COST OF LIVING INDEX as a means of mitigating the effects of INFLATION. In practice, indexation favors borrowers over lenders and savers.

Indicative planning Using a broad consultative process, this is planning that seeks agreement from all affected parties.

Indicator Measurable variable that has proven a reliable clue to performance or potential. Indicators are used in economics, psychology, and statistics. Macroeconomic indicators include the money supply, prices, income, exports, and imports.

Indifference curve Graphic representation linking the benefits to the risk of any venture. At any given point in the curve, the benefits are available only if the risk is taken.

Indirect costs Overhead that is not directly assignable to a product or service. In accounting, such costs are generally assigned to various centers of production.

Indirect demand Need for an unfinished product that is a component of another product.

Indirect discrimination De facto discrimination that results from meeting certain regulations and working conditions, such as frequent transfers that handicap married couples.

Indirect labor Workers not covered by an employment contract but who are employed by contractors for the duration of a project.

Indirect taxation Taxation of persons or organizations that is transferred or passed through to others, such as customers.

Individual retirement account (IRA) Pension plan for individuals that allows a set amount of nontaxable income to be set aside annually and that accumulates in a fund that pays interest when the funds are withdrawn at retirement, at which point the income taxes are also paid.

Industrial action Coordinated effort by an industrial union to force an employer to settle a labor dispute by threatening any of several means, including strike, work-to-rule, go-slow, and sit-down.

Industrial democracy Introduction of democratic principles of governance in an organizational setting. This includes worker participation in management decision making, representation on corporate boards, profit sharing, and worker councils that resolve industrial disputes and grievances.

Industrial disease Occupational-related health problem prevalent in certain professions, such as miners and construction workers.

Industrial dispute Labor disagreement regarding wages, terms of employment, or benefits.

Industrial dynamics Introduced by systems scientist JAY FORRESTER, a concept used to describe the behavior of industrial systems and to demonstrate how interrelated policies, decisions, structures, and delays influence growth and stability.

Industrial engineering 1. Applied science concerned with the planning and improvement of operational efficiency and quality. 2. Application of work-study techniques and the laws of physics, medicine, anatomy, and psychology to create ideal mechanisms, tools, and machinery on the floor of the workshop as a part of TOTAL QUALITY MANAGEMENT.

Industrial espionage Use of spies and spying devices to gain access to trade secrets so as to gain competitive advantage.

Industrial medicine Healthcare methods provided by employers for their employees, including occupational safety and improvements in the work environment that reduce stress. Also includes routine physical checkups and encouragement of physical activity.

Industrial organization economics Branch of MICROECONOMICS that studies the strategic behavior of firms in a state of imperfect competition. It explores the different approaches of industrialists and how markets behave under conditions of MONOPOLY, OLIGOPOLY, and MONOPOLISTIC COMPETITION and their competing strategies in areas such as pricing, production, marketing, and advertising. It also studies the effects of government regulations on market forces and is influenced by GAME THEORY and BEHAVIORAL FINANCE.

Industrial park Site established for selected types of factories and industrial plants with some common facilities, usually as part of a development strategy.

Industrial psychology Application of psychological principles and concepts to the study of business problems, especially recruitment and training of employees, decision making, leadership, and worker welfare and motivation. Also termed *organizational psychology.*

Industrial relations Linkage between labor and capital, represented by management in the conduct and evolution of productive sectors of the economy. It governs the environment in which products are manufactured or built and the climate of goodwill or ill feeling generated as a result of actions by the workforce or management.

Industrial revolution Transformation of the economy from one based largely on agricultural production and farm labor to the production of consumer goods and manufacturing by machines that began in England in the late 18th century and has spread around the world.

Industrial sabotage Actions by workers engaged in a dispute with management that deliberately delays or destroys production.

Industrial sociology Study of social relationships in the light of industrial development and the effect that industry has on society, and vice versa.

Industrial tribunal Court that decides labor disputes, employment conflicts, discrimination cases, and pay disputes; the court has mandatory jurisdiction.

Industrialization Process of transition from an agricultural economy to one based on manufacturing, which began with the industrial revolution in Great Britain.

Industry 1. Organized activity toward a goal. 2. A sector or organization in which labor and management work together to produce goods. 3. A group of companies engaged in similar production activities.

Industry structure Way in which a discrete industrial sector is organized in terms of its opportunities or barriers to entry, degree of competition, infrastructure (suppliers, importers, and exporters), types of needs the produced goods meet, and the labor force and skills needed to produce those goods.

Inertial marketing Reliance on consumer inertia to continue the sale of products, with no active canvassing for customer loyalty. For example, book clubs that send books monthly to customers unless they cancel the order.

Infant industry Fledgling group of companies that needs government tariff protection to enable it to survive foreign competition.

Inflation Economic period in which prices and interest rates rise, accompanied by lower purchasing power and fallen value of money. Varying in degree, inflation when severe often leads to a dysfunctional market or economic collapse.

Inflationary bias Tendency of a market to focus on INFLATION for political reasons, forcing policymakers to adopt ad hoc measures not sanctioned in traditional economic thinking.

Inflationary gap Difference between the amount of public and private spending in an economy and the spending required to sustain full employment.

Inflationary spiral Repeated periods of INFLATION fueled by wage and price increases, which in turn lead to further inflation.

Inflation targeting Monetary policy that sets a target rate of inflation in the medium term, as measured by an index, and then uses various means to achieve this rate.

Inflection point Stage at which important organizational changes take place in a company.

Infobahn Another name for the information superhighway, patterned on Germany's *Autobahn.*

Infomediary Intermediary business whose income derives from supplying businesses with detailed profiles of consumer groups that have been developed from market studies.

Infomercial Television commercial of more than 30 minutes that simulates regular television programming but is actually promoting a product or service.

Informal communication Exchanges of information via rumor and the grapevine, as well as casual office conversation.

Informal economy Underground economy run by unlicensed businesses and conducted largely OFF THE BOOKS.

Informal organization Casual group within an organization that conducts its activities largely through informal and unrecorded communications, such as the grapevine and outside the formal hierarchy.

Information acceleration Virtual reality system that simulates a real-life buying environment to study how consumers make purchasing decisions, measuring their preferences, intentions, and perceptions.

Information age General term for the period beginning at the end of World War II and continuing into the present. The period is marked by the increasing proliferation of information resources and communication technology and the emergence of information as a commodity, albeit a nonmaterial one.

Information industry Sector of the economy in advanced societies that assembles and communicates information as a basic resource for innovation and change. Also termed *knowledge industry.*

Information management Executive control of the flow of accurate information to all those entitled to it, and also provision of disinformation to those who would use it for negative purposes.

Information overload Situation in which the amount of information in a pipeline is more than can be easily absorbed, controlled, or processed, thus creating bottlenecks.

Information revolution Big change in the creation, use, and transfer of information, marked by the speed and volume of information flows.

Information technology (IT) Processing and distribution of information electronically, through satellite links, telephone lines, and cellular networks. In addition to communication channels, IT enables the electronic transfer of funds, automated trading in stocks, and online sales such as Ebay. By substituting labor, IT helps reduce the cost of operations and time, while increasing efficiency. It has become so powerful that it is the principal managerial and decision-making tool, integrated throughout business activities both horizontally and vertically and linking customers, managers, and suppliers. IT helps to streamline operations in the factory as well as in distribution. It allows entire layers of management to be deleted from the hierarchy. Intercompany and international transactions are also handled by IT, virtually abolishing geographic borders and time zones, and accelerates cross-border flow of goods and services.

Infrastructure Complex of facilities, physical installations, and public works that undergird a nation's economy, especially industry. These include roads, electric grid, railways, airports, and communications networks.

Initial public offering (IPO) Process by which a private firm sells shares of stock to the public for the first time. It is a rite of passage that marks an important phase of corporate growth, as well as providing access to public capital markets, enhancing the company's visibility, and establishing its credit rating. The process is overseen by the U.S. Securities and Exchange Commission, which has rigorous registration procedures, including audit. IPOs are usually handled by large investment banks, which sometimes share the risk.

Innovation New approach or breakthrough in design or structure, or new idea that adds value to a product or makes its production simpler and faster. Innovation is an organizational enhancement that can be used within an existing process, distinguished from *invention*, which represents a radical concept that has not been done before.

Innovation-intensive industry Industrial sector such as electronics or biotechnology, which depends on continuous innovation to sustain its growth.

Innovation management Stimulation of creative technology, leading to the discovery of new products with commercial potential.

Innovative efficiency Efficiency in creative

and proactive marketing, which anticipates needs and offers products that best meet those needs.

Inorganic growth In business, the expansion of a business from takeovers and mergers, rather than from internal innovations.

Input-output analysis Set of marketing statistics that analyze patterns of buying and selling, so as to establish patterns and trends over time.

In-service training Training of staff during working hours by their associates or supervisors, using informal training methods.

Inside director Employee of a company who is named to the board of directors.

Insider trading Dealing in securities by using price-sensitive information not available to outsiders. It is a prosecutable offense under U.S. Securities and Exchange Commission rules.

Insight learning Form of education that relies on sudden bursts of understanding, rather than gradually through study and analysis of data. Opposite of INCREMENTAL LEARNING.

Insolvency Inability to pay one's debts or meet financial obligations, preliminary to BANKRUPTCY or LIQUIDATION.

Insourcing Use of in-house personnel to execute specific jobs, rather than outsourcing them to external providers or foreign suppliers.

Institutional investor Large organizations, as distinguished from private individuals, such as pension funds, endowments, or labor unions. They generally employ their own investment advisers and because of their size, are able to influence market trends and share prices.

In-store promotion Sales offer within the premises of a retail store, advertised through signs and posters.

Insurance Contract that guarantees a stipulated party against a known peril or risk, in return for a premium. Distinguished from ASSURANCE, which is a guarantee against an event that is certain to take place at some time (such as death).

Intangible asset Something of value that has no physical existence, such as goodwill, copyright, patent, or trademark.

Integration Merger of two companies or systems and a pooling of resources for the purpose of reducing competition, capturing a larger market share, cooperating on research and development, and/or combining physical facilities In HORIZONTAL (lateral) INTEGRATION, businesses that produce the same products and services combine forces to create a near MONOPOLY. In VERTICAL INTEGRATION, a company obtains control of its suppliers (BACKWARD INTEGRATION) or its buyers (FORWARD INTEGRATION).

Integrative bargaining Negotiation with a view not of gaining absolute advantage and victory at all costs but of arriving at a win-win settlement in which both sides gain something.

Integrative growth Expansion of a firm's operation through acquisition of its suppliers, customers, or competitors.

Intellectual capital Knowledge and know-how, information systems, brand names, reputation, and related intangible assets. It is an amalgam of HUMAN CAPITAL (competencies, expert knowledge, and experience), STRUCTURAL CAPITAL (IT, communications technology, and databases) and RELATIONAL CAPITAL (customer bases, brands, trademarks, and reputation). Often, in the case of companies like Google or Microsoft, the intellectual capital may be four or five times the market capitalization or value of physical assets.

Intellectual property Intangible assets of a company, including copyrights, trademarks, patents, trade secrets, inventions, and computer programs, which are protected by law against piracy or misuse. Intellectual property may be licensed in return for appropriate royalties.

Intensive distribution Strategy for distributing consumer products, aimed at obtaining maximum exposure at as many retail outlets as possible.

Interactive communication Two-way computer system that allows the viewer to respond to prompts or questions and thus encourages respondent participation.

Interactive planning Forethought that en-

visions a desirable future and then marshals the resources to achieve it within a given time frame.

Interdependence Condition of co-dependence, mutual assistance, or reciprocal reliance, essential for growth and survival.

Interest In finance, the cost of borrowing money, usually expressed in a percentage per annum. Interest may be simple or compounded. Rates of interest are set by the lending institutions, based on the current money supply, economic regulations, the demand for money, risk of default, and period of the loan. In Islamic banking systems, interest is prohibited but the ban is usually circumvented.

Interest rate Amount charged for a loan of money, usually expressed as a percentage on an annualized basis. INTEREST-RATE FUTURES guarantee protection against adverse movement of interest rates and higher costs of borrowing.

Interest-rate future Financial derivative such as a futures contract with an interest-bearing instrument as its asset. They are used to hedge against the risk that interest rates will move high.

Interest-rate risk Potential risk associated with or resulting from volatility in interest rates, especially when bank loans are tied to fixed rates despite rising interest rates generally.

Interests In marketing or human resources, the personal or occupational likes and dislikes of a customer or candidate, as revealed through questionnaires.

Interlocking directorate Complex situation that occurs when some members of boards of directors of related companies hold multiple directorships and have controlling interests in more than one company.

Intermediary Firm in the distribution pipeline that buys and resells goods, or firm that helps manufacturers find customers.

Intermediate goods In manufacturing, goods used as input in a manufacturing process and that do not have an independent status.

Intermediation Role of a bank or other financial institution acting as a go-between in a transaction and taking on some of the associated risk for a fee.

Internal audit Review of accounting that is initiated by a company for reasons other than state regulations. The goal is to ensure that a transaction has not resulted in a breach of protocol and that there has been no theft of property or funds by employees.

Internal control Measures enforced by a company to prevent or minimize fraud and embezzlement and to ensure integrity in intramural affairs. These controls may include the use of more than one signature on documents, security checks, special passwords, and enforcement of professional standards of conduct.

Internal customer Unit, division, or employee that receives products, information, or services from another unit in the same organization, and is treated in the same manner as external customers in terms of communications and billing.

Internal growth Means by which a company tries to expand the scope of its territory and product range. Internal growth is achieved through increased market share at the expense of competitors, new product development, and new applications and markets for existing products. Internal growth is driven by innovation and sensitivity to market needs.

Internal labor market In a large company, the pool of talent that can transfer from one unit to another.

Internal marketing Application of marketing principles to sell ideas and directives to the staff of an organization.

Internal Revenue Service (IRS) Federal revenue collection agency in the United States, concerned primarily with income tax. It is comparable to Inland Revenue in the United Kingdom.

International Accounting Standards (IAS) Any of the accounting standards issued by the International Accounting Standards Committee (IASC), which were supplanted in 2001 by the International Financial Reporting Standards, issued by the International Accounting Standards Board.

International Accounting Standards Board (IASB) Successor to the International

Accounting Standards Committee, an independent, privately funded body that serves as the watchdog for the accounting profession worldwide. Its stated goal is to develop a single set of transparent and comparable protocols and rubrics in financial information and reporting.

International Bank for Reconstruction and Development (IBRD) The full name for what is popularly known as the World Bank, set up by the Breton Woods Conference of 1944 to help governments finance public projects, make loans to governments, and guarantee loans from private banks. The World Bank includes the International Finance Corporation and the International Development Association. Its funds are raised in commercial markets and it makes long-term loans on subcommercial terms. It is owned by the governments of 185 countries but the dominant partner is the United States, which makes all crucial decisions.

International Monetary Fund (IMF) International organization established in 1947 to enhance the convertibility and stability of the international monetary system. The IMF assists any member country that experiences a BALANCE OF PAYMENTS shortfall by supplying its own funds in HARD CURRENCY in return for a small fee. High levels of borrowing are conditioned on the implementation of IMF-devised monetary policies that usually dictate austerity and leaner budgets. The IMF is financed by subscription, and the level of subscription determines the extent of voting rights.

International Securities Exchange Electronic market for securities and securities options, launched in 2000 and comprising a stock exchange, options exchange, and alternative markets platform. It is owned by EUREX.

Interpolation Estimation of the value of an unknown quantity that lies between two known values, as for example the population of an intercensus unit from two broader census figures.

Interpretive research In marketing, analysis of buying consumer behavior against the backdrop of consumer lifestyle.

Interstitial Something that occurs within two cycles or work periods.

Intervention In organizational development, an action that brings about purposeful change.

Intervention price Guaranteed minimum price that triggers government action, such as purchase, usually regarding agricultural products.

Interventionism Managerial philosophy that permits top-level managers to continuously monitor the performance of subordinates and to intervene when necessary.

Interview In human resources, a structured, one-on-one meeting designed to assess a person's suitability for a job, judged by the interviewee's responses to appropriate questions.

Intranet Computer network within a company that can be accessed only by employees using a password.

Intrapreneur Executive or senior manager of a company allowed to launch new initiatives, sharing in both the risk and the profit. These initiatives may, if they are successful, later develop into profit centers for the company.

Intrinsic In human resources, relating to rewards, motivations, or values that originate within a person or group, marked by self-fulfillment.

Intuitive management Supervisory style that calls for flying by the seat of one's pants rather than following methods presented in textbooks and manuals.

Inventory 1. A business's stock or supplies, whether raw materials or finished goods, available on hand or in transit at any given time. Inventory is shown on the balance sheet as CURRENT ASSETS. 2. Total and accumulated resources or materials within an operating system, including those locked up in works in progress. Of these, there are five types of inventory: (1) *anticipatory inventory,* or goods in low demand produced in anticipation of a later spike in demand; (2) *uncoupling inventory,* or raw materials that are moving within the operating system; (3) *buffer inventory,* or materials held in reserve as insurance against variations in supply; (4) *pipeline inventory,* or materials in transit or those locked up in the system; and (5) *cycle inventory,* or the economic or-

der quantity calculated on the basis of the JUST-IN-TIME principle.

Investment Purchase of capital goods or durable assets for the purpose of leveraging them into a profitable enterprise.

Investment analyst Economically savvy person employed as an adviser to study equities to help identify the most profitable stocks and bonds. The analyst uses TECHNICAL ANALYSIS to single out companies that outperform the market and FUNDAMENTAL ANALYSIS to predict future market movements related to the underlying state of the economy.

Investment bank Banking institution that advises customers on mergers and acquisitions and provides finances for large corporations. Called MERCHANT BANK in the United Kingdom. Distinguished from COMMERCIAL BANK.

Investment club Group of investors who pool their resources to make large-scale investments.

Investment grade Status of a bond that is given a high credit rating by one of the major credit agencies (generally above BBB), such as Standard and Poor's, Fitch's, or Moody's.

Investment intensity Net value of a company's plant and equipment, plus its working capital less current liabilities, expressed as a percentage of sales revenue or a percentage of the value added by the business.

The RETURN ON INVESTMENT drops sharply as investment intensity increases.

Investment trust Company that invests funds on behalf of other investors, in a wide variety of securities, thereby spreading the risk.

Investomer Investor who is also a customer.

Invisible hand From early economist ADAM SMITH, a term to describe the self-regulating nature of the marketplace. The pursuit of self-interest is deemed to lead, when aggregated, to achievement of social benefit and prosperity.

Invisibles Earnings from abroad that contribute to the BALANCE OF PAYMENTS resulting from services and transactions other than trade, such as insurance, shipping, and tourism.

IPO INITIAL PUBLIC OFFERING

IRA INDIVIDUAL RETIREMENT ACCOUNT

Iron law of oligarchy Principle regarding organizations and institutions, in which power tends to rest in the hands of an elite few.

Iron law of wages Principle that wages tend to remain tied to subsistence level, leaving no room for advancement, and that capitalism survives on the exploitation of workers.

Irrational exuberance Artificial escalation of asset values in a stock market without any basis in economic theory or past experience and driven by speculation and greed. Term coined by Alan Greenspan, former chairman of the Federal Reserve Board.

Ishikawa, Kaoru (1915–1989) Father of the QUALITY CIRCLE movement and author of *Guide to Quality Control* (1982) and *What Is Total Quality Control?* (1985).

Issue Number of shares or amount of a stock offer at any given time, at an offering price.

ISO Series Internationally recognized quality standards developed initially by the International Standards Organization. The 14000 series is designed to regulate the environmental impact of industrial activities. It is a management system standard rather than a performance standard, and can be adapted to any national economic system. The 9000 series defines quality of financial services, setting out consistent procedures and policies to achieve measurable outcomes.

IT INFORMATION TECHNOLOGY

Iterative design Practice of making continuous improvements in the design of a product, based on testing, evaluation, and feedback.

J

January effect Phenomenon in which companies with lower capitalization outperform large companies in the first month of the year.

Jaques, Elliott (1917–2003) Canadian psychoanalyst and organizational psychologist. He developed the notion of requisite organization from his stratified systems theory. He developed the concept of social systems as a defense against unconscious anxiety. He is also known for his concept of time-span of discretion, a measure of how much discretion an employee has. His books include *The Changing Nature of a Factory: A Study of Authority and Participation in a Industrial Setting* (1951), *Measurement of Responsibility: A Study of Work, Payment and Individual Capacity* (1956), *Equitable Payment* (1963), *Product Analysis Pricing* (1964), *A General Theory of Bureaucracy* (1976), *Executive Leadership: A Practical Guide to Managing Complexity* (1994), and *Social Power and the CEO: Leadership and Trust in a Sustainable Free Enterprise System* (2002).

Jargon Terminology or lingo used by a professional group, containing technical words and usage peculiar to that group.

J-curve In economics, a curve on a graph that depicts a small decrease in a variable, followed by a large increase.

JIT Just-In-Time

Job 1. Discrete and identifiable piece of work with a beginning and completion, for which the worker is rewarded monetarily or otherwise. 2. Task assigned to a worker.

Job analysis Detailed study of a specific job, the tools and equipment needed, and the qualifications, experience, and aptitudes of the person best suited for it.

Jobber Distributer of goods, a middleman.

Jobbing Process by which small numbers of products are made to order, as distinguished from mass production.

Jobbing backwards Looking back on a transaction or event, weighing the alternatives not taken, and examining the deficiencies in information that resulted in problems.

Job component method In job evaluation, ranking of jobs on a hierarchical scale depending on the behavioral demands they impose.

Job description Official wording that states the title of a job, the qualifications of the job holder, its tasks and duties, the performance objectives, the reporting chain of command, remuneration, working hours, skills, and attributes required.

Job design General scope of a job from the perspective of the employer, including the competencies and personality traits required and the specific sequence of tasks. It reflects a balance between the personal needs of the employee, such as a healthy environment and work ethic, and the corporate needs of the employer, such as a well-defined responsibility, efficiency, and cost-effectiveness.

Job enlargement JOB DESIGN that focuses on the enhancement of motivation horizontally, by increasing the number and variety of tasks, and vertically, by giving the employee more autonomy and responsibility. Also JOB ENRICHMENT.

Job enrichment Change in the various component tasks of a job description so as to make the job more fulfilling and productive.

Job evaluation Assessment of the work, responsibilities, skills, and experience of workers on the basis of objective standards, with a view to setting proper and fair

remuneration so that comparable tasks are rewarded comparably.

Job lock Situation in which benefits more than pay are the main attraction for an employee.

Job rotation Sequence of work that reduces boredom through the alternation of tasks, enabling workers to learn new skills and broaden their competence.

Job satisfaction Key element in personnel development and industrial relations through empowerment, motivation, and job enrichment. It also reduces accident rates and absenteeism. Objective scales are used to calibrate the subjective content of work to determine its satisfaction level, measuring teamwork and esprit de corps, as well as worker input.

Johari Window Technique created by JOSEPH LUFT and Harrington Ingham in 1955 to help people discover and understand better their relationships and environment. Subjects are given a list of 56 adjectives and asked to pick five or six that best describes their self. These adjectives are then mapped on a grid. Subjects may also plot the scores from the Personal Effectiveness Scale.

Johnson, Spencer (1940–) Physician and popular management guru. Author of *One-Minute Manager* and *Who Moved My Cheese* (1998), a parable on CHANGE MANAGEMENT.

Joint stock Shares of a public limited

company that exists between a partnership and a corporation, in which shareholders pool their stock and conduct business but are liable for its debts.

Joint venture In multinational business, a strategic alliance with domestic firms with or without equity participation. Although they have a high rate of failure, joint ventures are an effective way of entering a new and untested market, especially in developing countries where local contacts are necessary, access to distribution is difficult, and there are political roadblocks. Joint ventures are symmetric by nature because one partner has political clout and the other has technological expertise.

Despite their many advantages, joint ventures suffer from serious dangers. First, they are difficult to integrate into a global strategy that involves substantial cross-border trading, especially in regard to pricing and export sources. Second, they militate against the trend toward centralized financial management, which may limit the impact of the domestic partner. Third, there could be a clash of cultures and goals, which creates conflicts in reaching normal business decisions. Fourth, the cultural clash can extend to personnel selection, especially in developing countries where nepotism and corruption are rampant. Lastly, tax laws in a developing country may inhibit the maximization of initial losses, and what is advantageous to the foreign partner may be disadvantageous to the domestic partner.

Journeyman Skilled worker who has completed a trade apprenticeship but is not yet a self-employed master craftsman.

Judgmental sampling In market research, a sample based not on statistical data but on the researcher's personal judgment in assembling a pool of respondents.

Junior management Employees who are hierarchically subordinate to senior management.

Junk bond Bond that offers a higher rate of interest than other bonds because of its higher probability of default.

Juran, Joseph Moses (1904–2008) Romanian-born management consultant associated with quality management For many years he was in Japan where his ideas were very influential, His Juran Trilogy was an approach to cross-functional management composed of three processes: quality planning, quality control, and quality improvement. Among his books are *Quality Control Handbook* (1951), *Management Breakthrough* (1964), and *Quality Planning and Analysis* (1980).

Jurisdiction The scope of authority held by an official or person in power.

Just-in-time (JIT) Computer-aided manufacturing and inventory-management technique of Japanese origin, in which the raw materials needed for manufacturing are available just prior to use. This system reduces the need for large inventories, which tie up capital and can create bottlenecks in the pipeline. It gives managers the leeway to achieve quality, speed, dependability, and flexibility while bringing down costs. Set-up times are reduced, efficient plant layout eliminates transit time, product designs are standardized, maintenance is preventive rather than reactive, and suppliers are integrated with the production schedules. Of necessity, the workforce is trained to be flexible and innovative. JIT also makes extensive use of robots.

In the Japanese system, decisions normally undertaken in the West by management are, instead, made by workers. Virtually everyone is involved daily as a member of QUALITY CIRCLES. Decision making is by consensus rather than confrontation and generalists get as much say as specialists. Excess capacity is jettisoned. Suppliers take responsibility for quality, so that producers do not have to. Components are standardized, as are production schedules. Control is also established by AUTOMATION, or *jikoda,* and production lines come to a halt at the first sign of a defect.

K

Kahnemann, Daniel (1934–) Israeli-American psychologist and winner of the Nobel Prize in Economic Sciences for his work on PROSPECT THEORY. He was Professor Emeritus of Public Affairs at Princeton University's Woodrow Wilson School. He is noted for his work on the psychology of judgment, decision making, behavioral economics, and hedonic psychology. He established a cognitive basis for common human errors using heuristics and biases.

Kaidanren Japanese Business Federation, the most powerful of Japanese business associations.

Kaiser plan Adopted by the Kaiser Steel Corporation and the Steel Workers Union, an agreement to guarantee employees against possible loss of wages or employment as a result of technological changes.

Kaizen Japanese concept of CONTINUOUS IMPROVEMENT that undergirds JUST-IN-TIME, TOTAL QUALITY MANAGEMENT, and KANBAN. Its key is to put out any fires as soon as they are noticed and to exploit opportunities for improvement not episodically but continuously. Employees are encouraged to bring problems before management without any bureaucratic red tape and without barriers to communication.

Kaizen has three dimensions: management, group, and individual. Management *kaizen* uses seven statistical tools, including PARETO CHARTS/DIAGRAMS, CAUSE-EFFECT, HISTOGRAMS, CONTROL CHARTS, SCATTER DIAGRAMS, graphs, and checklists. It also involves waste elimination. Group *kaizen* identifies problems, analyzes them, implements and test new practices, and establishes new standards. Groups also learn from other groups; many of these groups are integrated into the workforce and help to set goals, build team spirit, improve labor-management relations, heighten morale, and develop skills. Individual *kaizen* involves suggestions that contribute to overall savings, idea pools, improvements in tools, and better customer relations and services.

Kaldor-Hicks efficiency In economic theory, any alteration in the allocation of resources. An extension of the PARETO EFFICIENCY, in which one person is made worse off when another is made better off, the Kaldor-Hicks efficiency, those who are better off are asked to compensate those who are worse off, thus restoring parity to the system. Developed by economists Nickolas Kaldor and John Hicks. Also termed *Kaldor-Hicks criterion*.

Kamikaze pricing Predatory pricing strategy of Japanese origin, in which goods and services are offered at a loss in order to capture a market and drive out all competition.

Kanban (Japanese, "visible record") Card developed by businessman Taicho Ohno of Toyota, which records the supply and use of parts and is thus part of the Just-in-time system.

Kansei engineering Product design that places great importance on aesthetics and the evocative qualities of a product.

Kanter, Rosabeth Moss Management expert best known for her work on organization structures, globalization, and the empowerment of employees.

Kaplan, Robert American management guru who developed, with David Norton, the Balanced score card, which includes consumer satisfaction as an intangible asset for corporations.

Karoshi In Japan, death by overwork.

Keiretsu In Japan, a group of companies with cross-holdings and family as well as professional connections based on and descended from the prewar Zaibatsu family-based groups, which were banned after World War II. It is an industrial organization occurring in both vertical and horizontal forms. Today there are six main horizontal *keiretsu*: Mitsubishi, Matsui, Sumimoto, Sanwa, Fuji, and Dai Ichi Kangyo. There is a vertical relationship between the core company and its subsidiaries, in each of which the parent group has a controlling interest. All *keiretsu* contain financial service companies that provide financial and insurance services, as well as investment banking. Each group also contains a trading company known as *soga sosha.*

Cross-shareholding makes it virtually impossible for outsiders to take over the companies. *Keiretsu* continually diversify to maintain their broad-based dominance over a swath of the economy, and they lose no op portunity to exploit new technologies. Members help each other both through financial aid and through personnel redeployment. Within each group, there is a presidents' council, or *shacho kai,* that forms the supreme command. This council meets regularly and sets the path for the group to follow.

Kelly repertory grid In market research, a technique to obtain opinions from respondents about multiple products, thereby discovering what appeals most in terms of quality and affordability. Developed in 1955 by clinical psychologist George Kelly.

Kepner, Charles Higgins Management consultant whose book with Benjamin Tregoe, *The Rational Manager* (1981), described procedures for decision making.

Kepner-Tregoe method Systematic problem-solving method and retrospective problem analysis developed by management consultants CHARLES KEPNER and Benjamin Tregoe.

Kerb market Exchange that deals in shares of companies not listed on the stock exchanges.

Keynes, John Maynard (1883–1946) British economist, one of the most influential in the 20th century. Father of Keynesianism, the foundation of modern macroeconomics. His work dealt with business cycles and the use of fiscal and monetary measures to mitigate the effects of economic recessions and depressions. Author of *The Economic Consequences of Peace* (1919), *The End of Laissez Faire* (1926), *Treatise on Money* (1930), and *The General Theory of Employment, Interest and Money* (1936).

Keynesian economics Economic policies, programs, and theories associated with JOHN MAYNARD KEYNES. It is a macroeconomic school of thought that has been influential in the 20th century. It argues that the private sector in a free market economy is inefficient and needs to be corrected by active policy responses by the public sector, particularly monetary policy actions by the central bank and fiscal policy actions by the national government to stabilize output over the business cycle. It was first presented by Keynes in his book, *The General Theory of Employment, Interest and Money* (1936) and stands in sharp contrast to the classical economics that preceded it

and the SUPPLY-SIDE ECONOMICS that followed it. It advocates a mixed economy based on the private sector with a strong role for government interventions during recessions. It asserts that production is influenced by aggregate demand and that aggregate demand is influenced by a host of irrational factors including employment and inflation. *Keynesian unemployment* results when there is insufficient demand in the economy.

Kickback Colloquial term for a bribe.

Killer app Effective and successful smartphone application, or APP.

Killer bee Investment banker hired to repel a takeover attempt by devising strategies to make the company less attractive to investors See also POISON PILL, PORCUPINE PROVISION.

KISS Acronym for "Keep it simple, stupid," a maxim for effective communication.

Knight, Frank H. (1885–1972) Professor of Economics at the University of Chicago and champion of classical economics that extolled the virtues of economics freedom and a free market.

Knockdown 1. Product supplied or shipped in kit form, to be assembled by the customer. 2. Something offered at a temporarily reduced price.

Knockoff Poor imitation or unauthorized copy of a designer product.

Knowledge management Creation, sharing, and transmission of information or expertise, designed to foster employee creativity and risk-taking within established parameters, with the goal of gaining competitive advantage. Also termed *knowledge engineering*.

Knowledge triangle Conjunction of research (which creates knowledge), education (which diffuses knowledge), and innovation (which applies knowledge) as one of the drivers of corporate growth.

Knowledge worker Professional in the information industry, including scientists, educators, and information-system designers. This expert must possess factual and theoretical knowledge, be able to find and access information, and apply information to solve problems and communicate these solutions to peers.

Kolb, David A. (1939–) American educational theorist and proponent of experiential learning. He was Professor of Organizational Behavior in the Weatherhead School of Management at Case Western University. In the early 1970s he and Ron Fry developed the experiential learning model, which comprised four elements: Concrete experience, observation and reflection, formation of abstract concepts, and testing and repetition. He is also known for his Learning Style Inventory in which there are four types of learners: converger, accommodator, assimilator, and diverger.

Kolb's learning cycle Management training technique developed by consultant DAVID KOLB, which breaks up the learning process into different stages, such as doing, reflecting, conceptualizing, and experiencing.

Kondratieff, Nikolai Dmitriyevich (1892–1938) Russian economist and proponent of New Economic Policy, which promoted small business in the Soviet Union. He is best known for his theory known as the Kondratieff Cycle, or long-term (50 to 60 years) cycles of boom followed by depression, which he first proposed in his books, *The World Economy and its Conjectures During and After the War* (1922) and *The Major Economic Cycles* (1925)

Kondratieff cycle Hypothesis first developed by Russian economist NIKOLAI KONDRATIEFF that the international economy rises and falls in 50-year cycles.

Kotler, Philip (1931–) American marketing expert. He is Professor of International Marketing at the Kellogg School of Management at Northwestern University. His ideas on marketing appear in his classic text *Marketing Management* as well as in the nine-volume *Legends in Marketing*.

KSA Acronym for "knowledge, skills, and abilities," key attributes for career development and professional growth.

K-strategy Management system indigenous to South Korea.

Kyoroku kai In Japan, a supplier association.

Labeling theory Sociological explanation for deviance from the norm, as not a condition inherent in something itself but because others have labeled it as such.

Labor intensive Description applied to an industry or production process in which labor costs are so high that they form the lion's share of the costs.

Labor stability index Measurement showing degree of labor turnover in relation to length of time on the job.

Laboratory training In human resources, a form of relatively unstructured group dynamics in which participants learn to resolve conflicts. The emphasis is on interpersonal skills.

Laches In law, an unreasonable delay that prejudices the opposing party in a claim.

Lady Macbeth strategy In takeover or acquisition battles, a third party that tries to act as a WHITE KNIGHT but eventually joins the predator.

Laffer, Arthur Betz (1940–) American economist best known for the LAFFER CURVE, an illustration of the theory that there exists a tax rate between 0 and 100% that will result in maximum tax revenues. He was a professor at the University of Chicago Graduate School of Business.

Laffer curve Graph pattern based on economist ARTHUR LAFFER's principle that higher taxation ultimately results in decreased revenue.

Lagging indicator Economic measurement that trails behind other indicators in a cycle. See also LEADING INDICATOR.

Laissez-faire Descriptive of a free-market economy, in which government involvement is kept to a minimum and the market essentially regulates itself.

Laissez-faire leadership In management, when the apparent leader relinquishes the right to set standards and regulate behavior and allows members the freedom to do as they please.

Lame duck In business, a company that faces intense foreign competition and is unable to survive without government subsidies or support.

Lanchester, Frederick William (1868–1946) English polymath and engineer who made important contributions to automotive engineering and operations research.

Lanchester strategy From British polymath and engineer FREDERICK WILLIAM LANCHESTER, the application of military strategy to business operations. The approach includes two linear equations, known as the *linear law* and the *square law*. The Japanese made use of Lanchester's ideas to study business competition and competitive advantage. Market share was predicated on the strength of the sales force; the strategic elements were pricing, advertising, and product development; and the goal was to "capture" customers. With 26% of the market share, a company was vulnerable, whereas with 74% it was considered safe.

Last in, first out (LIFO) 1. A method of costing units of raw materials or finished goods issued from stock by using the latest unit value for pricing, until all stock at that price is used up. The next earliest price is applied to the next batch, and so on. 2. In human resources, ranking employees by the length of tenure; in case of redundancies or layoff, letting go of those with the least tenure first.

Late-entry strategy Trying to gain competitive advantage by introducing products after the competitors, so as to learn from their mistakes.

Lateral thinking From Maltese physician

and consultant EDWARD DE BONO, used to describe a bold approach to problem solving by attacking it sideways rather than frontally, considering unorthodox solutions.

Laundering Processing of illegal or tainted money though a legitimate, usually foreign, bank or other facility so that the origin cannot be quickly traced.

Law of Contracts Law that governs agreements entered into voluntarily by two or more parties with the intention of creating a legal obligation, either orally or in writing. In equity, the remedy can be specific performance of the contract or an injunction. Contract law varies greatly from one jurisdiction to another including the difference between common law and civil law.

Law of diminishing returns Theory that if one factor of production increases while the others remain constant, the extra output generated by the additional input will eventually fall.

Law of the situation Developed by management theorist MARY PARKER FOLLETT, theory that conflict between two parties should be resolved by reference to the facts of the situation and not through a power struggle.

Law of triviality From British historian C. Northcote Parkinson, theory that the amount of time spent on any task will be in inverse relation to the monetary sum involved.

Layoff Suspension or termination of

workers because they have become redundant or the production of goods has become unprofitable.

LBO Leveraged buyout

LCS Life-cycle strategy

LDC Less developed country.

Lead time Amount of time needed to complete a cycle of work, a project, or an activity.

Lead users First users of a product, who test it to determine its strengths and weaknesses in relation to its competitors.

Leadership Position, traits, and characteristics associated with the principal managers and executives who exercise authority and power, set the trends, influence and motivate their peers and subordinates, and determine the goals and fortunes of an organization. There are many styles of leadership, and each has a mode of operation: Authoritarian, Democratic, Charismatic, Laissez-faire, Transactional, Transformational, and Bureaucratic. Some leaders are disciplinarians or martinets, while others are more permissive and tend to delegate power to subordinates. The test of leadership is the quality of the performance of the organization as a whole, as evidenced by the desired outcome.

Leadership theories In industrial and organizational psychology, a taxonomy of theories that define leadership qualities and styles: (1) traits, or focus on certain key personality characteristics as decisive, including confidence, communication skills, and organizational ability; (2) behavior, or focus on motivation, such as task-motivated or relationship-motivated activity; and (3) cognition, or focus on the ability to transmit ideas, values, and perceptions as performance drivers.

Leading indicator 1. Economic measurement that precedes and heralds other indicators in a cycle. See also Lagging indicator. 2. Indicator in a time-series analysis that changes in the same direction but in advance of company sales.

Leading and lagging Techniques used to bolster a company's cash position and reduce its debt by collecting amounts payable and delaying payments of amounts due.

Leading from strength Idea that a company should concentrate on its strengths when fashioning strategies.

Lean Descriptive of an efficient and wasteless operation, with no fat or unnecessary frills. Also known as Toyota production system or Just-in-time.

Lean back Period of cautious inaction before a government agency intervenes to correct an anomaly in a market.

Lean supply model Supply chain example developed by economist L. R. Lamming, in which the flow of materials moves from suppliers to producers in an efficient way.

Learning curve Relationship between productivity and manufacturing time and costs so that as productivity rises, manufacturing time and costs decline.

Learning organization Company that places a high premium on CONTINUOUS LEARNING by employees as a means of ensuring the firm retains its competitive advantage.

Learning plateau Stage in learning at which there is pause to allow for assimilation of the lessons, resulting in a flattening of the learning process.

Least-preferred co-workers scale Measurement to identify the extent to which a leader is predominantly task-motivated or relationship-motivated.

Leavitt, Harold (1922–2007) American management psychologist and writer whose research explored patterns of organizational communications; author of *Management Psychology* (1956).

Ledger Record of all financial transactions by an individual or a firm that shows income and revenue and profit and loss.

Left-brained 1 Of or relating to the thought processes, such as logic. 2. Of or relating to a person who is less creative and emotional and more analytical.

Leg In finance, one element in a complex set of transactions.

Legitimacy Acknowledgment of the legality of a person or institution, confirming authority by law and custom, and not in violation of any rules.

Letter Legal document that confirms or states a specific intention or plan. A *letter of comfort* is sent to a bank by a parent company, supporting the loan application of a subsidiary; a *letter of credit* is sent by a bank to a sister bank, authorizing the payment of a specified amount to the person named; a *letter of indemnity* states that the issuing organization will compensate the person to whom it is addressed for a specified loss; a *letter of identification* is issued by a bank to a customer to whom a letter of credit has been issued; a *letter of intent* sets out a person's intentions to do something specified; a *letter of license* is sent from a creditor to a debtor who is having trouble raising money to pay a debt; a *letter of regret* is sent denying an application; a *letter of renunciation* is sent when a person who has been allotted shares in a new issue renounces those rights.

Level of aspiration Degree of ambition that drives a person to do his or her best to achieve defined goals.

Level-output strategy Regulation of production at a constant level, regardless of fluctuations in demand. This strategy helps to maintain a stable workforce and reduces the optimum use of capacity.

Leveraged buyout Acquisition of a company in which loan capital is used to finance the purchase and when management buys out the existing shareholders, thus becoming the owner. The debt used is secured with the assets of the target company, and the purchase is financed by standard high-yield securities known as Junk bonds. The market value of the company is reappraised, and the expected cash flows are based on dramatic savings through the Cannibalization of assets and cutbacks in employment. Management ends with a sizable share of the equity, and the investment bankers pocket a large fee. Much of the actual financing comes through what is known as Mezzanine financing, whereby the investors are wealthy venture capitalists and pension funds that resell their shares in a few years to realize substantial capital gains.

Leveraged firm Company with a high level of debt.

Leveraged marketing Marketing strategy in which a company capitalizes on existing products and processes to create new products at minimal cost.

Levitt, Theodore German-born management guru and Harvard professor who taught that the central preoccupation of corporations should be to satisfy customers and not merely to produce goods. See also Levitt's total-product concept.

Levitt's total-product concept Marketing concept devised by Theodore Levitt, recognizing the gap between a producer's evaluation of a product or service and the user's or consumer's perception of it.

Lewin, Kurt (1890–1947) German-born psychologist who pioneered the field of Group dynamics and the human relations school of management. He developed Force-field analysis, Change management, Action research, and Sensitivity training.

Lewin model Portrayal of human behavior based on an equation, in which behavior is determined by environment and personality. From psychologist Kurt Lewin.

Liability 1. Responsibility assumed according to law or equity or obligation pertaining to a funciton or office. 2. Pecuniary debt incurred in the course of a business transation that must be legally discharged.

Liberalization Loosening of regulations and accompanying expansion of markets for free trade.

LIBOR London Inter-Bank Offered Rate, a widely used benchmark for short-term interest rates used in interbank transactions, fixed by the British Bankers' Association. It is derived from a filtered average of interbank deposit rates for large loans with maturities between overnight and one year.

Licensing Act of permitting use of a trademark or product, manufacturing process, copyright, or patent in exchange for a fee or royalty.

Lien Legal right to retain or claim possession of property or goods owned by another until the possessor's claims have been satisfied. A lien may be general, where the goods are held as security for all outstanding debts;

or particular, where the claim is against a specific property; or possessory, where actual possession is not required; or equitable, where the claim is independent of the possession.

Life assurance Insurance policy that pays a specified amount of money on the death of the life that has been insured, or at the end of a specified period. See also INSURANCE.

Lifeboat In finance, a fund set up to rescue traders in an exchange in the event of a market collapse or insolvency.

Life-cycle costing Expenses for a fixed asset, based on the amount of money required to purchase it and its operating cost over its estimated lifetime.

Life-cycle segmentation Marketing strategy that recognizes the shifting needs of consumers based on the stages of their life.

Life-cycle strategy (LCS) Competitive strength of a business, represented by six categories (dominant, strong, favorable, tenable, weak, and nonviable). An alternative to the growth-share and market-attractiveness models developed by management consultant Arthur D. Little, in this view, every corporation is segmented into independent business units, then the life-cycle position of each is assessed and its competitive position determined. Each unit becomes a *strategy center* (SC), similar to a STRATEGIC BUSINESS UNIT. SCs are described in terms of competitors, prices, customers, quality, substitutability, and divestment or liquidation;

that is, they could survive as independent businesses if divested. The position of an SC within its industry life cycle is determined by eight factors: market growth rate, market growth potential, breadth of product line, number of competitors, distribution of market share, customer loyalty, barriers to entry, and technology. *Embryonic businesses* are characterized by high growth and a fluid market, whereas *natural markets* are characterized by stability. The competitive position of a business is determined by qualitative factors rather than by quantitative factors, such as market share. A dominant position results from a near monopoly.

For portfolio balance, using a lifestyle model offers a balanced mix of activities, with mature businesses generating positive cash flow and enjoying a solid dominance in as many markets as possible. For developing a strategy to achieve dominance, the lifestyle model has a concept known as *families of thrusts,* with four forks: natural development, selective development, proven viability, and withdrawal. Growth is measured by start-up momentum, gradual gain, aggressive gain, defensive tactics, and harvesting. For a generic strategy, LCS presents 24 measures, including market production, new products, backward and forward integration, development of overseas business, licensing, rationalization of distribution and production, technological efficiency, cost cutting, and market strategies. The level of risk associated with LCS is identified by a number of factors, such as maturity and competitive position, past performance, management, and current performance.

The stages of a life cycle vary widely in terms of time; markets change and the nature of competition differs from industry to industry. Innovation and the nature of entry barriers can also affect life-cycle outlooks.

LIFO LAST IN, FIRST OUT

Lifespace Human nature and physical space within which people conduct their activities.

Lifestyle In marketing, the activities, interests, opinions, and values of consumers as they impact their purchasing decisions. In turn, consumer lifestyles are an important element in marketing strategies and profitability. *Lifestyle segmentation* is the division of a market based on consumer lifestyles, useful in customizing marketing strategies.

Lifetime customer value Estimate of the business, and consequently the profitability, that an individual customer brings to a company over a specified length of time, based on the assumption that the customer will continue to buy those products during that time.

Lifetime employment Guarantee of full employment throughout a person's working life.

Likert, Rensis (1903–1981) American psychologist noted for his contributions to the study of management and organizational theory, including the concepts of HUMAN ASSET ACCOUNTING, LIKERT SCALE, LINKING-PIN MANAGEMENT STRUCTURE, and SYSTEM FOUR.

Likert scale Collective results of a questionnaire widely used in attitude studies, developed by psychologist RENSIS LIKERT. Respondents indicate how much they agree or disagree with a series of statements, graded on a three- or five-point scale in lieu of either/or responses.

Limit In finance, the maximum number of fluctuations allowed in certain markets during one trading day.

Limited company Business in which the liability of its members with respect to the company's debts is restricted to the value of their shares or by guarantee. Some partnerships may also operate under this principle.

Limited liability Condition in which shareholders are not personally responsible for the debts of the company in which they hold shares.

Line and staff System of management with two hierarchies: LINE MANAGEMENT is responsible for deciding policies and running the company's main activities; STAFF MANAGEMENT is responsible for providing support services such as accounting, personnel management, and warehousing.

Line extending Increasing a line of products by adding variations, as for example when a soft drinks producer adds a diet drink under the same brand name.

Line filling Adding products to an existing product line in order to leave no opportunities for competitors. Line filling may be horizontal, whereby the manufacturer adds features to an existing product and produces expensive as well as cheaper models; or vertical, whereby the manufacturer produces a wide variety of brand names within a single product line.

Line management Classification of supervisors in a business, in which each manager fulfills a discrete function and is responsible for a particular department within the organizational chain of command.

Line of command See of CHAIN OF COMMAND.

Line production Mass production, in which high volumes of identical or similar products or product parts are made in a set sequence of operations. Good product design and efficient plant layouts make it possible for lower skilled workers to operate the machinery.

Linear time Time viewed as an independent entity governed by its own laws and moving in a straight line to a goal. Opposite of CYCLICAL TIME.

Linear trend Data presented in a time sequence, represented on a graph by a straight line.

Linking-pin management structure Way of conceptualizing management structure, developed by psychologist RENSIS LIKERT. In this model, an organization consists of a series of interlocking groups connected to a coherent whole, with individuals as the key links having overlapping responsibilities.

Lipstick effect Indicator of adjusted consumer purchasing behavior, based on the economic situation. Reference to the sale of lipstick; that is, during hard times, sales of lipstick increase as consumers indulge their buying habits by buying cheaper items rather than more expensive ones such as designer dresses or handbags.

Liquid market Financial market in which the spread between asking and selling prices is narrow, with many sellers and buyers at hand and where market prices are not affected by large transactions.

Liquid ratio The relationship between liquid assets and current liabilities, used to assess the liquidity of a company.

Liquidation Distribution of a company's assets among its creditors prior to its dissolution; usually handled by a *liquidator*.

Liquidity Ability of an asset to be easily converted into cash, with little or no capital loss.

Liquidity trap In the *liquidity preference theory* of economist JOHN MAYNARD KEYNES, the concept that when interest rates are low and savings are high, investors favor cash over bonds, in anticipation of higher interest rates.

List renting Sale of a mailing list of potential customers to a direct-mail company, usually for one-time use.

Listed company Business that is listed on one of the stock exchanges and whose stock is publicly traded.

Listening Flip side of speaking, including *recall listening* and *empathic listening*. The former focuses on memory and the latter on overt expressions of approval or disapproval.

Livery company (chiefly British) One of 80 trade associations in the City of London, descended from the medieval guilds.

Living company Business that is managed for long-term success rather than for short-term profits and is sensitive to changes in the business climate.

LLDC Least less-developed country

Lloyd's of London Corporation that is a group of independent brokers and underwriters grouped into syndicates. Begun in London in 1689 and named after its owner, Edward Lloyd, its original business was mainly maritime insurance during Britain's role as a mercantile power in the 19th century. It still publishes the *Lloyd's Register of Ships*.

Loan Money lent on the condition that it is repaid, usually with interest, at the end of a given period.

Local Regional branch of a labor union.

Localism Development approach using different strategies for different localities, based on varying cultural and environmental conditions.

Location strategy Process and mode of choosing an industrial or commercial location, important for large corporations with multiple locations for production and distribution.

Lockheed model Management form that identifies relevant variables for establishing SPANS OF CONTROL, coordination of subordinates, and direction of supervision.

Lockout Action taken by an employer in the course of an industrial dispute, denying workers access to the workplace. It is a management response to a strike.

Locus of control Center of gravity in an organization that conveys a sense of control over events.

Locus poenitentiae (Latin, "opportunity to repent") Time and opportunity to back out of a deal before it becomes a legal document.

Logistics Detailed plan for a complex operation, usually involving physical transport and assignment.

Long position Owning shares in a company with the intention of selling them in the future, after some appreciation in value; opposite of SHORT POSITION.

Long tail 1. In marketing, the sale of a broad range of products, each in modest quantities but with large collective volume. It is common in niche marketing, in which a company makes a profit by selling small quantities of a very large number of items. 2. In economics, a situation in which a large number of companies are performing below par because of a depressed economy.

Long term 1. Description of a contract that spans two or more accounting periods. 2. Name for a debt that need not be paid for at least 10 years. 3. Classification for a bond that does not fall due for at least one year. 4. Category of unemployment that lasts for more than a year.

Longitudinal design 1. Marketing research approach that measures consumer or audience preferences over a long time, sometimes over a generation. 2. In strategic planning, projections of past events to develop future plans and scenarios.

Lorenz, Max Otto (1876–1959) American economist who developed the Lorenz curve in 1905 to describe income inequalities. His principal work is *Methods of Measuring the Concentration of Wealth* (1905).

Lorenz curve Graphic representation of the distribution of income and wealth in a target population. Developed in 1905 by economist MAX OTTO LORENZ.

Loss leader Product or service offered to the public at cost or below cost in order to entice customers who may buy other products over the long haul.

Low-hanging fruit 1. Metaphor for a good short-term opportunity for profit without much effort. 2. Term for consumers who are easy targets.

Low-involvement product Cheap product that calls for little or no deliberation on the part of the purchaser and is largely an impulse purchase.

Loyalty Faithfulness to a brand or service provider, built up as a result of repeated positive experiences over the years. Loyal customers are the mainstay of good business because they do not require costly persuasion. Loyalty may be reinforced through coupons and discounts offered to frequent buyers.

Luddite Person who opposes new machines, processes, and technologies, often feeling threatened by them. Evolved from Ned Ludd, a leader in the 19th-century English protest movement by textile artisans against increasing industrialization of cloth production.

Luft, Joseph U.S. psychologist who devised the JOHARI WINDOW along with Harrington Ingham in 1955. He is the author of *Group Processes: An introduction to Group Dynamics* (1984) and *Of Human Interaction* (1969).

Lutine bell Hanging in the underwriting room of Lloyd's, this bell is rung only on rare occasions, but to mark important events; formerly it was rung once for bad news (such as the sinking of an insured ship) and twice for good news.

M

Ms The different types of money in the FEDERAL RESERVE SYSTEM, classified in a range from M0 (narrowest) to M3 (broadest). For example, *M1* is money held in banks; *M1-A* is cash held in bank accounts excluding deposits by foreign-owned banks and nonbank depositories; *M1+* is the basic money supply; *M1-B* is M1-A money plus other checkable deposits at all depository institutions; *M2* is M1-B money plus savings and time deposits under $100,000 and money market funds; *M3* is M2 money plus savings and time deposits over $10,000 and institutional money market funds.

Maastricht treaty Legislation signed in 1992 that created the EUROPEAN UNION. It led eventually to the creation of the ECONOMIC AND MONETARY UNION.

Machiavellian From *The Prince* by Niccolo Machiavelli, used to describe political actions whereby the ends justify the means, however immoral they may be.

Machine bureaucracy Organizational structure that places a premium on punctuality, standardization, and efficiency.

Macho management Style of management that is aggressive in protecting its rights and is dismissive of the rights of employees and unions.

Macroeconomics Branch of economics that studies large functioning economic structures and trends rather than the behavior of particular economic agents or phenomena. It is largely concerned with such factors as money supply, employment, interest rates, government spending, investment, and consumption. See MICROECONOMICS.

Macroenvironment Large national and international forces that indirectly influence corporate decisions and affect their profitability and viability. These forces include political violence and unrest, environmental disasters, social anomie, political instability, demographics, labor force composition, and legislative and regulatory actions. See MICROENVIRONMENT.

Macrorisk Potential harm associated with major economic changes that affect an entire economy.

Magnuson-Moss Warranty Act 1975 U.S. law requiring written guarantees and warranties to be made available to buyers at the time of purchase, specifying in clear language the who, what, when, and how of the warranty.

Mail order Direct sale to a customer by the producer through catalogs sent by mail, with orders received either by phone or mail. The Internet has supplanted mail order in many cases.

Makework Work devised to kill time and keep workers busy, or superfluous work engaging more workers than needed. See FEATHERBEDDING.

Managed currency Money supply that is controlled by a CENTRAL BANK as part of an overall monetary policy with political overtones.

Managed float System of floating exchange rates with CENTRAL BANK intervention to reduce currency fluctuations. Also *dirty float*.

Management 1. Control of a company or organization with the goal of making it profitable and sustainable. The operation requires organizational and human relations skills that are different from entrepreneurial skills. Management is responsible for setting goals, overseeing change and growth, measuring performance, planning, cost control, pricing, conflict resolution, and quality control. 2. People involved in the operation of a company or organization, es-

pecially the higher echelons, known as TOP MANAGEMENT. Managers are accountable to the owners or shareholders for the conduct of business affairs. 3. Academic discipline dealing with the study of management as a science and the ways and means of administering an institution or corporation.

Management audit Systematic assessment of a management's methods and policies and the use of its resources. It involves an analysis of the management performance and effectiveness in the light of their strategic objectives.

Management buy-in Acquisition of a company from a group of outside managers, backed by a team of VENTURE CAPITALISTS.

Management buyout (MBO) Acquisition of a company or subsidiary by the existing management, usually following divestment of noncore operations by the owner.

Management by crisis Approach to management that looks on crises as opportunities, but only provides short-term, ad hoc solutions. This style deals with symptoms rather than root problems, but achieves quick successes.

Management by exception Approach to management by which a decision that cannot be made or a problem that cannot be solved at one level is passed on to the next higher one.

Management by objectives (MBO) Approach to management by which managers are encouraged to specify quantitative and qualitative objectives to be achieved within a given time period and they are judged on the basis of their success in achieving those objectives.

Management by walking around (MB-WA) Approach to management that entails maintaining a constant presence on the floor, meeting regularly subordinates and associates, and engaging in candid discussions of problems.

Management capitalism Form of operation in which the dominant administrative role falls on the salaried executives rather than on the owner or owner's immediate family.

Management consultant Professional adviser engaged by a company to guide management in improving efficiency and profitability. These consultants generally are outsiders who study existing work practices, and their reports generally span decision making, policies and planning, use of resources, division of labor, and critical assessment of industrial relations, production, marketing, and sales.

Management development Program by which managers are trained to hone their skills in real-life situations. The program often includes mentoring, team-building, work studies, systems analysis, and role-play.

Management grid Tool to evaluate management styles, based on concern for peo-

ple and concern for production; original five styles were identified by ROBERT BLAKE and JANE MOUTON; model was revised in 1999 to reflect nine styles, with optimum being THEORY Y.

Management information system (MIS) Comprehensive computer system for providing financial and quantitative information to all levels of management. Access to the data is by need to know and is restricted to areas regarded as useful for particular managers; confidential information is restricted to top management.

Management letter Correspondence from an auditor to the management of a client company at the end of an annual audit, usually suggesting improvements that could be made to the accounting system and internal controls.

Management philosophy Guiding principles of good management that forms the framework for decisions.

Management science Application of scientific methods and quantitative methodology to the practice of management.

Management services Department in a company concerned with improving overall quality and productivity, usually through work studies and systems analysis.

Management style Approach to management generally based on the individual's personality traits. It varies from democratic to authoritarian.

Management succession planning Strategy to ensure that there is a pool of talented junior managers trained and ready to fill senior positions as they become vacant.

Manager Senior executive, usually the chief of a department or agency, who is responsible for planning and decision making and who heads one or more project teams.

Managerial psychology Branch of industrial psychology dealing with the role of managers in human relations and decision making.

Managing director Title of the principal executive or operational head, just below the chairman. Equivalent to the CEO.

Mandate Order or commission given to a specific person, a department, or an organization to carry out the wishes of the grantor; a higher authority issues a mandate to a lesser agent.

Manual Document explaining the workings of a machine or procedures for completing a process.

Manual labor Work done by hand, such as ditch digging, vegetable harvesting, or construction.

Manufacturing management Branch of management that deals with manufacturing processes and machinery.

Maquiladora Mexican name for a factory operating in a free trade zone in Mexico, near the U.S.–Mexican border; used by U.S. companies to take advantage of lower manufacturing costs and looser regulatory compliance.

March, James Gardner (1928–) Professor emeritus at the Stanford University School of Education best known for his research on organizations and organizational decision making. He worked on the systemic-anarchic perspective of organizational decision making known as the garbage can model.

Margerison, Charles Professor of Management at the University of Queensland in Australia and Cranfield University School of Management in the United Kingdom. Along with DICK MCCANN, he developed the Team Management System.

Margin 1. Difference between production costs and income from sales constituting profit, often expressed as *net margin* or *gross margin* 2. Difference between the buying and selling price or between rates of interest.

Margin call Broker's demand for additional money or securities in a margin account. It occurs when the value of the stock is depressed.

Marginal costing Approach to costing that separates expenses into two categories: fixed and variable or adjustable. Also termed *direct costing, incremental costing, variable costing.*

Marginal pricing System of pricing products based on MARGINAL COSTING, which allows future cost variations.

Marginal revenue Additional revenue derived from the sale of one additional unit of production.

Marginality In management, state of being excluded from the mainstream because of a lack of influence on other individuals or groups.

Margin of safety Extent to which revenues exceed the breakeven point.

Markdown Reduction in the price of goods in response to poor demand or to create more shelf space.

Market 1. Arena in which traders, buyers, and sellers gather to exchange goods and services, with money as the medium of exchange. 2. Demand for a particular product, measured by the number of buyers.

Market challenger Company whose goal is to supplant the market leaders by increasing its market share.

Market development Actions to enlarge the market territory or constituency by actively soliciting new customers and introducing new products.

Market entry strategy Deliberate plan to enter a foreign market and establish a presence in manufacturing or selling based on factors such as amount of capital, degree of risk, ease of entry, cultural penetration, infrastructure, and profitability. The most common strategies are (1) assembly operations that use low-cost labor; (2) contract manufacturing using domestic facilities and marketing channels; (3) exports, which present less risk than other strategies; (4) joint ventures with a host-country partner with different levels of equity participation; (5) franchising the trademark, product, or process; (6) licensing, a variant of franchising; (7) manufacturing based on the host country's capabilities and the availability of skilled labor; (8) piggyback exporting, whereby one company markets through the distribution channels of another; (9) wholly owned subsidiaries, where considerable investment is required and company employees are subject to frequent transfers.

Market failure Loss of purchasing power by consumers, leading to a loss of business and inefficiencies and caused by any number of disfunctions.

Market follower Company that is content to take its cues from trendsetting market leaders, following in their wake.

Market forces Events, factors, and trends that influence business activities in a FREE MARKET economy, especially the laws of SUPPLY AND DEMAND.

Market niche Small, specialized segment of a market suitable for exploitation.

Market leader Company with the largest

market share, or the bellwether in innovation and distribution.

Market maker In finance, an intermediary who creates a market for a financial obligation.

Market overhang Situation in which sellers, worried by falling prices, postpone their sales until there is a market recovery.

Market penetration 1. Extent to which a company's product satisfies a demand or felt need, as determined by its share of that market. 2. Process of entering a market to establish a new brand or product, often supported by a low pricing strategy and extensive promotion.

Market power Ability of a company to influence the prices in a market on the basis of its large market share.

Market research Systematic collection and analysis of data on the size of a market, consumer behavior and preferences, the extent to which current products meet consumer expectations, and social trends that might impact sales.

Market risk Chance of failure in a market subject to wide price fluctuations, often moderated by HEDGE trading.

Market segmentation Breakdown of market demand by homogeneous groups of consumers, each of which responds best to a different marketing approach. The traditional segmentation is by age, sex, income, family size, ethnic group, occupation, social class, and lifestyle.

Market share Portion of the total sale of all brands of a product competing in one market captured by one product, usually expressed as a percentage. It is a critical factor in determining competitive position and profitability. Market share may denote absolute share or relative share. ABSOLUTE MARKET SHARE is per capital income. RELATIVE SHARE is the share of business divided by the sum of the shares of its three leading competitors. Market share also is subject to definition because it may pertain to a global market, national market, or local market.

Market shares may be described as high, medium, or low, and the strategies in regard to each are different. For *high-share competitors*, the three most effective strategies are (1) building barriers against entry by raising the cost of entry; (2) introducing alternative brands; (3) maximizing price range offering; (4) broadening the product line; and (5) increasing production volume. For *medium-share competitors*, the strategies are different because they do not have the resources to take on larger companies; instead, they focus on customer segments ignored by the leader, supplying the needs of specialized markets, catering to customers who demand and can pay for superior quality, and maintaining a sufficient speed to keep pace with the leader.

Market skimming Setting the price at a level that maximizes sales, irrespective of the costs of production, targeting those consumers who are willing to pay a higher price.

Market value Dollar worth of a company obtained by multiplying the number of its issued ordinary shares by their market price.

Marketability Extent to which a product is suitable for commercial sale and the extent to which it can be easily bought and sold.

Marketing 1. Planning and implementing innovation, pricing, promotion, and the distribution of goods and services to the widest possible clientele. It consists of anticipating demand, supplying felt needs, conducting research and promotion, and ensuring quality and availability. 2. Distribution of goods to consumers through a wide variety of channels.

Marketing environment External climate in which MARKETING takes place, including social, ethnic, and cultural ethos; technology; depth of competition; political stability and its pro-business policies; distribution facilities; infrastructure; and transportation.

Marketing information system (MIS) Organized and focused collection of information and its timely dissemination and transmission to the personnel of evaluation and analysis. The information covers the business environment, customer base, suppliers and distributors, government agencies, and competition.

Marketing management Planning and oversight of a company's marketing operations and the efficient implementation of a marketing plan.

Marketing mix Four factors (called the FOUR Ps) that together influence sales: product, pricing, promotion, and place. This is based on findings of the company's own market research.

Marketing objectives Elements of a marketing plan that specify the targets to be achieved within a given time frame and the resources needed.

Marking to market In accounting, valuing financial obligations and products according to their current market prices, considered controversial in some contexts.

Marketing warfare Aggressive marketing plan based on military strategies and tactics, where marketing terms are borrowed from the military lexicon and are designed to overpower or outwit the competitor, though direct confrontation is avoided in favor of guerrilla-style campaigns.

Marketization Introduction of markets and marketing into developing economic systems or into the public sector.

Markowitz, Harry Max (1927–) American economist and winner of the Nobel Prize in Economic Sciences in 1990 and the John von Neumann Theory Prize in 1989. He was Professor of Finance at the Rady School of Management at the University of

California, San Diego. He is best known for his pioneering work in modern portfolio theory studying the effects of asset risk and return.

Markowitz model Method of selecting the optimum investment portfolio, devised by Nobel economist HARRY MAX MARKOWITZ. It assumes that investors are risk-averse and should diversify by mixing the proportions of their portfolio.

Markup Dollar amount by which the production costs of a product or service are hiked to arrive at the selling price.

Maslow, Abraham (1908–1970) American psychologist whose contributions to management science include the concepts of hierarchy of needs (see below), PEAK EXPERIENCE, and SELF-ACTUALIZATION.

Maslow's motivational hierarchy Model of human motivation developed by ABRAHAM MASLOW. The model posits a hierarchy of human motives and needs, with five levels: physiological (food and sleep), security, love and affection, esteem and recognition, and meta needs (fulfillment, aesthetics, and intellectual achievement). Of these, the physiological make up the primary and the other four constitute the secondary.

Mass marketing Marketing of products with the same pricing, customer base, and packaging so as to bring down prices.

Mass production See LINE PRODUCTION.

Massify Produce a good for the mass market.

Master of business administration (MBA) Postgraduate degree in business and management, awarded after four years of training in a business school.

Material fact Information that influences a decision and the suppression of which in a legal document constitutes a crime.

Materiality Extent to which any piece of information is crucial in decision making and affects the veracity of the statements attested to in a document.

Materials management Optimum utilization of materials for the efficient flow of production without loss of manpower or time.

Matrix departmentation Hybrid management structure that combines product departmentation and functional departmentation leading to employees reporting to two supervisors.

Matrix management Organizational structure in which vertical and horizontal links between managers are active at the same time.

Matrix organization Task-oriented management structure in which an employee reports to more than one manager in different departments.

Matrix structure Organizational structure

based on vertical and horizontal relationships, found mostly among multinationals. The production facilities are localized but industrial policies are set by the global office. Each country is treated as a profit center, but the management of taxes is important and profitability is calculated globally. Executives report to more than one central unit; below the country manager level, operations are divided by product group, which takes precedence over country managers. The headquarters, managed primarily by home-country nationals, sets the strategies for overseas subsidiaries and in doing so may impose its own values. For example, the Japanese coordinate their matrix structure by product, geography, and function, thus cutting across divisional boundaries and eliminating rivalries.

Mature economy Developed economy that has reached a high level of sophistication and stability, and in which growth is accompanied by accountability and transparency.

Maturity grid Organizational structure conceived by Philip B. Crosby with five levels of maturity: Uncertainty, Awakening, Enlightenment, Wisdom, and Certainty.

Maturity stage Longest period in the life cycle of a firm, industry, or product during which sales peak and start to decline. In macroeconomics, the final stage of economic growth characterized by a high level of mass consumption.

Maximax criterion Positive approach to financial decision making under conditions of uncertainty.

Maximin criterion Pessimistic approach to financial decision making under conditions of uncertainty.

Maximum slippage Period between the date when a new company's venture capital runs out and the date it starts receiving earnings from sales.

Mayo, Elton (1880–1949) Austrian psychologist and management expert whose seminal contributions to the field of industrial psychology bore fruit in the HAWTHORNE STUDY. He stressed the importance of human relations and interpersonal relations, and encouraged management to meet one-on-one with workers on the shop floor.

MBA MASTER OF BUSINESS ADMINISTRATION

MBO 1. MANAGEMENT BUYOUT 2. MANAGEMENT BY OBJECTIVES

MBWA MANAGEMENT BY WALKING AROUND

McCallum, Daniel (1815–1878) As general superintendent of the Erie Railroad, McCallum developed principles of management that included discipline, division of labor, detailed job descriptions, and merit-based promotions. He also developed organizational charts and sophisticated information-management systems using the telegraph.

McCann, Dick Australian management expert who, with Charles Margerison, developed the Team management wheel.

McClelland, David American psychologist and leading contributor to the study of motivation. He elaborated on the concept of the Need for achievement as a driver of human performance, especially in entrepreneurs. He also stressed the Need for power as an essential ingredient of management.

MCDM Multiple-criteria decision making

McGregor, Douglas (1906–1964) American psychologist and leading contributor to Organizational theory. He rejected Theory X in favor of his own more hopeful Theory Y.

McKinsey 7S Model Framework developed by management gurus Robert Waterman and Tom Peters, linking shared values (all starting with S): structure, systems, style, staff, skills, strategy, and shared values. These broad areas are integrated to achieve overall successful strategy implementation. At the core of the model are superordinate goals and shared values around which the firm pivots, and which define corporate culture. Transformation of a company requires a change in these values.

McLuhan, Herbert Marshall (1911–1980) Canadian philosopher of communication theory and one of the most influential thinkers in the 20th century. He coined the terms *medium is the message* and Global village and predicted the World Wide Web 30 years before it was invented. His major works include *The Mechanical Bride* (1951), *The Gutenberg Galaxy* (1962), *Understanding Media* (1964), *The Medium is in the Message* (1967), and *War and Peace in the Global Village* (1968).

MD Managing director

Mechanistic organization Company characterized by rigid hierarchies, largely vertical command modes and interactions, and clearly defined roles and boundaries. Term coined by management consultants Tom Burns and George Stalker.

Media analysis Investigation into the relative effectiveness and costs of mixing various formats and media in an advertising campaign to achieve maximum impact.

Mediation Intervention by a neutral state-sponsored agency or person to settle an industrial dispute. This generally results in a compromise solution that is acceptable to both sides. If the mediation results in a binding award, it is known as Arbitration and if it is a nonbinding award, it is known as Conciliation.

Medium-size Relating to a second-tier company based on its net worth, turnover, and number of employees.

Medium-term Relating to the period of

time when liabilities or maturities become due and are payable, varying according to the nature of the obligation.

Megacorporation Large corporation with multinational offices and thousands of workers.

Megatrend General and widespread current thinking or paradigm affecting large countries and markets.

Meltdown From nuclear energy, a fatal disaster that cannot be repaired and that causes enormous losses.

Membership group In social psychology, a group in which people are enrolled as members, as distinguished from a REFERENCE GROUP.

Memorandum 1. Document providing essential information on the structure and purposes of an association or organization, its rationale, and officers. 2. Brief office communication.

Mensualization Of French origin, term describing the transition of BLUE-COLLAR workers to STAFF status, with monthly salary.

Mentor Senior employee who is training a junior employee and providing guidance and encouragement, especially with the intricacies of corporate culture and protocols.

MEPT Managerial, executive, professional, and technical (staff).

Mercantile law Commercial law as it applies to banking, contracts, copyrights, insolvency, insurance, patents, sale of goods, shipping, trademarks, transport, and warehousing.

Merchandising Promotion of goods being sold by a retailer or merchant, especially through discounts, rebates, and free samples, so as to persuade customers to patronize the establishment.

Merchant Trader in goods and services or a middleman.

Merchant bank Bank dealing in derivatives, hedge funds, venture capital, takeover bids, credit cards, new initial public offerings, investment portfolios, and unit trusts. Formerly specialized in lending to merchants engaged in foreign trade. Because of its access to large amounts of capital, it is willing to take more risks than a COMMERCIAL BANK. Also INVESTMENT BANK.

Merger Combination of two or more businesses with equal standing, resulting in the creation of a new company. Unlike in an ACQUISITION, no one party acquires the other, and the management of the new company has representatives from both entities. Only equity shares are exchanged, rather than a sale. True mergers are rare where the resulting union is not lopsided, however.

Merit rating Calibrated system of rewards based on performance, used cumulatively to assess an employee's contribution to an organization.

Meritocracy Social system in which advancement is based on ability and skills, rather than on birth and privilege.

Metcalfe, Henry (1847–1917) Management expert who, as manager of the Frankford Arsenal, developed a system of controls. His book, *The Cost of Manufactures and the Administration of Workshops, Public and Private,* was published in 1885.

Metcalfe's law Principle that the value of a network of people using the same Internet sites increases with the square of the number of participants. Attributed to Robert Metcalfe in 1980.

Method study Critical examination of work practices and protocols in an effort to single out employees who are more efficient, productive, and cheaper.

Metrocorporation Corporation with responsibilities that transcend those to the shareholders and extend to several other social sectors.

Metropolitan statistical area (MSA) Geographic unit of the U.S. Census Bureau, marking either a city with 50,000 or more inhabitants or an urbanized area with at least 100,000 inhabitants.

Mezzanine finance Funding provided by specialized institutions, constituting a mix of equity and secured or unsecured loans

and with varying interest rates. This is a tool used in MANAGEMENT BUYOUTS.

M-form Organizational structure, known also as *multidimensional structure*, consisting of a relatively large number of relatively small semi-autonomous units, each with its own budget and financial target set by the main office.

Microcredit In the developing world, the lending of small amounts of money at non-commercial rates to encourage initiatives such as cottage industries and rudimentary capitalism.

Microeconomics Analysis of economic behavior at the detail level, consisting of individual households or small businesses, often reacting to MACROECONOMIC forces such as taxation and cost of living.

Microenvironment Situation where a local company flourishes, affecting the health and well-being of its employees and its immediate customers.

Micromanagement Form of over-management characterized by excessive controls and intensive attention to details, usually translating to constant interference in the work of subordinates.

Micromarketing Marketing focused on the needs and behavior of a small segment of the population.

Midcareer plateau Dead-end stage in a

career, where opportunities for further promotion do not exist.

Middle management Level of management below senior management but above junior management. Middle managers exercise very little decision-making power but have significant supervisory functions.

Middleman Intermediary in the flow of goods and services who makes a profit by facilitating or reselling the goods.

Miles, Lawrence Delos (1904–1985) American engineer. He created the concept of VALUE ENGINEERING in his book *Techniques of Value Analysis and Engineering* (1961).

Milestone scheduling Use of set markers to monitor progress.

Milgram, Stanley (1933–1984) American psychologist noted for his contributions to social psychology, especially his concept of conformity to authority by passive subordinates.

Milk round Annual visit to universities at graduation time by personnel managers, using job fairs to find new employees.

Mindmap Graphical tool for visualizing and clarifying ideas; it resembles a tree, with a central trunk and spreading branches.

Minimax strategy In GAME THEORY, a strategy of minimizing loss rather than maximizing gain.

Minimum wage Legal floor for wages for workers on the bottom rung of the employment ladder. It is revised upward periodically based on the cost of living.

Minority interest Small proportion of shareholders in a company where control of more than 50% is held by a dominant group or holding company.

Minority protection Legal protections, including audit and inspection of accounts, afforded to minority shareholders against abuses by majority rule, such as STEAMROLLER TACTICS during annual meetings.

Mintzberg, Henry Canadian management theorist known for his empirical observations on managers at work, especially the differences between what they are supposed to do, what they actually do, and what they think they are doing.

MIS MANAGEMENT INFORMATION SYSTEM

MIS MARKETING INFORMATION SYSTEM

Misery index Measure of economic distress, calculated by adding the unemployment rate to the inflation rate. Sometimes the index also incorporates the number of bankruptcies and annual gross domestic product.

Misperceptions theory In economics, the concept that business cycles are caused by imperfect information rather than structural flaws.

Mission creep Expansion of a project beyond its original scope, often without planning or an exit strategy.

Mission statement A simple and direct expression of a company's goals and objectives, as well as the vision animating its products and activities. Mission statements define what a company stands for.

Missionary sales Information by salespersons who tout the company products to prospective customers but do not take orders.

Mixed capitalism Imperfect capitalist system with both FREE MARKET and state-run sectors.

Mixed economy Economy in which the private and public sectors coexist and in which the state has no overriding commercial interests to protect. It is an intermediate economic status, between a COMMAND ECONOMY and a LAISSEZ-FAIRE economy.

MNC MULTINATIONAL COMPANY

Mobility Freedom to move upward, downward, or horizontally in a profession or industry (*occupational mobility*) or from one geographical location to another (*geographical mobility*). In stratified societies and in command economies, there is little or no mobility.

Model Representation of a process or program that includes all the necessary ele-

ments in the proper order, which can be used as a template or to extrapolate data. Models may be physical, mathematical, descriptive, solution-driven, or deterministic.

Model-embedded decision-support system Method of decision making based on mathematical models.

Modus vivendi Arrangement whereby two parties in a dispute settle on the terms of engagement and work out a compromise.

Mojo Slang for magical or special powers to achieve a desired goal or to influence people to act in a certain way.

Moller, Claus Danish management consultant and advocate of effective customer relations to promote products; he originated the concept of putting people first.

Monetary policy Procedures available in a regulatory toolbox to control and affect MACROECONOMIC conditions by adjusting the flow of money. There are four main tools in the toolbox: (1) using open-market operations to buy or sell government debt; (2) raising or lowering the reserve requirements of banks; (3) through short-term funds; and (4) lowering or raising interest rates or rates on Treasury bills. Generally a tight monetary policy is used as a means of controlling inflation. KEYNESIAN ECONOMIC theory holds that monetary policy is a blunt instrument with indifferent results.

Monetary system Network of mechanisms

and institutions governing the supply of money and exchange of currencies.

Money Medium of exchange that serves as a unit of account, a store of value, and a means of deferred payments. Currencies replaced barter in the early stages of economic history.

Money laundering See LAUNDERING.

Money market Wholesale exchange for short-term loans and debt instruments, consisting of money brokers, discount houses, and banks. The main vehicles are bills of exchange, Treasury bills, and trade bills. Money market funds generally earn higher rates of interest than bank deposits.

Money supply Total amount of money in the MONETARY SYSTEM, under the authority of the CENTRAL BANK. The types of money are as follows: (1) MO notes and coins in circulation; (2) M1 notes and coins in circulation plus private-sector current accounts and deposit accounts that can be transferred by check; (3) M2 notes and coins in circulation plus non-interest-bearing deposits; (4) M3, M1, plus all other private-sector bank deposits plus certificates of deposit; (5) M3C, M3, plus foreign currency bank deposits; (6) M4, M1, plus most private-sector bank deposits, plus holdings of money market instruments as T-bills; and (7) M5, M4, plus bank deposits.

Moneyness Relationship between the strike price of an option and the current trading price. When the settlement is financial, the difference between the strike price and spot price determines the moneyness.

Monochronic culture Organizational culture where the norm is to divide time sequentially into segments and dedicate each segment to a particular task. The main instruments of such a culture are timetables and the main emphasis is on punctuality. Distinguished from POLYCHRONIC CULTURE.

Monopolistic competition Market for a particular product or service in which there are many competing sellers offering similar but nonidentical goods. There are few barriers to entry, and there is a multiplicity of buyers and sellers as in PERFECT COMPETITION, but each product is unique and can be obtained from only one producer. In effect, each product is a MONOPOLY on its own.

Monopoly Market in which there are multiple buyers but only one seller, who is thus able to control the terms of trade, especially pricing. There are natural monopolies, as for example public electric utilities and water supply.

Monopsony Market in which there are many sellers but only a single buyer, who thus is able to control the price and availability of the goods offered.

Monte Carlo simulation Generation of random data from specified distributions that are then used as input into predictive models. In finance, such simulations are used to price complicated derivatives and portfolios and to calibrate risks.

Moonlighting Holding down a second job in addition to a primary day job.

Moore, Gordon (1929–) American cofounder and chairman emeritus of Intel Corporation. He is the author of MOORE'S LAW, which governs the rate of innovation in computers.

Moore's law Named after GORDON MOORE, cofounder of Intel, law that computing power will increase every two years exponentially through the production of new microchips.

Moral hazard Situation in which a person has no incentive to act honestly or with diligence or prudence.

Moral suasion Regulatory body's appeal to morality and the use of persuasion rather than legislative authority to induce a company to act in conformity with legal requirements.

Morale Collective motivational energy of a group; known in French as *esprit de corps*. It determines the sense of well-being and satisfaction that employees demonstrate, and it is the basis for auditing the ability of a company's leadership to provide employees with comfort regarding company activities and policies.

Morgenstern, Oskar (1902–1977) German-born economist who, in collaboration with JOHN VON NEUMANN, founded the mathematical field of GAME THEORY and its application to economics in the Neumann-Morgenstern Utility Theorem. His major works include *On the Accuracy of Economic Observations* (1950), *Predictability of Stock Market Prizes* (1970), and *Mathematical Theory of Expanding and Contracting Economies* (1976).

Mortgage Loan extended for purchase of real estate, with the real estate serving as security, for a specified number of years and on mutually agreed-upon interest terms and conditions.

Most-favored-nation clause Portion of a trade agreement between two or more nations under which each party gives the other the same favorable conditions as regards tariffs and quotas.

Motion study Business efficiency technique combing the time-study work of F. W. TAYLOR and the motion study of FRANK and LILLIAN GILBRETH. It is a part of Taylorism. It has evolved into a technique for improving work methods. Also TIME AND MOTION STUDY.

Motivation The drive in human beings that causes them to act in a certain way; in business, this is often in the form of inducements and appeals to self-interest. Motivation is related to other drivers, such as purpose, desire, need, preference, perception, attitude, recognition, and sense of achievement. Sometimes motivation is expressed in monetary terms and sometimes as psychic income. It is one of the key elements in understanding consumer behavior, and it also plays a role in human resources. Autonomy and responsibility add to the motivational menu of employees, while discounts, low prices, and perquisites add to the motivational menu of consumers. Dissatisfaction stifles motivation and thus inhibits ability to respond appropriately.

Motivation-hygiene theory Developed by theorist FREDERICK HERZBERG, a principle that identifies working conditions as leading to either employee dissatisfaction or satisfaction.

Motivational research Inquiry designed to discover the psychological drivers of human actions, especially in the consumer world.

Mousetrap, build a better To build a better and more efficient product; presumably, build a better mousetrap and the world will beat a path to your door.

Mouton, Jane Srygley (1930–1987) American management theorist who developed the MANAGEMENT GRID MODEL with ROBERT R. BLAKE.

MRP Manufacturing resource planning.

MSA METROPOLITAN STATISTICAL AREA

Multidimensional scaling Technique used by marketers to assess consumer perceptions of competing brands.

Multidomestic company Company where each division operates independently.

Multilateral netting Centralization of international payments and receipts in different currencies, so as to reduce the cost of processing.

Multinational company (MNC) Conglomerate operating in more than one country and having plants and offices in countries outside its home base. Multinational enterprises have a different setup from national companies, with efficient, cost-effective operational networks and the ability to exploit the cheapest labor, take advantage of tax loopholes, and bypass protectionist barriers. They are also the agents of technology transfers across borders. Because they are more concerned with the bottom line than with the welfare of the countries in which they operate, they are often guilty of corrupting local officials, contributing to high pollution levels, and flouting employment safety regulations. Also termed *transnational enterprise*.

Multiple-criteria decision making (MC-DM) Polygonal approach to decision making and problem solving that takes into account all the factors that have impacted the problem directly or tangentially. It is an advanced field of operations research devoted to the development and implementation of decision support tools and methodologies when confronted by needs and goals of conflicting natures. VILFREDO PARETO was the first to place the aggregation of such conflicting data into a single evaluation index.

Multiple niching Marketing strategy in which several offers of sale are made for a product, each designed to appeal to a particular segment of the consumer public.

Munsterberg, Hugo (1863–1916) Father of INDUSTRIAL PSYCHOLOGY. In 1893, he established the Harvard Psychological Laboratory, which became the center of the industrial psychology movement. He studied telephone operators, trolley drivers, and naval officers to find out how to match people with the right kind of work, where they could function effectively. In 1913, he wrote *Psychology and Industrial Efficiency*.

Muth, John Fraser (1930–2005) American economist, considered the father of the rational expectations revolution. He was a professor at the Graduate School of Industrial Administration at Carnegie Mellon University.

Mutual Company owned by its members or depositors, where all profits are distributed to the stakeholders.

Myers-Briggs type indicator Psychometric questionnaire of personality, in which the subject answers personal questions.

Myopia Cognitive bias that screens out undesirable information that contradicts previously held biases. From nearsightedness, extended to imply a lack of foresight.

N Ach NEED FOR ACHIEVEMENT

N Aff NEED FOR AFFILIATION

Nader, Ralph American lawyer and consumer advocate; the father of CONSUMERISM. His early investigation of the safety of GM's Corvair automobile gave birth to the consumer movement and made the safety of consumer products a national issue.

NAFTA NORTH AMERICAN FREE TRADE AGREEMENT

NAICS NORTH AMERICAN INDUSTRIAL CLASSIFICATION SYSTEM

NAIRU NONACCELERATING INFLATION RATE OF UNEMPLOYMENT

Naive quantitative method Technique used to forecast future trends, using historical data plotted in a time series. It displays the underlying trends, seasonal and cyclical variations, and random elements that are then decomposed to reveal underlying patterns.

Narrow market Market that is sensitive to changes in supply and demand, resulting in fluctuations in price.

Narrow money Informal name for M0 or M1, or that part of the money supply used as a medium of exchange.

NASDAQ National Association of Securities Dealers Automated Quotations System, an electronic marketplace for securities, founded in 1971.

Nash, John Forbes, Jr. (1928–) American mathematician who made important contributions to GAME THEORY, differential geometry, illustrating the forces that govern chance and events in daily life. His theories are used in market economics, computing, artificial intelligence, and military theory. He was a co-recipient of the Nobel Prize in Economic Sciences in 1994.

Nationalization Takeover by the state of companies and utilities that have a vital national interest and their operation henceforth under government control. Nationalization generally occurs in a socialist economy and reflects the view that private enterprise is more interested in profits than in public welfare. Nationalization is more a political move than an economic one. Opposite of PRIVATIZATION.

Natural capital Land as a factor of production.

Natural wastage Reduction of the workforce through attrition rather than layoffs.

Near-market research Scientific research with commercial potential.

Near money Assets, such as bills of exchange, that are immediately transferable and may be used to settle some, but not all, debts. Also termed QUASI MONEY.

Need Any of several drivers in human psychology, such as the need for achievement, need for affiliation, need for power, and need to make sense.

Need for achievement Concept developed by social psychologist DAVID MCCLELLAND, describing the human need for achievement as a strong driver of performance, especially in entrepreneurs and managers.

Need for affiliation Concept in social psychology developed by DAVID MCCLELLAND, referring to the basic human need for company and a sense of belonging, which enable us to thrive in a corporate environment.

Need for power Concept in social psychology developed by DAVID MCCLELLAND, describing the thrill of exercising power over others, which can cause aggressive and antisocial behavior. The need for power stems from an inherent sense of insecurity and is an effort to affirm one's own worth.

Need to make sense Basic human need for relevance, a sense of purpose, and validity that can come only from the external environment and the projection of one's own values onto the world.

Need-pull Unmet need, or a new regulation or opportunity that creates a new need or demand.

Negative equity Difference between the value of a property and the outstanding amount borrowed against that property, where the latter is greater than the former.

Negative income tax Income redistribution program by which the state pays those with income levels below a stated amount a subsidy.

Negotiability Characteristic of a document entitling its owner to pass on legal ownership by endorsing it. Bills of exchange and checks are negotiable when they are signed on the back by the endorser.

Negotiate To confer with a view toward arriving at mutually acceptable terms for a contract or agreement.

Nellie, sitting next to Informal training program, whereby the learner sits close to an older worker and learns how he or she operates.

Nemoto's principles of leadership From Masao Nemoto, managing director of Toyota, his ideas of CONTINUOUS IMPROVEMENT, coordination among divisions, better communication, rotation of best employees, setting deadlines, action following inspection, and rehearsal of presentations.

Nenko Human resources management system used in Japanese organizations.

Neoclassical economics School of MICROECONOMICS developed in the late 19th century, focusing on the allocation of capital and individual-level supply and demand. In combination with NEO-KEYNESIAN ECONOMICS, it was a dominant school of economic thought in the 20th century.

Neo-Keynesian economics Application of the MACROECONOMIC theories of KEYNESIAN ECONOMICS to the postwar period. It was combined with NEOCLASSICAL ECONOMICS to form the *neoclassical synthesis,* which became the mainstream economic approach until the latter part of the 20th century and the introduction of CHICAGO SCHOOL monetary theories.

Nepotism showing favoritism in employment or promotion, based on family ties rather than merit.

Net Amount remaining after specific deductions are made, as in *net assets, net earnings, net dividends, net income, net investment, net profit, receipts, net value,* and *net worth.*

Net national product GROSS NATIONAL PRODUCT less capital consumption.

Netiquette Informal rules and regulations that govern Internet communications.

Network Arrangement of parts, as in an organization, with interconnecting lines of communication and support, but functioning independently and simultaneously.

Network analysis Use of a network to plan a series of activities, to make the best use of resources, or to ensure control over a schedule.

Network marketing Selling of products or services through a network of self-employed agents and representatives.

Neumann, John von (1903–1957) Hungarian-American mathematician and polymath, considered a towering intellect and one of the greatest mathematicians of modern times. His contributions straddle many disciplines, including mathematics, physics, economics, computer science, and programming and statistics. He was a principal member of the Manhattan Project and a member of the Institute of Advanced Study at Princeton.

Neurotic organization Dysfunctional organization that exists at the whim of its top executive, whose capricious demands create instability at all levels. Ford Corporation under Henry Ford is an example.

New economics See KEYNESIAN ECONOMICS.

New product development Marketing strategy by which new and untried ideas are developed and converted into marketable innovations and inventions, through tests and analysis of their profitability, viability, and need. Prototypes are then made, tested, refined, and then test-marketed.

New York Stock Exchange (NYSE) Principal U.S. stock exchange, founded in 1792. It moved to Wall Street in 1793.

Next in, first out (NIFO) Method of valuing raw materials or finished goods issued from stock, using the next unit price at which consignments will be received. Compare FIRST IN, FIRST OUT; LAST IN, FIRST OUT.

NGT NOMINAL GROUP TECHNIQUE

NIC Newly industrializing countries.

Niche market Tightly defined market with relatively few customers, who support high levels of demand for a specific product or service.

Niche width Size of a niche market in terms of the number of customers and the depth of their demand. Generally, this is divided into *broad niche markets* and *narrow niche markets*.

NIH For "not invented here," a derogatory term applied to foreign inventions and ideas, reflecting reluctance to benefit from globalization.

Nikkei stock average Index of prices on the Tokyo Stock Exchange, launched in 1949.

Noise 1. In communication theory, disruption in communications through chatter and background static. 2. In statistics, random fluctuations in data. 3. In finance, excess volatility in stock prices induced by nonstandard techniques for analyzing and valuing stocks.

Nominal group technique (NGT) Group problem-solving technique in which each member of a group is asked to write down ideas without consulting colleagues. These ideas are then discussed, without awareness of the origin. Similar ideas are grouped or merged, and the remaining ideas are ranked on the basis of potential. The individual rankings are combined mathematically and the ideas at the top are adopted. NGT avoids the distortions associated with GROUPTHINK, caused by deference to authority, peer pressure, office politics, and personal idiosyncrasies.

Nominal price Minimal price, fixed for considerations other than market value and generally a concession to a most favored party.

Nominee Person named to act on someone's behalf, generally to conceal the identity of a stakeholder.

Nomothetic Approach to the study of human behavior that emphasizes general or universal principles. Opposed to IDEOGRAPHIC.

Nonaccelerating inflation rate of unemployment (NAIRU) Rate of unemployment that does not affect wage inflation.

Nonadjusting event In accounting, an event occurring between the date of the balance sheet and the date of the financial statements reflected on the balance sheet.

Nonaka, Ikujiro (1935–) Influential Japanese writer and Professor Emeritus of Hitotsubashi University Graduate School of International Corporate Strategy. He was also a Distinguished Scholar at the Drucker School and Institute, Claremont Graduate University and Distinguished Scholar at the University of California, Berkeley. He is best known for his study of Knowledge Management, a field that he founded with his book, *The Knowledge-Creating Company*.

Noncompete agreement Contract in which one party agrees not to compete with the other or to divulge any secrets to a third party. Such agreements are most common in employment contracts or in licensing agreements.

Nondisparagement clause Agreement that bars a present or past employee from criticizing the employer, especially on the Internet.

Nonequity share Share in a company, whereby the shareholder receives payment for a limited amount without reference to the company's assets, profits, or dividends; or whereby the share is redeemable on the request of the issuer.

Nonexecutive director Executive of a company not involved in its day-to-day management but, rather, to provide independent and objective advice and counsel.

Nonfinancial performance Measure of performance that cannot be quantified and does not appear on the company books. It incorporates an array of techniques, such as defect rates, response times, and delivery commitments, that serve as strategic weapons, differentiating one firm from another.

Nonmonetary considerations Relating to aspects of an employee's hire, including commuting time, boredom, morale, work environment, recognition, and self-fulfillment.

Nonnegotiable Relating to a negotiation's demands or points that are outside the purview of discussion, and therefore where no concession is likely.

Nonprobability sampling In marketing, a sampling procedure in which the sample is chosen on the basis of personal preference rather than at random, and where bias in selection is likely to skew the responses.

Nordstrom, Kjell Anders (1958–) Swedish economist. Writer of popular business books, including *Funky Business: Talent Makes Capital Dance* (2000) and *Karaoke Capitalism:Management for Mankind* (2003).

Normal distribution In Gaussian terms, the symmetrical or bell-shaped frequency curve that appears when a range of values is plotted on the vertical axis and the values of a random variable are on the horizontal axis. The bell shape results because extreme values are infrequent toward the ends while median values are clustered around the middle.

Normative Conforming to an ideal or desirable standard, as in work behavior.

Norming Process by which an individual melds into the group and adopts the attitudes and values that are exhibited by the majority in the group, thus contributing to a cohesive corporate culture.

North General reference to the developed or industrialized countries of the Northern Hemisphere, including Japan, the United States, Canada, and Europe, as well as Australia in the Southern Hemisphere. Compare SOUTH.

North American Free Trade Agreement (NAFTA) A commerce trade agreement among Mexico, the United States, and Canada.

North American Industrial Classification System (NAICS) Taxonomy of business establishments according to the type of economic activity that replaced the older Standard Industrial Classification System. Its numbering system employs a six-digit code at the most detailed industry level. The first five digits are common to Canada, Mexico, and the United States. The last digit designates national industries. The first two digits designate the largest business sector, the third digit designates the subsector, the fourth digit designates the industry group, and the fifth digit designates the industries.

Norton, David P. American founder of the Palladium Group and co-author of *The Execution Premium: Linking Strategy to Operations for Competitive Advantage* (with ROBERT KAPLAN).

Nostro account Domestic bank's account in a foreign bank, in the currency of that foreign country; used primarily to settle money exchanges.

Nostro and Vostro (Italian, from Latin, *noster*, ours and *voster*, yours) Accounting terms used to distinguish an account from an account held by another entity. The entities in question are almost always banks.

Not-for-profit Classification of charitable or public service institutions that are not designed to create profit and that therefore enjoy tax-exempt status.

Novation Replacement of one legal agreement with a new obligation, done with the consent of the parties involved.

Numeracy Ability to understand and work with numbers and statistical data.

NYSE NEW YORK STOCK EXCHANGE

O&M ORGANIZATION AND METHODS

Object-oriented programming (OOP) Programming that focuses on grouping, simplification, streamlining, and standardization.

Objective(s) Goal, or the end toward which an effort is directed and resources and strategies are focused.

Objective and task method Procedure for preparing a promotional budget, setting out the OBJECTIVES and the budget required to achieve those objectives.

Objectivity Accounting concept that eliminates or minimizes bias and subjectivity in the examination of accounts and ensures full comparability and consistency over time.

Obligation In financial transactions, the assumption of responsibility with regard to the payment or repayment of legal and financial dues.

Observation research Market research without the intervention of a physical interviewer.

Obsolescence Fall in the value of an asset as a result of the passage of time and wear and tear, rather than from a breakdown. It has special application to CONSUMER DURABLES, which are built to endure for a certain period of time but will need to be replaced with newer models that are more efficient. The concept has applicability to manufacturing as well, where it has given birth to PLANNED OBSOLESCENCE. Most products continue to function reasonably well after they have become technically obsolete, and it is in the interests of the manufacturer to maintain consumer demand by making sure that consumer durables have a short lifetime.

Occupational hazard Risk of accident or illness at a place of work, or injury or illness directly or indirectly caused by working conditions. Occupational hazards are governed by government regulations and supervised by OSHA.

Occupational segregation Informal discrimination in employment, based on the traditional dominance of certain jobs by privileged ethnic communities.

Odd-even pricing Pricing of a product that ends in 9, as in $4.99; a psychological gimmick to lead consumers to think that they are paying less than a full dollar price.

OECD Organization for Economic Cooperation and Development

Off the books Accounts that are not recorded in the financial ledgers or reported to the authorities or shareholders.

Off-balance sheet Relating to a company's accounts and finances that do not appear on the official balance sheet. It is also known as Creative financing because it creates illusory profits by adding transactions that are bogus, such as factoring and consignment stock that inflate profits and conceal liabilities. Many of these transactions are legal, but they are the result of the manipulation of numbers (Cooking the books) and concealment of debt obligations. Off-balance sheet accounts are particularly designed to hoodwink shareholders and the stock market.

Office politics Juggling for power and influence in a corporate office, often by manipulating the information channels and creating a climate for personal advancement.

Offshore account Company, fund, or bank account set up in a foreign country, such as the Cayman Islands, Switzerland, or the Channel Islands, with the goal of evading the tax laws of the home country. Also Tax haven.

Offshore operations Deals involving a company not registered in the same country as its principal stakeholders, executives, or investors.

Offshoring Locating a company's operations or offices in countries outside the home country. Compare Outsourcing.

Ohmae, Kenichi Japanese management consultant, whose book *Mind of the Strategist* (1982) introduced Japanese production techniques to the West and popularized such concepts as innovation, creativity, and strategic planning.

Ohno, Taiichi (1912–1990) Japanese business executive who is considered the father of the Total Production System, known as lean manufacturing in the United States. He wrote several textbooks about the system including *Toyota Production System: Beyond Large-Scale Production* (1988) and *Workplace Management* (1988).

Okun, Arthur Melvin (1928–1980) American economist who served as chairman of the Council of Economic Advisers (1968–69). He is the author of Okun's law.

Okun's law Concept developed by American economist Arthur Okun that relates declines in the idleness rate of workers to increases in the Gross national product, using data that exclude the first two quarters of every economic recovery.

Old Lady of Threadneedle Street Nickname for the BANK OF ENGLAND, coined by Restoration playwright R. B. Sheridan.

Old-boy network Social and business connections, generally the alumni of prestigious state and private schools, who dominate a firm or institution.

Old-school ties Networking based on class, status, and wealth derived from childhood and early adult friendships and partnerships.

Oligarchy Organization controlled primarily by an elite or clique; in business, a company with senior management making all decisions and whose personal interests often override those of the company.

Oligopoly Market in which relatively few sellers supply multiple buyers, and who thus control the supply and the prices. Generally, it is a market in which the largest four players control more than 40% of the market.

Oligopsony Market in which there are numerous sellers but only a limited number of buyers, especially in soft commodities, where the buyers have the advantage in setting prices and choosing sellers.

Ombudsman Official charged with handling grievances and acting as go-between for both parties in an attempt to reach a resolution satisfactory to both.

Omikoshi In Japanese, bottom-up management.

Omnibus research Marketing surveys that are broad in scope and that ask wide-ranging questions.

On approval Allowance for potential buyers to receive goods for inspection and trial before deciding to purchase.

One-pack giveaway Gift given with the purchase of a good, designed to encourage further purchases.

On-the-job training Informal job training, in which colleagues serve as teachers and actual work experience is counted as education.

One-two-three bank Member of the secondary banking sector, whose status is only slightly above that of a moneylender.

OOP OBJECT-ORIENTED PROGRAMMING

Open-door policy 1. Relating to imports from all countries, without discrimination or favoritism. 2. Management philosophy that is receptive to ideas from subordinates.

Open economy Economy in which a large portion of the national income is derived from exports and imports, rather than from domestic industry.

Open-ended Activity without an assigned termination date or an exit strategy.

Opening Job vacancy for which applications are being accepted.

Opening bell Bell that marks the opening of a trading day on a stock exchange. It is usually rung by a celebrity.

Open market Purchase or sale by a CENTRAL BANK of government bonds in exchange for money, with the intention of influencing liquidity in the private banking sector and thus controlling the money supply.

Open-plan office Large single room for employees that has been divided into workstations, with no fixed halls or partitions.

Open position Situation in which a trader had stock on hand that is unhedged or unsold, and thus is vulnerable to sudden fluctuations in price.

Open system Management system that is continuously receiving inputs and producing outputs.

Operant conditioning Systematic program of rewards and punishments to influence behavior. It grew out of B. F. SKINNER's theory of BEHAVIORISM, which states that actions have consequences and that awareness of consequences can be used to motivate performance.

Operating cycle Average time, expressed in days, between the purchase of materials and receipt of payment.

Operating statement Financial and quantitative statement outlining key performance indicators, especially providing comparative data for a selected budget period.

Operating system Configuration of activities through which management maintains control of the business activities that transform resources into assets, trying to achieve an optimum match between capabilities and outcomes.

Operation Activity encompassing the transformation of inputs into outputs, the harnessing of resources, and the aggregation and oversight of responsibilities, skills, and functions for achieving stated goals and objectives.

Operational research Element of scientific management that designs models and scenarios representing best possible solutions and strategies to real problems, especially those outside the textbook. It makes use of GAME THEORY, CRITICAL-PATH ANALYSIS, and SIMULATION.

Operations manager Manager entrusted with responsibility for a particular operational division or department and synchronizing that operation with that of the entire company.

Operations strategy Conversion of production blueprints and objectives into deliverable products, ensuring acceptable quality and costs.

Opinion leader A person whose opinions are highly valued by his or her peers so that they subscribe to them.

Opportunity cost Economic cost of non-action, measured in terms of the benefits lost by not pursuing a course of action, as when returns on an investment are judged against the potential profits of other investments using the same amount of money.

Optimization Process by which all factors affecting a decision or plan are weighed to produce the most effective outcome.

Optimized production technique Manufacturing control based on the elimination of bottlenecks in getting the materials to the output stage.

Optimum bias In management psychology, the tendency of planners to underestimate risks and overestimate benefits, based on their own biases or past experiences. It leads them to take increased risks, overlook uncertainties, ignore the need for exit strategies, make unfounded assumptions, underestimate costs and overestimate benefits, and fail to heed critics.

Option Right to buy or sell a fixed quantity of a commodity, currency, or security at a particular date at a particular price. A *traded option* may be bought or sold at any time on any exchange, as opposed to a *traditional option*, which once bought cannot be resold. An option to buy is called a CALL OPTION and an offer to sell is a PUT OPTION. Options allow traders to hedge against the risk of wide variations in prices; they also allow dealers and speculators to gamble for large returns with limited initial payments. Traders purchase combinations of options to cover a variety of expectations and con-

tingencies. With a European option, the buyer can exercise his or her rights only on the expiry date, whereas with an American option, this right may be exercised at any time up to the expiry date, thus giving the holder more chance of buying at the most favorable price. An option is distinguished from FUTURES, which do not bind the purchaser by bid and may lapse.

Option to purchase Right of a shareholder to buy shares at a reduced price in certain specified circumstances.

Ordinary activity Activity that furthers the normal business of a company designed to increase its profits or help it comply with the regulatory environment.

Ordinary share Fixed unit of the share capital of a company.

Organic organization Company structure with the freedom to reinvent itself in response to emerging needs; it is open, flexible, and informal, with control and decision making decentralized, little reliance on authority as the final arbiter, and interactions both vertical and horizontal.

Organismic theory Developed by Hungarian-American psychiatrist ANDRAS ANGYAL and applied to business, the concept that the link between producer and individual consumer or group of consumers is organic.

Organization Structured corporate entity

operating under defined rules, protocols, roles, and responsibilities, with a stated goal. It may be for profit or nonprofit.

Organization and methods (O&M) Form of work study involving procedures and controls, and management oversight involving efficiency and productivity.

Organization behavior Discipline concerned with the study of human behavior in the corporate setting. It integrates performance, attitude, commitment, and leadership.

Organization for Economic Cooperation and Development (OECD) Group of developed countries that act in concert to protect their economic interests and to assist developing countries to bridge the economic divide.

Organization hierarchy Vertical layers of management within an organization and the echelons that constitute the pyramid of authority.

Organization man Title of William Whyte's classic 1956 novel of a man totally devoted to the corporate culture and to the advancement of his career within it. The book led to critical examination of the idea of lifelong commitment to an organization.

Organizational agility An organization's capacity to anticipate changes in marketplace conditions and trends and preemptively adapt policies and technologies to continuously add value. It involves strategic visioning and planning.

Organizational analysis Development of models and theories that provide a basis for how an organization functions and how it can initiate change.

Organizational audit See MANAGEMENT AUDIT.

Organizational chart Diagrammatic representation of an organization in the form of a family tree, showing the flow of authority, chain of command, titles, and functions.

Organizational behavior Social behavior determined by the interaction of individuals in a corporate environment and shaped by a corporate culture.

Organizational climate Atmosphere created by a mode or style of management, determining the degree of teamwork, cohesion, commitment, creativity, and employee participation.

Organizational commitment Psychological devotedness to a company's culture and a desire to remain attached to it. It is normally measured by attitudinal vectors and identification with the goals and values of an organization.

Organizational culture Norms and protocols by which an organization conducts its business and the codes of communication and behavior that govern interpersonal relations and individual responses to corporate values. Organizational culture is of three kinds: (1) integrative culture, which emphasizes consensus and consistency, predictability, and clarity; (2) differentiated culture, which tolerates subcultures with some variations in values and behavioral vectors; and (3) fragmented culture, which allows diversity to be the rule rather than the exception.

Organizational design The flow of authority within an organization, outlining the duties, tasks, privileges, and responsibilities of each member, the chain of command, and the resulting hierarchy of relationships.

Organizational development Long-term, systematic, and prescriptive approach to planned organizational change. Each organization is similar to a social or biological unit, which responds in rational ways to external stimuli. Organizational development tries to modify these responses to maximize output.

Organizational ecology Biological principles at work in an organization, determining its evolution and response to change, stress, and natural selection.

Organizational knowledge Knowledge shared by a group and based on its common values and experiences. It encompasses all knowledge resources within an organization. In professional terms, it is communal knowledge embedded in the structure of the mission of the firm.

Organizational learning Culture of learning and constant improvement within an organization, marked by the pursuit of excellence.

Organizational life cycle Evolutionary model of a corporation from founding to growth to maturity; and the organizational structure, leadership style, and strategy that support each stage of growth.

Organizational mirror Technique by which each group in a corporation is critiqued by other groups, in order to explore weaknesses and to learn from each other.

Organizational multiplier Factor by which a primary change in a particular sector of an organization is multiplied to determine the total change to the whole organization.

Organizational pathology Factors taken together that affect the health of an organization and the climate in which it functions, such as reality testing, adaptability, identity, and unity.

Organizational planning Design of the structure of an organization and the division of its responsibilities and chains of command.

Organizational structure Framework of responsibility and the chain of command in an organization to achieve optimum efficiency.

Organizational theory Study of the design,

structure, and process of decision making in an organization and the sociology of its organizational system. It focuses on the ways in which decisions are made and how they are influenced by reason and the bottom line, rather than by altruism or abstract theory.

Orientation Induction training or a refresher course for a new task or new set of working conditions.

Orphan product Drug that is not developed for commercial use because the number of prospective users is not sufficient to justify its high production costs.

Osborn, Alex Faickney (1888–1966) American advertising executive and pioneer of brainstorming. Along with Sidney Parnes, he developed the Osborn-Parnes Creative Problem Solving Process. He wrote extensively on creative advertising. His books included *A Short Course in Advertising* (1921), *Wake Up Your Mind* (1952), *Applied Imagination* (1953), and *The Goldmine between Your Ears* (1955).

OSHA Occupational Safety and Health Administration, a federal agency that oversees safety in the workplace and regulates industrial policies regarding accidents.

OTC Over the counter

Ouchi, William G. (1943–) American expert in business management and a professor at the Anderson School of Management at the University of California at Los Ange-

les. His first successful book was *Theory Z: How American Management Can Meet the Japanese Challenge* (1981). It was followed by *The M Form Society: How American Teamwork Can Recapture the Competitive Edge*. He described three types of organizational control: bureaucratic, market, and clan.

Outbound logistics Movement of materials from a production center comprising storage, transportation, and distribution.

Outplacement Counseling of laid-off employees to help them find work.

Outsourcing Contracting out work to foreign or domestic companies for the production of materials, spare parts, or services such as telemarketing. This is an effort to reduce the workforce or downsize a company's production facilities, invariably leading to considerable savings, especially when the work is outsourced to countries like China and India where labor costs are lower. The downside is that outsourcing leads to or reinforces domestic unemployment and creates dependence on foreign expertise. It also leads to a general weakening of industrial dominance in the countries that outsource.

Outwork Work by generally poorly paid workers, done outside a company's premises by freelance workers. Also termed *telework*.

Over the counter (OTC) Market in which financial obligations are bought and sold outside the jurisdiction of recognized financial markets or stock exchanges. The OTC markets are specifically designed for DERIVATIVES.

Overachiever Person who exceeds the expectations of peers in terms of performance and rise to positions of authority.

Overall reciprocity Unrestricted trade concessions, as among members of trading blocs.

Overcapitalization Condition of having too much subscribed capital, caused by an overestimation of financial needs.

Overhead Recurrent daily expenditures incurred in running a company, apart from labor costs and materials. Included in overhead are rent, repairs, heating, and lighting. These overhead costs are due and payable whether the company makes a profit or not.

Overheated economy Situation whereby very high aggregate demand leads to higher prices but not necessarily higher output.

Overpositioning Attempt to give investors a narrow and skewed profile of a company's strengths.

Overshooting In financial markets, the tendency for a security, commodity, or currency to experience extremely volatile ups and downs before settling into equilibrium.

Oversubscription Situation in which subscribers are willing to invest more in shares than the company's required capital. In such cases, applications are scaled down or shares are allotted by ballot.

Owens, Robert (1771–1858) Scottish industrialist, believed to be the first manager of a manufacturing firm. He was concerned with management problems such as motivation, productivity, and attitudes.

Own brand Product sold under the name or trademark of the distributor and through its own outlets at a price considerably less than the manufacturer's brand. Chain stores and grocery outlets have their own brands that compete directly with a known manufacturer's brand. Also known as *house brand*.

P

P2P Peer-to-peer

Paasche, Hermann (1851–1925) German statistician and economist. He is best known for his Paasche index, which provides a calculation of the Price Index.

Paasche index Pricing index invented by German economist HERMANN PAASCHE that compares prices of goods bought by a specific population during one year to the prices of the same goods in a base year.

PABLA PROBLEM ANALYSIS BY LOGICAL APPROACH

PACE Price, assortment, convenience, entertainment; an acronym for the benefits of e-commerce.

Pacing The amount of time required for the performance of a task.

Packaging 1. Design of wrappers or containers for goods, as part of marketing. 2. Delivery of a finished product, combining all the downstream activities.

Packard, Vance (1914–1996) American journalist and social critic. In his *Hidden Persuaders* (1957), he explored the use of consumer motivational research and subliminal advertising to manipulate expectations and induce demand for wasteful products. He followed up in later years with a number of other books examining social trends. Among them were *The Status Seekers* (1959), *The Waste Makers* (1960), *The Pyramid Climbers* (1962), *The Naked Society* (1964), *The People Shapers* (1977), and *The Ultra-Rich: How Much is Too Much?* (1989).

Pacman defense After the pocket calculator game, a technique by which a company threatened with a hostile takeover counters with a bid to take over the challenger.

Paired comparison Rank order of elements by comparing their relative values.

Panic In business, a condition of irrational thinking in which participants fear the worst and overreact, leading to further problems; usually applied to stock market, divestment and devaluation, and decisional paralysis.

Panoptic view Perspective of an entire operation from a strategic vantage.

Paradigm Example or pattern; a set of values and norms that constitute a stable state. A change in paradigm leads to a *paradigm shift*.

Paradox of community size Principle that small groups have more active and committed members, who participate in community activities for the greater good.

Paradox of thrift Theory developed by British economist JOHN MAYNARD KEYNES, that efforts to increase the level of savings have the opposite effect.

Par banking Practice, enforced by the FEDERAL RESERVE SYSTEM, of one bank's honoring checks drawn on other banks at full face value, with no check-cashing charge.

Paralysis by analysis Inability of managers to make decisions as a result of being preoccupied with meetings, writing reports, collecting statistics, and analyzing data.

Parenting As applied to business, nurturing of a subsidiary company by the directors of a parent company, with the degree of control and support extended vertically.

Pareto, Vilfredo (1848–1923) Italian economist who is noted for the PARETO RULE, or 80-20 principle.

Pareto chart Chart, named after VILFREDO PARETO, containing bars and a line graph where individual values are represented by bars in descending order and the cumulative total is represented by the line.

Pareto efficiency From Italian economist VILFREDO PARETO, the name for an alteration in the allocation of resources that leaves at least one person better off and nobody worse off.

Pareto rule From Italian economist VILFREDO PARETO, and commonly called the 80-20 rule, states that 80% of national income comes from 20% of the population. The rule can be extrapolated to apply to a number of proportional situations: 80% of systems failure is a result of 20% of possible causes; 20% of a population is responsible for 80% of that nation's progress; 80% of a company's profits come from 20% of its products; 20% of a company's problems take up 80% of a manager's time. Also termed *Pareto principle*.

Paris Bourse French stock exchange.

Parity Equity in pay between different groups of employees and the absence of discrimination in determining pay scales.

Parity of authority Management principle that a superior has the right to issue orders and the employee has the responsibility to obey them.

Parking securities Hiding the real ownership of stocks by buying and holding them under an assumed name.

Parkinson's laws Observations attributed to humorous British writer Cyril Northcote Parkinson, which state that work expands to fill the time available, that expenditures rise to meet income, and that the number of employees multiplies independent of the amount of output. See also PETER PRINCIPLE, DILBERT PRINCIPLE.

Participant observation Research technique in social science whereby an observer joins the group being studied in order to acquire a stake in their activity.

Participating interest Controlling interest in a company through ownership of more than 20% of its shares, entitling the holder to a seat on the BOARD OF DIRECTORS.

Participative management Style of management that encourages worker participation on governing boards, as in an INDUSTRIAL DEMOCRACY.

Partnership Association of two or more persons for the operation of a business under existing commercial laws. Partners are generally liable for the debts of their company, unless it is a limited partnership where the liability is limited to the extent of the investment.

Pascale, Richard Tanner American management guru who developed the MCKINSEY 7S MODEL. He originated the concept of ORGANIZATIONAL AGILITY.

Passing a name Disclosure by a firm of brokers of the names of the principals on whose behalf they are acting, without guaranteeing their solvency.

Passive management Portfolio management that involves holding assets over the long term, aligned to a market index; see INDEX FUND.

Patent Grant of an exclusive right to exploit an invention registered with the U.S. Patent Office or under appropriate INTELLECTUAL PROPERTY laws.

Paternalism Authoritarian management philosophy whereby a manager acts as a benevolent dictator.

Paterson method Job evaluation technique devised by business consultant Thomas T. Paterson, which classifies jobs according to the degree of decision making involved. Also termed *Paterson grading*.

Pathfinder prospectus Initial prospectus for a new company that does not include details but is designed to test-market reactions and to garner support.

Path-goal theory of leadership Management approach that sees the task of senior management as primarily setting goals for junior managers, outlining the paths to reach those goals, and giving them sufficient responsibility to achieve the goals.

Patriarchal management Close management style, usually found in family-owned businesses where the senior-most member of the family is also the chief operating officer or chairman with absolute powers.

Pattern bargaining Negotiating tactic that brings pressure to bear on one party by citing other agreements made in similar cases.

Paula principle Belief that women employees are always held below their level of competence. See also PETER PRINCIPLE.

Pay secrecy Company policy maintaining confidentiality about salaries and perquisites.

Payday loan Small, short-term unsecured loan, also known as cash advances, that carry high interest rates.

PDCA PLAN, DO, CHECK, ACT

Peak experience Transpersonal and ecstatic state, especially one characterized by euphoria, harmonization, and ineffable peace. Term coined by ABRAHAM MASLOW. It is generally associated with religion but may also be induced pharmacologically.

Pecking order Hierarchic status in an organization, showing the relative importance of individuals and their associated status symbols.

Peer group People who are of equal age and standing and have similar tastes and attitudes.

Penalty 1. Compensatory payment required for breach of contract or agreement,

as a result of which the injured party has suffered damages. 2. Fee assessed for a violation of rules, late payment, or disregard for procedure.

Penetration pricing Introduction of a new product to a market at a low price so as to attract new customers, with the intention of raising the price after the product gains acceptance.

Per proc (short for Latin, *per procurationem*) Denotes an action by an agent not on his own authority but on that of a principal who has assumed responsibility for the action.

Perceptual mapping Use of mathematical psychology to understand the structure and behavior of a market; the track records of competing products are shown on a map or graph, and success or failure is charted to show how each fares relative to the others.

Perfect competition Market operating under ideal conditions, in which no product or company has an undue advantage over others. For such a market to exist, there would be no barriers to entry and there would be equilibrium between SUPPLY AND DEMAND. Perfect competition does not exist in the real world, but it serves the comparative purpose of exposing the inadequacies of real-world markets.

Perfect information In a state of PERFECT COMPETITION, information on products and their benefits is available to all, so that no one has to act on the basis of misinformation or incomplete facts.

Perfect storm Unusual conjunction of severe circumstances, whose cumulative effect is disastrous.

Performance Overall quality of work, judged in terms of standard norms and the completion of stated goals over a period of time.

Performance appraisal Formal review of an employee's performance for purposes of training or review of remuneration, using accepted standards, indicators, or a calibrated scale applied without partiality.

Performance bond (p-bond) Bond that indemnifies one party against losses caused by the failure of the second party to perform to specified specifications.

Performance management Style of management that enables employees to reach their optimum level of performance, indicated by setting clear markers and standards.

Performance measurement Tool for judging an employee's suitability for the work assigned, based on objective indicators. These indicators are (1) strategic, related to efficiency and compatibility; (2) operational, related to success and profitability, product mixes, and productivity; (3) physical, relating to income per member of staff, per customer, per offering, per outlet, per square foot, returns on investment, product durability, and longevity; (4) behavioral,

relating to staff and management, attitudes and values, strikes, disputes, absenteeism, turnover, and accidents; (5) confidence, relating to company reputation, shareholder satisfaction, customer satisfaction, and contributions to community welfare; and (6) ethical, relating to the behavioral standards and how they have been met. Distinctions are sometimes made between financial indicators, such as return on capital and economic value added, and nonfinancial indicators, such as the company's ranking in compliance with legal regulations and ethical standards and employee welfare.

Performance standard Level of work required or expected, spelled out in company memoranda relative to the level of remuneration.

Performance tolerance Acceptable level of variance from professional standards tolerated during job evaluation.

Perishable dispute Industrial dispute that becomes moot because the primary issues being contested have grown irrelevant or have been overtaken by recent events.

Perks Short for PERQUISITES.

Permalancer Blend of the words *permanent* and *freelancer;* basically, a freelancer who has no exit date.

Perpetual succession Continued existence of a corporation as a legal entity until it is legally dissolved.

Perquisite Benefits to which an employee is entitled, over and above the salary. These may include free housing, free medical care, and free tuition.

Person-job fit Extent to which a person's skills, interests, and personal characteristics are consistent with the job description.

Person-organization fit Extent to which a person's skills, interests, and personal characteristics are consistent with the objectives of the company.

Personal space In social psychology, the physical space immediately surrounding a person, regarded as inviolable; a violation of this space is considered an invasion of privacy. Also used figuratively to denote a person's ingrained interests and beliefs.

Personality promotion Advertising campaign utilizing a celebrity.

Personnel Human resources department of an organization, as distinguished from its material assets.

Personnel management Business function covering the recruitment, employment, training, placement, promotion, and welfare of the company's employees.

PERT Program evaluation and review technique

PEST Political, economic, social, and technological; an acronym used in analysis.

PESTLE Political, economic, social, technological, legal, and environmental; an acronym used for external issues affecting the development and viability of a company apart from its markets and products.

Peter principle Devised by educator Laurence Peter and Raymond Hull, in their book *The Peter Principle* (1969), a humorous observation that every employee eventually rises to the level of his incompetence. See also Parkinson's laws.

Peters, Thomas J. (1942–) Popular writer on management. His best-selling book, *In Search of Excellence* (1982), inspired a whole generation of corporate executives. Later, he wrote *Thriving on Chaos* (1987), *The Pursuit of Wow* (1994), and *Leadership* (2005).

Philadelphia lawyer Legal professional skilled in finding loopholes in a law.

Phishing Fraudulent act of obtaining bank account numbers, credit card details, Social Security numbers, and other sensitive details via bogus e-mails and text messages.

Physical distribution Warehousing and moving of goods from one point to another, planning the logistics of controlling the flow of materials to markets, and managing the supply chain.

Piece rate Payment to an employee for each unit of work or a set output, sometimes combined with a base salary and bonus.

Piggybacking Selling the complementary goods of another manufacturer.

Pigou, Arthur Cecil (1877–1959) English economist who built up the influential Economics department. His contributions covered welfare economics, unemployment, public finance, index numbers, and measurement of national output. He was a member of the Cunliffe Committee on Currency and Foreign Exchange (1918) and the Royal Commission on Income Tax.

Pigou effect Conceived by economist ARTHUR CECIL PIGOU, the concept that output and employment is stimulated as a result of higher consumption brought about by an increase in wealth.

Pilot production Small-scale production of a new product so as to check its physical specifications and its functionality.

Pilot study Marketing research concerned with making sure that there are no surprise problems when introducing a new product to consumers.

PIMS PROFIT IMPACT OF MARKETING STRATEGIES

Pin-drop syndrome Stress caused by eerie quietness and/or silence in a work space.

Pink-collar Relating to jobs traditionally reserved for women. Compare BLUE-COLLAR, WHITE-COLLAR.

Pink slip Metaphor for a notice of termination of employment or layoff; dates back to 1929, when these notices were slipped into pay envelopes and were on pink paper.

Pipage Distribution of liquid materials through pipes.

Pipeline 1. Materials in transit after they have been purchased but not yet entered in inventory. 2. Process of goods through stages of production, as in "in the pipeline."

Piracy Illegal copying, distribution, and sale of INTELLECTUAL PROPERTY, especially software, books, and music, across borders.

Pit Trading area of a traditional stock exchange, where traders congregate to buy and sell stocks.

Pitch Sales presentation, usually made in person.

Plain vanilla In finance, a simple and straightforward instrument, without any frills or bells and whistles.

Plan, Do, Check, Act (PDCA) A four-stage supervisory technique for continuous improvement of work procedures. The *plan* involves defining goals, *do* involves practice, *check* involves feedback control, and *act* calls for modifications in the light of experience.

Planned obsolescence Strategy in manufacturing of shortening the lifetime of a product through built-in inadequacies, and often matched by bringing out new and im-proved models featuring improvements.

Planning Act of anticipating future needs and resources and matching them, with a view to maximizing output and profits. Planning can be either long term and strate-gic or short term and mostly for scheduling.

Planning fallacy Demonstrated tendency of underestimating the time required for completion of a task. The fallacy derives from natural optimism combined with the assumption that all things will go accord-ing to plan, with the result that there are no provisions made for unintended conse-quences and roadblocks. There is a further tendency to screen out potential or un-pleasant details, so as to reinforce the feel-ing that everything is under control.

Planning, organizing, staffing, directing, coordinating, reporting, and budgeting (POSDCORB) Management functions and roles defined by economist HENRI FAYOL.

Plateau Career stage at which an employee has paused at a particular level of achieve-ment and there is little or no prospect for further promotion.

Plough back To reinvest profits, convert-ing them into capital assets.

Pluralistic ignorance Common belief held by an employee that he or she is an excep-tion to the general rules that apply to eve-ryone else.

Pluralistic theory In industrial psycholo-gy, the existence of common and divergent interests among employers and employees.

Poaching In business, the unauthorized recruitment of employees or customers from a competing company, or a raid on another's sales territory.

Point method Analytical means of job eva-luation, in which jobs are scored on fea-tures such as skills, responsibility, and work conditions, and then used as a basis for cre-ating a graded pay structure.

Point of equilibrium When supply equals demand.

Point of ideal proportion In a production process, the point at which profitability is at its optimum because of the ideal conjunc-tion of labor and overhead.

Point of indifference When revenues bar-ely cover expenses.

Poison pill Tactic of repelling an unwel-come or hostile takeover by ensuring that a successful bid will reduce the value and attractiveness of the company, and will trig-ger developments detrimental to the new owners. Poison pill strategies have multi-plied since the middle of the 20th century. They include:

1. *Flipover rights plan*. The holders of common stock of a company re-ceive one right for each share held, allowing them the option to buy more shares.

2. *Flip-in rights plan.* The holder has the right to purchase shares in the target company at a discount, when a potential acquirer accumulates a specified percentage.

3. *Poison debt.* The target company issues debt securities under conditions designed to discourage the hostile takeover.

4. *Put rights plan.* The target company issues rights in the form of dividends.

5. *Voting poison pill plan.* The target company issues a dividend of securities conferring special privileges to stockholders.

Poka-yoke (In Japanese, "mistake-proofing" or "fail-safety") Range of techniques used in Japan for avoiding human errors; developed by Shigeo Shingo. It consists of three strategies: (1) source inspection to detect errors at their source; (2) one hundred percent inspection for defects using sensing devices; and (3) immediate actions to stop operations when an error is detected.

Political correctness Consciousness of and adherence to popular attitudes and beliefs, without differing or questioning of assumptions.

Political credit risk Chance that a sovereign foreign nation will fail to honor its legal obligations and commitments, for political or other reasons. The principal forms of political risks are (1) confiscation, (2) contract repudiation, (3) currency in-

convertibility, (4) discriminatory taxat. (5) embargo, (6) expropriation of proper (7) war, (8) nationalization, and (9) exces sive fees for bonds or guarantees of performance. Also termed *sovereign risk.*

Polluter pays Principle that the company responsible for violating environmental laws, and consequently adding to the pollutants in water, land, and air, must take full responsibility for cleanup, as well as payment of damages to those adversely affected. See also CAP AND TRADE.

Polychronic culture Society in which time is organized horizontally, so that people engage in various activities at the same time and not sequentially. In such a culture, interpersonal relationships are more important than time-conscious punctuality.

Polyspecialist Person who is neither a GENERALIST nor a specialist, but is knowledgeable in a broad range of subjects.

Ponzi, Charles See PONZI SCHEME.

Ponzi scheme Fraud in which investors are enticed into investing via promised high returns, and sometimes are asked to recruit other investors. In this PYRAMID SCHEME, the money obtained from the later investors is used to pay the early ones. Named after Charles Ponzi, an Italian-born American swindler.

Pooled interdependence Relationships among parts of an organization that have the same goals but different functions and structures, and that cooperate in working toward a common outcome.

Population Group of people sharing common characteristics and who, for marketing purposes, may be considered homogeneous from which a marketing sample can be taken.

Population hypothesis In market research, the assumed characteristics of a target population, based on studies conducted on their suitability as consumers.

Porcupine provision Form of POISON PILL by which the management of a takeover target company hopes to deter unwelcome or hostile takeovers. Also termed *shark repellent.*

Portal-to-portal Relating to pay for time spent in traveling to and from place of work.

Porter, Michael Influential Harvard Business School writer on strategy, especially concerning COMPETITION and COMPETITIVE ADVANTAGE. See also PORTER'S FIVE FORCES.

Porter's five forces Framework developed by business professor MICHAEL E. PORTER for analyzing the balance of power within a particular industry and its profitability. the five forces in the MICROENVIRONMENT that drive competition and weaken a firm's profitability are (1) rivalry among existing competitors, (2) threats of new entrants,

(3) threats of alternative substitutes or comparable products, (4) strength of the consumer public, and (5) strength of the supplier power. COMPETITION and rivalry are considered under this paradigm as negative forces in business growth.

Portfolio career Career spanning a succession of short-term freelance jobs, as opposed to a career that shows progression up the ranks as a full-time employee.

Portfolio theory Developed by HARRY MAX MARKOWITZ, the theory that rational investors are averse to taking increased risk unless the risk is accompanied by potential increased income. Most investors prefer safe investments and a lower level of risk.

Portfolio worker Worker who works for several employers and holds several jobs.

POSDCORB PLANNING, ORGANIZING, STAFFING, DIRECTING, COORDINATING, REPORTING, AND BUDGETING

Position audit Systematic assessment of the current situation of an organization, especially its strengths, weaknesses, opportunities, and threats.

Position trading In finance, holding a long-term OPEN POSITION, with an eye toward achieving profits from calculated risks.

Positioning Marketing strategy by which a company plans to carve out for itself its

space in a field of competitors and build a suitable image among its consumers. To achieve and maintain this positioning in a crowded field, a strategy must include (1) cost leadership, which is achieved through lower costs of production and distribution and higher productivity per worker; (2) differentiation, enabling competitors and consumers to see the company's distinguishing characteristics; (3) focus, or concentration of strengths and historical expertise, rather than dilution of efforts into too many areas.

Post-hoc segmentation Process of segmenting a market after penetration.

Postindustrial society Propounded by economist DANIEL BELL, the service-sector-dominated economy that will replace the manufacturing-dominated era brought about by the INDUSTRIAL REVOLUTION.

Potential market Group of consumers who profess interest in a new product or service.

Poverty trap Situation in which an employee finds him- or herself when an increase in employment benefits is cancelled out by an increase in payroll taxes.

Power 1. Ability to make things happen and exert influence on people, based on one's hierarchic standing, acquired authority, knowledge, or charisma. Power is neutral by nature, and may be used for good or evil. Power is also corrosive and tends to abuse and excess. 2. Relating to power or influence, as in a *power nap* or a *power lunch*.

Power and influence theory of leadership Concept that leadership is based on consensus and relationships, rather than personal qualities and abilities, and that leadership flows from networking and interactions.

Power distance Employee acceptance of the span between the highest level of power in a company and the lowest rung in an organization.

Power style Characteristic ways in which managers influence and massage the behavior of their employees, overcome opposition, and achieve goals. These ways may be classified as consensus, confrontational, or transactional. *Confrontational style* consists of controlling and manipulating information and disinformation through spin and is designed to turn employees into people who rubber-stamp ideas from above. *Consensus style* encourages participative decision making and collective groupthink and problem solving, using the manager's persuasive powers to guide employees and inspire them toward a shared vision. *Transactional style* involves negotiation, incentives, and cooperative undertakings to bring people together without making them feel coerced.

Prahalad, C. K. (1941–2010) Indian-born academic who, together with GARY HAMEL, developed a new theory of competitiveness, strategy, organizations, and core competencies in their book *Competing for the Future* (1994).

Prairie-dogging Working in an OPEN-PLAN OFFICE, divided into cubicles with little privacy.

Preapproach Selling or learning process in which the target is studied in depth and information is gathered about tastes and habits before directly approaching the prospect.

Predatory pricing Strategy of pricing goods and services at such a low level that other firms cannot compete and are forced to leave the market, opening the door for raising the prices.

Predictive bargaining Approach to collective bargaining that tries to anticipate future demands.

Preemption Right of first refusal granted to a party, such as a shareholder, either as a courtesy or in compliance with a contract.

Preference (preferred) share Share in a company yielding a fixed rate of interest rather than a variable dividend. It is an intermediate form of security, between an ORDINARY SHARE and a DEBENTURE. Preferred shares confer some degree of ownership and their claims take precedence over ordinary shares in the event of a LIQUIDATION.

Presenteeism Situation in which an employee is physically present but slacking in work effort. See also ABSENTEEISM.

President Chief executive or CEO of a company, ranked below a CHAIRMAN.

Pressure group Interested parties who actively canvass private or public organizations for favors or benefits that are not available under normal circumstances.

Prestige price Artificially high price charged for a luxury product, conveying the impression that it is of high quality and implying that its cheaper competitors are of poor quality.

Prevention costs Expenses incurred in complying with regulations that enforce environmental standards or in keeping machinery in proper working order to maintain efficiency.

Price and incomes policy Program by a state authority to impose strict controls on market forces in order to rein in INFLATION and reduce or freeze wages. In a FREE MARKET economy, this is usually a temporary measure.

Price controls Restrictions on the prices of goods, enforced by the government during times of economic hardship or to control INFLATION.

Price discrimination Sale of the same products at different prices to different buyers, taking advantage of the needs of different markets but not necessarily related to quality.

Price/earnings ratio (P/E ratio) Current market price of a company share divided by the earnings per share of the company. The P/E ratio usually refers to annual earnings per share and is usually expressed as a number, called the multiple of the company. The multiple corresponds to the number of years it would take the company to earn an amount equal to its market value. High multiples, associated with low yields, indicate that the company is growing rapidly, while low multiples indicate the opposite. Most investment decisions are based on P/E ratios.

Price-to-sales ratio Relationship of a company's stock price to its sales for the past 12 months; used as a means of determining its market strength.

Price leader Dominant company in an industry, which sets the prices in the knowledge that competitors will follow suit. If the price leader has an insurmountable lead as in an OLIGOPOLY or CARTEL, its position will be challenged under antitrust laws.

Price support Government policy of providing subsidies for certain basic sectors or industries, for political or economic reasons; the goal is to shore up prices and prevent them from falling below set levels, to avoid having the sector or industry turn unprofitable. Such support may be either by purchasing, and sometimes stockpiling, surplus products or by cash payments directly to the producers.

Price war Severe competition between two or more firms in the same industry, each seeking to increase its market shares by cutting prices sharply.

Pricing strategy Historically, a method of pricing goods to get them to move out off the shelves and into the shopping carts. Companies use a number of pricing options, such as (1) markup pricing, (2) value pricing, (3) target pricing, (4) going-rate pricing, (5) sealed-bid pricing, (6) penetration pricing, (7) skimming pricing, and (8) experience-curve pricing.

Primary labor market Workers with a narrow range of skills who need retraining for any new type of technology.

Primary market In finance, the market into which a new issue of securities is launched.

Prime rate Rate at which banks lend to their first-class borrowers, based on the FEDERAL RESERVE interest rates.

PRINCE PROJECTS IN CONTROLLED ENVIRONMENTS

Principle of selectivity Maxim that, in any given situation, a minority of agents are responsible for the majority of results or outcomes.

Private enterprise Economic system that

allows or encourages citizens to own capital and property, run businesses, and accumulate wealth and profits without state interference. Also FREE ENTERPRISE. Opposite of COMMAND ECONOMY.

Private equity firm Investment firm that seeks to own and control public companies with a potential for high return. The firm turns these companies into private companies and subjects them to radical financial and organizational restructuring, usually by cutting unprofitable divisions and laying off employees. When the companies regain profitability, the firm sells them or floats them on a stock exchange. Most private equity investment is funded by debt and the acquisitions generally take the form of highly leveraged buy-ins or buyouts. In some views, private equity firms engage in asset stripping and industrial cannibalism strictly to maximize profits.

Private sector Part of an economy that is not under government control. In FREE MARKET economies, this sector is the largest and most efficient sector. See also PUBLIC SECTOR.

Privatization Process of selling a publicly or state-owned company or industry to the private sector, often for political reasons. This generally happens when a government moves from socialism to capitalism. The move is accompanied by increased efficiency and a broadening of stakeholders in the economy. Also gained are liquid funds for the state, thereby allowing it to reallocate resources. Sometimes the changeover is rapid;

other times it follows a gradual privatization, with steps such as DEREGULATION, LIBERALIZATION of regulations, and diversification. Also termed *denationalization*.

Proactive management Philosophy of management that emphasizes being ahead of the curve, in anticipation of problems and as a way of managing change.

Probability In statistics and mathematics, the likelihood that a particular event or result will occur, especially when represented on a chart or scale from 1 to 10.

Probation Trial employment period for verifying the ability and suitability of a new recruit before being entered on the rolls.

Problem analysis by logical approach (PABLA) A problem-solving method to improve design processes using cards.

Problem definition First stage in market research, consisting of composing a statement that identifies the nature of the problem and its probable causes.

Problem solving Act of using a systematic approach to overcoming obstacles in the management of an enterprise, including such techniques as BRAINSTORMING, FISHBONE CHARTS, and PARETO CHARTS. Problem solving is a seven-step process: (1) identification of the problem, (2) verification, (3) definition, (4) root-cause analysis, (4) evaluation of alternatives, (5) implementation of solution, (6) post-implementation review, and (7) institutionalization and control.

Process Specific, structured, and managed set of activities with known inputs, designed to produce a desired output; or a configuration of operational capabilities and restrictions that are designed to produce a desired result.

Process choice Selection of the type of process ideally suited to create a particular product or service, varying from one-off approach (in which third-party contractors are involved), to batch production, to continuous processing. Each option involves a different combination of skills, design, planning, control, and scheduling. The process also must be in sync with consumer needs and preferences. Process choice calls for costing mechanisms to be in place because costs are accumulated over the lifetime of the product and yield different unit costs, as well as sometimes normal or abnormal losses. Different processes also require different plant layouts in which resources will flow through different routes and workstations.

Process control Statistical and engineering tool that deals with architecture, mechanisms, and algorithms for maintaining the output of a process within a desired range. It is used extensively in industry to enable continuous manufacturing of oil, paper, chemicals, and electric power. It enables automation by which a small staff can operate a complex factory from a central control room.

Process departmentation Grouping of departments or subunits on the basis of their primary organizational operations. See MATRIX DEPARTMENTATION, GEOGRAPHICAL DEPARTMENTATION, FUNCTIONAL DEPARTMENTATION, and PRODUCT DEPARTMENTATION.

Process improvement Feature of organizational development consisting of a series of actions to identify, analyze, and improve business performance and processes to meet new goals and objectives and increase profits, reduce costs, and accelerate schedules. These methods include BENCHMARKING, capability maturity model, HOSHIN PLANNING, ISO SERIES, IT governance, JUST-IN-TIME, LEAN manufacturing, REENGINEERING, redesign, SIX-SIGMA, software process improvement, THEORY OF CONSTRAINTS, trillium model, and twelve leverage points.

Process management Integrating quality and performance excellence into strategic management, this is Category 6 in the BALDRIDGE AWARD. It includes process design, process definition, process documentation and description of existing processes, process analysis and control, and process improvement.

Process mapping Effort to present all the interdependent processes within an organization on a table or chart. A PROCESS is a coordinated set of activities that meets customer requirements. This is important, as many organizations undergoing BUSINESS PROCESS REENGINEERING change from a functional structure to a horizontal structure. Process mapping analyzes the flow of work across the functions and even within them. There are three phases in which process maps may act as a focus: (1) process capture and business modeling, (2) process redesign, and (3) process support. Companies are typically organized into functional and vertical hierarchies, such as marketing and finance, with a high degree of hierarchy in which status, power, control, and rank are more important than efficiency, cooperation, and service. Maps help companies to move into a cross-functional management structure.

Process principle Organizational concept defined by economist HENRI FAYOL, which describes the desirable traits of managers in the dealing with subordinates.

Process production Continuous and capital-intensive production cycle designed to fit the requirements of a process, as in chemicals, rather than mass production, as in an assembly line. Process production requires intensive planning, specifying the sequence and the nature of the end product.

Procurement Act of purchasing. It includes determining needs, identifying potential suppliers, conducting market studies, analyzing proposals, selecting suppliers, issuing purchase orders, negotiating with suppliers, administering contracts, checking the quality of received materials, and maintaining records. Also called *supply management.*

Product Anything that meets a need and yields measurable economic value, and that needs to be processed before the consumer can consume or utilize it.

Product bundling Sales of related products together at a combined price that is lower than when priced individually.

Product churning Flooding the market with new, similar products in the hope that one of them will become successful.

Product class Broad group of products that perform similar functions, meet similar needs, and provide similar benefits, although they may have distinctive features.

Product departmentation Organization and division of a firm on the basis of its product portfolio, placing a group or team in charge of each product or group of products.

Product development Strategy for company growth that relies on the generation of new ideas and concepts to get new products to new markets or new segments of existing markets.

Product differentiation Effort to stress unique features of a product. It is successful when there's a difference that convinces consumers that they are getting a better deal. Product differentiation may be generally only in packaging and design, but may sometimes extend to content and operability. Producers also offer new and improved versions to distinguish from earlier versions.

Product liability Legal responsibility assumed by the manufacturer and seller for any material loss or damage suffered by users of its products, often as a result of a defect in manufacturing or raw materials.

Product life cycle Lifetime of a product in terms of its use, sales, or profitability. A product has five distinct stages to its life cycle: (1) development, (2) introduction, (3) growth, (4) maturity, and (5) decline. Many products reappear in a reincarnation stage.

Product line Group of related products with similar functionality, comparable in price and utility, and sold through the same channels to the same markets.

Product management Development of products, including invention, design, production, and marketing.

Product-market strategy Marketing planning model in which companies try to achieve a optimum mix between existing products and new products. Using the ANSOFF MATRIX gives a choice of several models: (1) market penetration, in which companies sell more of their existing products in the existing markets through price manipulation and better advertising and promotion; (2) product development, by which companies modify or improve their existing products for their current customers; (3) market development, by which companies sell their existing products to new customers; and (4) product diversification, by which new products are developed for new markets.

Product mix Spectrum of product lines offered by one company, covering a variety of needs.

Product-process matrix Tool for analyzing the relationship between the product life cycle and the technological life cycle, a concept introduced by business consultants ROBERT H. HAYES and STEVEN C. WHEELWRIGHT.

Production Output in a manufacturing process that results in the creation of an identifiable and marketable product, by hand or machine.

Production orientation Goods produced for sale whose production determines the selection for consumers, rather than consumer demand.

Production system Management guru PETER DRUCKER's classification of production methods, including process production, mass production, and unique product production.

Production unit In accounting, a method of computing the depreciation charge for a given period on a piece of machinery, based on the number of units manufactured.

Productivity Measure of output per unit by input such as labor, raw materials, or capital; used as an indicator of profitability and efficiency.

Productivity ratio Measurement of the relationship of input to output, yielding output per person, per unit of raw material or unit of time.

Professionalization Introduction of professional standards into an occupation, so as to bring uniformity to the credentials of its members, institute requirements for training, evaluate performance, and standardize the claims and qualifications of the field.

Profile Collection of parameters on a subject or person or activity either as text or graphs.

Profit Revenues above and beyond the costs of producing and distributing a product, or income beyond expenditures for a business.

Profit-and-loss account Assignment of monies showing profits and expenditures. Profits may be classified further as *net profits* and *retained profits*.

Profit center Unit of an organization that is treated as a separate entity for purposes of financial control and that is allocated income targets for a specified period.

Profit impact of marketing strategies (PIMS) Widely used database that profiles characteristics of successful marketing strategies and products and brands. Also the name of a database examining the relationship between marketing outlays and profitability. At the heart of the PIMS program is a database of thousands of businesses with data on market environments, competitive situations, costs, asset structures, and profit performances. Key determinants include marketplace standing, market environment, differentiation from competitors, and capital and production structure.

Profit sharing Incentive plan in which companies distribute a portion of their profits to their employees in addition to their wages. There are three types of profit-sharing plans: (1) cash, (2) deferred, and (3) combination.

Profit variance Difference between standard operating profits in a budget and actual profits made.

Profit-volume ratio Sales revenue less variable costs, divided by sales volume; this shows which products are most profitable at which levels of sales.

Profit warning Official statement from a company that its profits may be less than expected for a coming quarter or year.

Profitability Return on capital employed and the ratio of net profit to sales.

Profitability Index Ratio of payoff to investment. It is a useful tool for ranking projects. Also *profit investment ratio* or *value investment ratio*.

Profiteer Person who makes excessive profits by charging inflated prices for a commodity in short supply.

Program Evaluation and Review Technique (PERT) Statistical tool used in project management designed to represent and analyze tasks. It is commonly used in conjunction with the critical-path method. It is designed as a decision-making tool for saving time in achieving goals and for measuring and forecasting progress in research and development.

Progress chaser Person responsible for monitoring the progress of a project and ensuring that it is completed on time.

Progressive consumer Prospective consumer who has an interest in buying newer and more advanced versions of the same product.

Progressive tax Tax in which the tax rate advances as the taxable base increases. It reduces the tax incidence of people with a lower ability to pay and shifts the incidence proportionately to those with a higher ability to pay. It also applies adjustment of the tax base by using tax exemptions or tax credits, as in the case of lower sales tax on food and higher taxes on luxury items. Opposite of REGRESSIVE TAX.

Project Set of activities or tasks designed to produce a desired result within a specified time. Since the activities are interrelated, they are prioritized and the tasks are assigned to specialists.

Project champion Manager in charge of a particular project, with full responsibility for bringing it to completion.

Project financing Money borrowed for a specific project, secured only by the project, and payable upon completion.

Project management Oversight of a project with time-limited objectives and a budget that crosses departmental boundaries; usually involves work with dedicated teams.

Projects in controlled environments (PRINCE) A method of project management in which the project moves through its cycle under predetermined and structured variables, using standardized procedures. The controlled environment enables the managers to concentrate on content rather than process.

Promoter Principal person involved in securing approvals and funding for a project, and in organizing the people who will take charge of it.

Promotion from within Policy of promoting junior staff to senior positions when the openings occur, rather than advertising and recruiting from outside.

Propensity to consume Proportion of income in an economy that enters the circular flow from consumer to producer, and that stays there and is not withdrawn into inactive savings.

Proportionate stratified sampling Probability sampling method for identifying different social and demographic strata, and the elements drawn from each stratum proportional to their numerical strengths.

Proprietary accounts Accounts showing assets and liabilities.

Prospect theory Developed by psychologists DANIEL KAHNEMANN and AMOS TVERSKY, the theory that improbable events are more frequent in real life than probable events, and that losses are more consequential than gains. This work seeks to explain how individuals make decisions when faced with uncertainty. It is an attempt to link psychology and financial decision making, and has three components: decision frames, mistakes in evaluating probabilities, and risk preference.

Prospector strategy Aggressive business strategy seeking large gains and taking significant risks. It is willing to bet on unproven technologies.

Prospectus Manifesto of a new organization or project, stating its goals and objects, its resources, its principals, its likely profitability, and a description of its principal markets.

Prosuming Situation whereby a company or person is both consumer and producer.

Protean career Career that involves frequent changes of organization, work profile, and job content; there's no pattern of loyalty to a single company or career path, but, rather, is shaped by an individual's own needs.

Protestant work ethic Belief in the virtue of thrift, hard work, and self-discipline. It is believed that this guiding principle was

instrumental in launching the INDUSTRIAL REVOLUTION and especially in the development of U.S. industrial strength.

Protocol Rules governing professional conduct, or the guiding principles of a field of study or particular discipline.

Prototype Preproduction model developed to evaluate the feasibility of new materials, technology, or design, as part of NEW PRODUCT DEVELOPMENT.

Provision Amount set aside out of profits for a known liability of an uncertain amount.

Prudence Concept that anticipated or expected revenues and profits should not be included in a company's accounts unless they have been realized in cash, lest they skew the financial information.

Psychic income Satisfaction derived from a job, over and beyond the salary.

Psychological contract Relationship based on expectations and implied assertions. They may take a number of forms: (1) *coercive contract*, such as between a public utility and its customers, where the corporate entity has the law on its side; (2) *alienative contract*, where the workers have no control over work procedures and quality; (3) *remunerative contract*, as between management and staff, which is based on monetary and quantitative terms; (4) *calculative contract*, where there is a direct correlation between worker skills and the remuneration and work satisfaction, as is between a doctor and a hospital; and (5) *normative contract*, in which there is professional camaraderie and ideological affinity between workers and the administration, as in religious organizations, trade unions, and political parties.

Psychological price Retail price that meets little consumer resistance because it appeals to the consumer's aesthetic sense.

Public company Company whose shares are available to the public through a stock exchange.

Public corporation State-owned business that operates as a branch of the government and is fully or partially funded out of the state's budget. It is generally accountable to the legislature.

Public limited company Company legally registered as corporation, but with limited liability and operating under the relevant regulations.

Public policy Decisions that advance the interests of a community, rather than particular segments of it.

Public relations Manipulation of images and information in the media, with the ostensive purpose of creating a favorable impression and softening a negative image. It is work done by professionals who maintain good relations with journalists and other information gatekeepers.

Public sector Part of the economy that is owned and run by the state, including na-

tionalized industries and public corporations. See also PRIVATE SECTOR.

Public utility In a mixed economy, the sector that is owned and run by the government or by utilities that serve basic public needs.

Publicity Use of the media to spread information about a company, product, or person in a favorable light or to mitigate the effects of wrong or misleading information. Publicity, in essence, is free ADVERTISING.

Pull manufacturing Systems, such as JUST-IN-TIME, in which production takes place only in response to demand from the customer.

Pull strategy Tactic that requires high spending in advertising and consumer promotion to build up customer demand.

Pulsing Scheduling of advertisements and commercials in short bursts over a short period.

Pumping Injection of money into the banking system by the FEDERAL RESERVE BOARD.

Punter Speculator in the financial market out to make a quick profit.

Purchase method Type of accounting in which cash and other assets are distributed as liabilities incurred. The net assets are recorded as acquired at fair value and any excess is recorded as goodwill.

Purchasing power Ability of a currency to be exchanged for goods and services. Monetary assets have less purchasing power in times of INFLATION, and companies with outstanding loans gain purchasing power while lenders recover money that has lost value.

Purchasing power parity Principle that the value of a currency is based on its purchasing power in terms of a consistent basket of goods and services.

Pure competition Ideal state in which there are no barriers to entry, and there is unlimited freedom for all traders.

Pure monopoly Market in which there is only one seller for each commodity or service.

Push manufacturing System in which production is driven solely by demand.

Push strategy Strategy by which a company creates demand for a product or need that did not exist before.

Put option Contract between two parties to exchange an asset at a specified price (strike price) by a predetermined date (maturity or expiry). The buyer has the right but not the obligation to buy and the seller has the obligation to buy.

Pygmalion effect The greater the expectation placed upon people, the better they perform. Named after the character in the play by George Bernard Shaw.

Pyramid hierarchy Organizational structure in which there are fewer people in each succeeding higher level of management. See TALL ORGANIZATION.

Pyramid scheme Nonsustainable and illegal business model that promises incentives for enrolling people in a scheme without involving any direct sale or products or investments. The most common pyramid scheme is the PONZI SCHEME.

Pyramid selling Method of selling franchises using an array of part-time entrepreneurs, with the principal instigator recruiting others who are required to take stock in the company. They may then resell to their associates on the same conditions, in a pyramid that broadens as it descends. It is a con job, comparable to a PONZI SCHEME, by which the principals take all the money while those lower down do all the work and never realize any return.

Q

Q ratio Devised by American economist James Tobin, a ratio of the total value of a company to the replacement value of its total assets. The ratio is used to measure the impact of intangible assets.

Qualified audit Review of a financial statement that is qualified either because the auditor has found some irregularities, the audit itself was limited in scope, or all details have not been disclosed but there is insufficient cause for a negative report.

Qualitative forecasting Predictions that rely on expert opinion rather than statistical data.

Qualitative marketing research Study of the beliefs, motivations, perceptions, and opinions of respondents, using in-depth interviews and group discussions.

Quality Totality of the features, characteristics, and traits that encompass the functionality and appearance of a product or service and its ability to satisfy the customer's need as intended.

Quality assurance Strategic corporate function charged with maintaining strict QUALITY CONTROL and compliance with specifications, targets, and procedures.

Quality circle Members of a workforce or team charged with solving problems and generating ideas for improving a process or product.

Quality control Monitoring a process or work operation so as to ensure it conforms to the desired output in terms of quality; this entails inspection at various stages and periodic sampling.

Quality engineering Branch of engineering that deals with a manufacturing system at all stages to improve the quality of the production process and the output.

Quality function deployment Technique for designing services or products based on consumer expectations, which are then built into the finished product.

Quality of life Nebulous concept embracing positive factors that affect one's overall physical comfort, sense of security, and well-being.

Quality planning roadmap Systematic effort to project goals and targets in a quality-driven campaign or program and note the milestones and benchmarks needed to achieve them.

Quango In the United Kingdom, short for *quasi nongovernmental organization*; an unofficial organization that serves the state, either directly or indirectly.

Quantitative easing Monetary policy that increases the money supply in an effort to promote increased lending and liquidity.

Quantitative forecasting Predictions stemming from statistical research and historical trends.

Question mark Marketing situation in the BOSTON MATRIX characterized by high growth but poor market position.

Quantitative marketing research Study involving collection of data gauging respondents' reactions to stimuli and perceptions of a product.

Queuing theory In business, the way

components arrive in the system, enabling study of the most effective ways to process them.

Quick fix A simple, fast-acting solution to a complex problem, usually without dealing with its root causes.

Quick ratio Relationship between existing liabilities and available funds.

Quit rate Speed at which workers leave employment, an indicator of employee dissatisfaction.

Quorum Required minimum number of persons for holding a meeting, especially to pass any motions or make decisions.

Quota 1. Set proportional share of a whole, often applied to a person or group qualified to be hired or considered for admission. 2. Limit on the number of exports and imports allowed.

Quotation In finance, the price of a security, usually the bid, asked, and the last prices of the day on a stock exchange.

R

Race to the top Competition among peers to achieve the distinction of being the leader, usually the market leader.

Radar chart Graphical method of displaying multivariate data in the form of a two-dimensional chart of three or more quantitative variables represented on axes starting from the same point. Also known as web chart, spider chart, start chart, cobweb chart, polar chart, kiviat diagram, or irregular polygon.

Radar mapping Device that permits management to see at a glance the financial status of the firm.

Radical innovation A new product that represents a quantum leap, rather than a sequential progression. Henry Ford's introduction of the assembly line is an example of a radical innovation in manufacturing.

Raider Corporation, or its representative (CORPORATE RAIDER), that attempts to take over another company that it has deemed having undervalued assets by making a hostile bid.

Rainmaker Well-connected person who can make things happen, especially in transactions with a government.

Rally Rise, extended or short term, in prices on a stock exchange, sometimes in reaction to positive news or after a fall in prices.

Ramping Attempt to boost the prices of a stock by artificially raising demand and purchasing large quantities, then selling them as soon as the price reaches a plateau.

R&D RESEARCH AND DEVELOPMENT

Rand formula In Canada, a way of ensuring employees pay union dues even when they decline membership; this is to avoid the situation whereby employees benefit from the gains achieved by the union but avoid paying dues.

Random variation Unplanned shift away from a normal level of performance, as a result of factors beyond control, such as weather or the quality of the input.

Rank-order scale In market research, tool

used by respondents to rank various products in terms of stated criteria on a progressive scale.

Rat race Common expression for the intense pursuit of career success.

Rate of return Annual amount of income from an investment, expressed as a percentage of the original investment.

Rating Work measurement technique for comparing data from a series of time studies against an accepted standard norm.

Rating agency In finance, an organization, such as Standard and Poor's or Moody's, that rates the creditworthiness of institutions, bond issues, and other forms of corporate or government borrowings.

Ratio analysis Use of accounting ratios to evaluate a company's operating performance and financial stability.

Ratio covenant Clause in a loan agreement stipulating conditions relating to GEARING ratio and interest that indicate the company's stability. Breach of the covenant enables the lender to request immediate repayment.

Rational appeal In marketing, the approach to potential customers using their basic interests and instincts of a company's promotional advertisement.

Rational expectation MACROECONOMIC

theory developed in the 1960s by economists JOHN F. MUTH and others, that economic transactions are made on the basis of all available information, and although the forecasts may turn out to be wrong, they were nonetheless legitimate because they were based on rational premises.

Rational management Style of management that is overly concerned with input and output, and not with human impacts of decisions.

Rationalization Reorganization of a company by cutting out the dead wood and streamlining operations, thereby making it leaner, more efficient, and profitable. This involves layoffs, closing some units while expanding others, merging stages of production, DOWNSIZING, RIGHTSIZING, and weeding out product lines that have low returns.

Reaction In finance, a reversal of a current market trend or sudden response to positive or negative news; usually means sudden selling in a BULL market and buying in a BEAR market.

Reactive Actions or approach to problems as they occur, rather than in anticipation of them. This is a policy marked by lack of advance planning.

Reactor strategy Strategy in strategic management that is limited to delayed responses to market conditions and opportunities.

Reaganomics Economic policies and philosophy associated with President Ronald Reagan, focusing on DEREGULATION, SUPPLY-SIDE ECONOMICS, and smaller government.

Real interest rate Actual interest rate less the current rate of INFLATION.

Real-time marketing Sale of goods and services customized to incorporate customer needs continuously, without input from customers or sales personnel.

Reality check Effort to ascertain whether something that works well in theory or on paper also works well in practice.

Realized profit/loss In regard to a completed transaction, the full amount either gained or lost, as opposed to a gain or loss on paper only. For example, if a stock is purchased at $50 and its price decreases to $40, the $10 loss in value is realized only when it is actually sold at that lower price.

Rebalancing In finance, adjustment of a hedge to reflect its effectiveness in a rapidly changing market and to its relative standing among various securities.

Rebate Partial refund on the price of a good or service, constituting a discount but paid after the sale.

Reboot Restart a computer or resume a project that has been dormant for any reason.

Rebundling Changing the product mix in a firm's portfolio to achieve sustainable growth, especially through mergers and acquisitions, thus leveraging economies of scale. It may also require unbundling or the divestiture of nonperforming divisions and subsidiaries.

Recall Manufacturer's announcement of a product defect that requires the consumers and dealers to return the affected product for repair, replacement, or refund.

Recapitalization Process by which the balance between debt and equity is adjusted without adding to total capital.

Receiver Manager handling the settlement of debts for a bankrupt business, with the authority to liquidate property.

Recency, Frequency and Monetary analysis (RFM) Marketing tool used to analyze customer behavior in terms of how recently they have made a purchase, how frequently they make purchases, and how much money they spend.

Recession Downturn in an economy that is less severe than a DEPRESSION but more severe than STAGNATION, a determination based on many economic factors. According to the National Bureau of Economic Research, a GROSS DOMESTIC PRODUCT for two successive quarters is commonly but erroneously considered to constitute a recession.

Reciprocity In business and trade, mutual

extension of favorable terms and conditions, as between friendly equals. There are four types of reciprocity: (1) identical; (2) affinity-based, as in a trading bloc; (3) overall or broad; and (4) sectoral, or limited to specific products or sectors.

Recognition dispute Industrial dispute that follows when a company declines to recognize a labor union as the legitimate representative of its workers.

Recommended retail price Suggested price of a product sold at retail, set by the manufacturer and not binding on the retailer, who is free to charge what the traffic will bear. For example, automobiles are listed with a suggested price but dealers negotiate with customers and offer discounts. Also termed *manufacturer's suggested listed price.*

Recourse Right of redress should the terms of a contract not be fulfilled to the satisfaction of the injured party.

Red circling Practice of protecting the salaries of employees whose jobs were downgraded during a RECESSION.

Reddin, William James (1930–1999) British-born Canadian management guru whose book *Managerial Effectiveness* (1970) explored THREE-DIMENSIONAL MANAGEMENT.

Reductionism Simplification or even oversimplification of a complex event or idea, either to demonstrate its fallacy or to examine its validity.

Redundancy Unnecessary or duplicated employment. This usually leads to loss of a job because it has become superfluous or has been eliminated for economic reasons. Often, this entails dismissal with or without notice, for any reason other than BREACH OF CONTRACT.

Reengineering Approach to introducing change in an organization from the top down, popularized by management experts MICHAEL HAMMER and JAMES CHAMPY. It focuses on processes other than traditional functions and makes extensive use of information technology to help rethink the business from scratch. It requires DELAYERING, DOWNSIZING, and EMPLOYEE EMPOWERMENT

Re-exports Goods that have been imported and then exported without material changes in their value or composition. Re-exports are the staple of the ENTREPOT TRADE.

Reference group Group with which a person identifies emotionally, without reference to membership.

Reference rate Base rate at which a bank offers loans relative to the interest rates prevalent in the financial markets.

Referent power Influence exerted on a subordinate by a powerful superior, by which the former adopts the mannerisms and style of the latter.

Refinancing Process of repaying some or

all of a loan or mortgage by obtaining a new loan at a lower rate of interest.

Reflation Policy of stimulating a sagging economy by government stimulus, either by government spending, lowering taxes, or increasing the money supply.

Refreezing State of an organization that has undergone radical changes, in which employees have to relearn their work and adjust to new experiences. Term introduced by German-American psychologist KURT LEWIN.

Regiocentric Focused on or promoting the interests of a region or bloc, as opposed to those outside the region.

Regression In statistics, a method for establishing functional relationships between variables.

Regression analysis Statistical technique that measures the extent to which one variable is related to two or more other variables, often for predicting the future of the dependent variable.

Regressive tax Taxation in which the rate decreases as income increases; more commonly, a tax that is based on consumption rather than income, such as a sales tax, which by default negatively impacts the poor much more than the rich. See also PROGRESSIVE TAX.

Regret rule In decision making, the choice of the option that causes least regret if it turns out to be the wrong one.

Reinforcement theory Process of shaping behavior by controlling its consequences, most often through a combination of rewards and punishments. It is also called OPERANT CONDITIONING because it establishes a relationship between action and consequence.

Related diversified strategy Expansion by a firm into activities that bear strong similarities to their current or original activities. Firms in technology and the skill-based industries were among the first to adopt this strategy.

Related party transaction Transfer of resources or obligations between related parties, regardless of a monetary nexus.

Relational capital Cumulative trust, experience, and knowledge that form the core of the relationship between a firm and its clients.

Relations analysis One of three techniques introduced by management guru PETER DRUCKER to analyze organizational strength. It examines the actual relations among key managers, rather than what their relations ought to be according to the textbooks.

Relationship 1. In marketing or banking, a long-term, sensitive, positive, and supportive relationship based on mutual interests.

2. In management, leadership concerned with avoiding causes of friction and lifting morale, treating subordinates as associates whose ideas and contributions are valued. 3. In banking, the extension of special privileges to long-term or most valued clients.

Relationship role Any of several roles on a team, such as encourager (who uses praise), harmonizer (who mediates opposing views), gatekeeper (who keeps channels of communications open), and comedian (who uses humor).

Relative share Ratio of per capita income to that of the rest of society.

Relevance Importance of particular information to those reaching decisions.

Relevance analysis Study of existing research programs to determine their effectiveness in advancing the company's core interests.

Reliability principle Belief that every piece of information is faithful to facts, neutral, complete, and free of error.

Reluctant manager Introduced by business consultants RICHARD SCASE and ROBERT GOFFEE, description of a manager who feels alienated from his or her peers because of being left out of key decision making. This alienation reduces the person's effectiveness as a team member.

Reorganization Process of restructuring a company that is in financial difficulties or is under CHAPTER 11 for bankruptcy.

Repatriation Return of capital from a foreign investment to its home country.

Replacement demand Need for second- and later-generation products, driven by the concept of model year and the annual introduction of new versions.

Representations Information given by one party to another in furtherance of a transaction.

Representative heuristic Quality of a product judged on the basis of its price or on its similarity to a familiar product.

Resale price maintenance Agreement between a manufacturer and wholesaler or retailer not to sell a specified product below a fixed price recommended by the manufacturer.

Rescission Right of the party to a contract to have the agreement set aside and conditions restored to the precontract position on the grounds that the contract is unfair and based on misrepresentation.

Research Scientific investigation with a purpose. It can be APPLIED RESEARCH or *pure research*, and it forms the basis for decision making. As a process, research begins with a question and a proposal is designed to answer that question. The research design may be experimental or nonexperimental, with the former conducted in the field or in the laboratory. The next stage is data collection, which may be primary or secondary; a survey design provides the methodology and parameters of the survey.

Research and development (R&D) Work to discover new applications of old ideas or new ideas based on technology, for commercial exploitation and particularly the gaining of new patents. R&D may be of the BLUE SKY type in pure science and technology, without immediate commercial potential, or it may be an extension of existing technology into new fields to satisfy new needs.

Reserve Part of the capital of a company other than the share capital, arising from retained profits or surpluses not yet distributed.

Residual Payment received by a person, such as an actor, musician, or producer of a movie or television commercial, every time the movie or commercial is played in a commercial setting.

Residual income Net income of a subsidiary or division after deduction of a certain percentage for the use of assets, facilities, or property owned by the parent company.

Residual unemployment Unemployable people, such as prisoners and sick people, as a segment of the population.

Resistance level Point at which a price for a good that represents the maximum

reached but never exceeded, and therefore is considered its ceiling.

Resistance to change Tendency to resist the forces of change and fear of the uncertainties brought about by change.

Resolution Binding decision adopted by the governing body of a corporation or organization.

Resource appraisal Management review of corporate resources available for making decisions about diversification, takeovers, and acquisitions.

Resource-based Relating to a strategy based on a company's internal resources, such as its assets, intellectual capital, patents, or managerial talents, rather than on external factors such as market conditions. The strategy holds that sustained competitiveness requires resources characterized by the VRIN criteria: valuable, rare, imperfectly imitable, and nonsubstitutable.

Restraint of trade Activity that restrains a person's right to carry on a trade or profession or to compete in the marketplace; often a clause in a contract but also part of ANTITRUST legislation.

Restrictive covenant Clause in a contract that restricts the freedom of one of the parties in some way, especially relating to competition or employment.

Restrictive trade practice Collusive

agreement between two or more parties with a view toward restricting prices, conditions of sale, quantities offered, processes, and territory, especially in a way that is prejudicial to the public interest and contrary to fair and nondiscriminatory dealings.

Résumé Document that outlines pertinent career and personal information of a candidate for employment, particularly in the context of a specific job opening.

Retailing accordion Manner in which the range of a product mix changes over the lifetime of the products.

Retention marketing Practices focused on keeping the loyalty of existing customers, rather than on acquiring new ones.

Retirement on the job Actions of an employee on the verge of retirement, who tries to do as little as possible or does his job perfunctorily.

Retrenchment One of the tools in company downsizing whereby the existing staff is reduced in number or their pay curtailed and expenses are scaled down.

Retrogressive consumer Consumer who values low prices and economy over quality and new features. Compare Progressive consumer.

Return on investment (ROI) Accounting ratio expressing the profit of a company as a percentage of the capital employed. In these calculations, *profit* is defined as that earned before interest and taxes, while *capital* is defined as fixed assets plus current assets minus current liabilities.

Revaluation 1. Rise in the exchange rate of a currency, especially in relation to foreign currencies. In general terms it is the calculated adjustment of a country's official exchange rate relative to a baseline. 2. Adjustment of a tax level to slow or stop the rise in tax revenue as taxable assets increase.

Revaluation of assets Accounting method to reassess value against new baselines or new accounting methods, so as to create a new set of values.

Revenue Form of income that is incorporated into the Profit-and-loss account.

Revenue management Use of sophisticated computer systems to analyze consumer behavior, forecast demand, and adjust pricing schedules; used in industries where the resources are fixed and perishable, such as theaters, airlines, hotels, stadiums, and restaurants, and where the loss of income from a particular flight or event is irrecoverable. It is an attempt to optimize yield through market segmentation, price discrimination, and differentiating the product.

Reverse culture shock Experienced by an employee who returns to his or her home country after an extended stay abroad; this is a sharpened perception of changes that have taken place during the period of absence.

Reverse engineering Act of taking apart a competitor's product and examining it to find what makes it work, then figuring out how to make it better. It is usually done to explore ways of redesigning without infringing on patents.

Reverse evaluation Evaluation of a supervisor by the subordinates.

Reverse takeover Purchase of a larger company by a smaller one, or the purchase of a public company by a private one.

Revolving credit Credit that can be drawn upon at any time, without limit as to the manner and amount of the DRAWDOWN.

RFM RECENCY, FREQUENCY, AND MONETARY ANALYSIS

Rhochrematics Method of seamlessly managing material flow covering production and distribution by using the most efficient combination and mix of options.

Ride the curve Taking advantage of a rapid growth in demand for a new technology as it becomes more widely adopted.

Rigging Attempt to make a big profit in the market by circumventing regulations and overriding normal market forces. This involves taking a long or short position designed to influence prices, and then selling or buying accordingly.

Right-brained Descriptive of people who are visual and intuitive, rather than analytical and verbal. Compare LEFT-BRAINED.

Right first time Concept integral to TOTAL QUALITY MANAGEMENT, whereby the production process does not have any room for mistakes or afterthoughts.

Rightsizing Restructuring and RATIONALIZATION to improve effectiveness and to cut costs without severely DOWNSIZING and only moderately reducing expenditures and staffing.

Rikutsupoi (Japanese, "the brash ones") Younger workers who are bright but pushy and short on experience or wisdom.

Ringelmann, Maximillien (1861–1931) Professor of Engineering who discovered the RINGELMANN EFFECT, which states that workers are more unproductive when working in groups. He is considered the founding father of social psychology.

Ringelmann effect After agricultural engineer MAX RINGELMANN, a principle that output grows proportionately with the growth in size, but productivity declines by a similar percentage, and that smaller groups are more efficient per capita than larger groups.

Ring-fence 1. To block off part of a company or group that goes into liquidation so that it survives and escapes receivership. 2. To earmark an amount of money for a specific purpose so that it cannot be used for any other purpose.

Ringi system Form of Japanese collective decision making in which all members affected by a decision participate in its forming.

Rising bottoms In regard to the stock market, a pattern in which low prices in a fluctuating market display a steady upward trend over time, presaging a coming Bull market.

Risk Possibility of a financial loss, in absolute terms or relative to expectations, that is built into a speculative endeavor undertaken for gain. Risk arises from uncertainty, the vagaries of nature, or human nature and cannot be forecast.

Risk analysis Consideration of the extent of a risk involving an enterprise, especially its identification, classification, and management.

Risk-averse Tendency to prefer safer opportunities or investments over those presenting greater chances of failure or ruin and lower returns.

Risk capital See Venture capital.

Risk management Understanding and evaluating the risk involved in a business proposition or transaction, so as to prepare for the eventuality of failure or loss and to moderate the effects of such a loss. Common forms of risk management include insurance, derivatives as a hedge against sudden market fluctuations, and higher interest rates to compensate for potential losses.

Risk matrix Method or framework of Risk analysis first developed by the U.S. military to identify operational risk under combat conditions; it was then applied to business and in that context involves Brainstorming to establish what needs to be saved during a crisis and what is expendable. The framework itself deals with the effects of a business decision on the company's assets.

Risk premium Difference between the expected rate of return on a risk-free investment and one in a risky investment, often serving as an added cost for a loan.

Robinson-Patman Act 1936 federal law intended to halt discriminatory pricing policies by specifying when a seller is permitted to charge different prices to different buyers.

Robotics Automated assembly of parts and products through the use of automation technologies and nanotechnology; intended to reduced the need for manual labor.

Robust design Design system, devised by Genichi Taguchi, that improves the fundamental function of a production process and facilitates flexible design and concurrent engineering. It reduces costs, improves quality, reduces development time, cuts down component deterioration, and enhances consumer satisfaction. Also TA-GUCHI METHOD.

Rogue product Manufactured good that suffers from a high degree of technical problems or is prone to malfunction.

Rogue trader In securities trade, an individual whose rash and unsupervised investment activities can cause irreparable damage or loss to the company or clients.

ROI RETURN ON INVESTMENT

Role Functional niche assigned to each member of a group, carrying the expectations of peers regarding individual contributions to that group. Roles are differentiated and should be unambiguous.

Role ambiguity Lack of clarity on the part of an employee regarding the expectations of team members concerning work or contribution to a joint effort.

Role culture Style of corporate culture described by management consultant CHARLES HANDY as a rational one where roles are clearly defined and stable.

Role-play Training technique in which subjects assume temporary identities in order to increase sensitivity or empathy.

Role reversal Training situation in which employees deliberately switch assignments to experience the differentiation.

Role underload Situation in which a per-son feels that his or her assigned role is undervalued or inadequate.

Romalpa clause Clause in a contract, in which the seller retains interest in the goods sold to a third party until they have been paid for. Named for a 1976 decision involving Romalpa Aluminum Company.

Root-cause analysis Problem-solving technique to identify the underlying reasons something has gone wrong and show ways it could have been avoided.

Rostow, Walter Whitman (1916–2003) American economist and political theorist. He developed important concepts in the theory of modernization of underdeveloped societies. His take-off model of economic growth was used by social scientists to illustrate development trends in emerging nations. In his book *The Stages of Economic Growth* (1960), he identified five stages of economic growth: traditional society, preparation for take-off, take-off, drive to maturity, and mass consumption.

Route sheet Document showing the succession of manufacturing processes through which a product passes.

Royalty Fee paid for permission to use a property or right that belongs to another, such as the work of an author or composer, a patent or other such INTELLECTUAL PROPERTY, or a landowner's mineral rights. Royalty is considered a WASTING ASSET because it runs out at the end of a specified period.

Rucker plan Gain-sharing scheme to increase the equitable share of labor in the profits of a company, usually through bonuses.

Run In manufacturing, the time span of a good's production, from start to finish.

Run-out time Length of time that will elapse before an item is out of stock.

Rust belt Former manufacturing zone, with many closed factories; usually refers to the upper Midwest in the United States, where automobiles formerly were built.

Sacred cow Inviolable traditional assumptions, ideas, and theories; reference to the animal that is venerated in Hindu culture.

Safety See Osha.

Sagacity segmentation Subdivision of a market to differentiate by stages of life, noting levels of income, demographics, and lifestyle.

Salary Fixed, regular payments to employees in return for their services, expressed in annual earnings.

Salary grade Bracket in which a person's salary falls, based on seniority and with a maximum and minimum but excluding bonuses, allowances, and perquisites.

Sale Transaction in which a good is purchased by a user or consumer from a manufacturer or merchant, following inspection, by description from a salesman, or by sample on the basis that the quality of goods received will be as good as the sample.

Sales orientation Sales strategy focused on selling existing products through aggressive techniques and advertising.

Sales representative Principal contact between manufacturer and retailer or consumer; usually works in an assigned sales territory, either as an employee or on commission. Responsibilities include disseminating product information, generating new sales leads through cold calling, and gathering information about competitors' products and activities.

Sales resistance Customer lack of interest in a product, particularly when confronted with the standard sales pitch or price adjustment.

Sample In market research, a representative selection of people or products with a certain characteristic that is assumed to be true of all members of the group.

Sandbag Stalling tactic used by an unwilling target company in a takeover bid. It consists of prolonging the discussions, making unreasonable requests for documents, and postponing the day of reckoning.

S&P 500 Standard and Poor's 500 Stock Index

Sapiential authority Aura of authority

invested in a person because of his or her superior knowledge, wisdom, or experience, rather than by management status.

Sarbanes-Oxley Act 2002 federal legislation to establish and enforce new standards in corporate governance, financial reporting, and auditing, passed in the wake of the Enron collapse.

Sacrificing behavior Action by a company or individual aimed at achieving a satisfactory immediate return in lieu of long-term growth.

Satisfaction Organizational morale that is not quantifiable in monetary terms.

Satisficing Situation in a negotiation or sales targeting in which the outcome is less than optimal but is the best possible under the circumstances.

Satisfier Frederick Herzberg's term for an activity that brings satisfaction to the worker beyond the wages.

Saving face Maintaining one's self-esteem and the respect of peers in a conflict or situation that is potentially humiliating.

Savings and loan association Financial institution that offers loans with a fixed rate of interest and greater investment flexibility.

SBU Strategic business unit

Scalar principle In management, theory that authority should flow from the imme-

diate superior to the immediate subordinate, and that there should be only one link at any given time.

Scanlon plan Cooperative relationship between management and labor, devised by and named after cost accountant and union activist Joseph Scanlon, in which labor receives a percentage of the profits resulting from increased productivity.

Scase, Richard Leading British business strategist and Emeritus Professor of Organizational Change at the University of Kent. Author of *Global Remix*.

Scatter diagram Mathematical diagram using Cartesian coordinates to display values for two variables in a set of data. The data are displayed as a collection of points, each having the value of one variable on the horizontal axis and the other variable on the vertical axis. Also, Scatter plot.

Scatter plot Mathematical diagram using Cartesian coordinates to display values for two variables in a set of data. The data is displayed as a collection of points with the value of one variable determining its position on the horizontal axis and the value of the other variable determining its position on the vertical axis. Also Scatter diagram.

Scenario analysis Forecasting technique similar to the Delphi technique, in which a battery of experts offer their views of possible and probable futures and identify major trends and challenges. The final integrated scenario examines strategic options and challenges existing assumptions and practices.

Scenario planning Method of visualizing alternative features and adopting strategies for achieving them. Many scenarios begin in the past and use past events and historical data to develop future plans. Scenario plans may be broad or narrow depending on the kind of data used and on the assumption that certain phenomena will continue to produce the same results as they did in the past. The process begins with a PEST analysis from which critical indicators are selected and future events are impacted against them using the DELPHI TECHNIQUE. A series of usually no more than three scenarios can then be developed on the basis of alternative predictions. A cross-impact analysis examines the effect of contrary variables. All scenarios must be internally consistent and they must be possible or plausible.

Schedule 1. Plan of work aligning resources with the tasks at hand and allocating them to the person or persons most qualified to handle them. 2. Tax classification system for returns that specifies details and sources.

Schein, Edgar Henry (1928–) Professor at the Sloan School of Management at MIT who coined the expression *management culture*. He also made important contributions to the study of group consultation and career development. He developed the concept of *career anchors*, which consist of talents, abilities, and values as they pertain to career development. He identified eight career anchors: Autonomy, Security, Technical Competence, Managerial Competence, Creativity, Dedication, Challenge, and Lifestyle.

Scheme of arrangement Compact between a company and its creditors on restructuring the business to avoid bankruptcy or a takeover.

Schumpeter, Joseph (1883–1950) Austrian-American economist who popularized the expressions "small is beautiful" and "creative destruction." From 1932 to 1950 he served on the staff at Harvard University.

Schumpeterian growth Endogenous economic growth driven by innovation, described as CREATIVE DESTRUCTION, as distinct from growth driven by exogenous factors, such as a growth in national income or government spending.

Scientific management Classic approach to management that emphasizes application of scientific principles and enhancement of efficiency, performance, and productivity through rational analysis of the components of production. Developed by F. W. TAYLOR in the 19th century, the theory forms the basis of what is now known as WORK STUDY. Also called *Taylorism*, it has the elements of responsibility, efficiency, planning, selection and training, and monitoring. Taylorism is credited with improvements in productivity, but by the same token, it made work boring and repetitive and dehumanized the workplace.

Scope economies Increase in efficiency and sales, resulting from ECONOMIES OF SCALE and MASS MARKETING.

Scorched-earth policy From the military, a tactic taken by a company under threat of takeover by which it makes itself less attractive, often by borrowing unnecessarily at an exorbitant rate of interest.

Scorekeeping In management accounting, the monitoring of managerial performance and its incorporation in periodic financial statements.

Scott, Walter Dill (1869–1955) A pioneer in motivational studies, Scott devised a system for classifying personnel and testing candidates.

Scrambled merchandising Sale of products in nontraditional outlets, such as the sale of financial services in supermarkets.

Scrap What is left of an asset at the end of its useful life.

Screwdriver operation Factory where only the parts of a product are assembled, especially prevalent in Third World countries where labor is cheap.

Seasonality Descriptive of predictable changes in certain economic phenomena, such as unemployment tied to harvests or holidays.

SEC SECURITIES AND EXCHANGE COMMISSION

Secondary market 1. In finance, an exchange for resale of stocks, bonds, options, and other financial instruments, distinct from the primary market, where these are purchased from the issuers. Sometimes called an *aftermarket*. Also, market in which mortgages are resold, as to FANNIE MAE. 2. In sales, an additional market for a product or good beyond its primary use.

Secondary sector Manufacturing sector of the economy, as distinguished from agriculture (primary sector) and services (tertiary sector).

Secondary worker Retired worker who is rehired for a seasonal job.

Secondment Transfer of personnel for a temporary period without affecting their seniority.

Second-tier market Exchange for riskier investments, often in new and developing companies, that are exempt from the complex regulations governing sale of primary investments.

Secular In finance, denoting a long-term trend, in contrast to seasonal or cyclical phenomena.

Securities and Exchange Commission (SEC) U.S. government agency created in 1934 and charged with the responsibility of overseeing compliance of public companies traded on the various exchanges. Its principal divisions are corporation finance, market regulation, enforcement, investment management, and compliance inspections and examinations. It enforces seven major securities legislation: Securities Act of 1933, Securities Exchange Act of 1934, Public Utility Holding Act of 1935, Trust Indenture Act of 1939, Investment Company Act of 1940, Investment Advisors Act of 1940, and Sarbanes-Oxley Act of 2002.

Securitization Process by which assets are turned into securities; one party sells a portfolio of assets, such as home mortgages or bank loans, to an issuer that finances the purchase off-balance sheet by packaging the cash flows from these assets as tradable financial instruments or securities, which in turn are sold to investors.

Security Asset against which a borrower receives money from a lender and which is forfeited if the borrower defaults. Also *collateral*.

Security of tenure Constitutional or legal guarantee that an officeholder cannot be dismissed or removed from office except in exceptional circumstances specified in a document.

Seed capital Amount of capital required to jump-start a company and draw up a business plan.

Segmental reporting Disclosure in the annual accounts of the results of subsidiaries of a diversified conglomerate; the report accurately reflects the quantitative performance of the subsidiaries.

Segmentation Business strategy of break-ing up a market into smaller units. *Geographic segmentation* may be region, size, density of population, or climate. *Demographic segmentation* may be by age, gender, family size, family life cycle, income, occupation, education, religion, race, or nationality. *Psychographic segmentation* may be personality, lifestyle, or social class, as well as by such characteristics as user status, usage rate, loyalty, attitude, and interests.

Self-actualization In psychology, the motivation that drives people to find satisfaction and meaning in their job and their needs for challenge, responsibility, creativity, variety, self-worth, and pride in accomplishment. It provides them with a self identity that is lost when they lose their job.

Self-concept Individual's perception of him- or herself and perception of others; one of the prime motivating drivers in a person's economic decisions.

Self-discipline Quality of a person that enables him or her to do a task at hand without distraction.

Self-fulfilling Descriptive of a prediction or statement, the tendency of a desire to actualize itself because the speaker or writer unconsciously creates the conditions that facilitate its fulfillment.

Sellers' market Situation in which demand exceeds supply, so that the seller can charge what the traffic will bear. See Buyer's market.

Selten, Richard (1930–) German economist

and professor emeritus at the University of Bonn. He won the Nobel Prize in Economic Sciences in 1994. He is well known for his work in bounded rationality and is considered the founding father of experimental economics. He also developed the game known as Selten's Horse.

Semantic differential Method of comparing the strengths and weaknesses of a product or company image by asking respondents to describe, in so many words, the qualities they associate with the product.

Semi-manufactures Semi-processed material, ready to use in a final manufacture.

Semi-variable Describing a cost structure that is part variable and part fixed, and in which the fixed cost remains even when the variable ceases to apply.

Sempai Kohai In Japan, the practice of mentoring junior managers by their more experienced seniors.

Senge, Peter Management guru who popularized the theory of the LEARNING ORGANIZATION, as described in his *Fifth Discipline: The Art and the Practice of the Learning Organization* (1990).

Senior capital Capital in the form of secured loans, which need to be repaid first in the case of LIQUIDATION.

Senior management Team of managers at the top of a hierarchy, generally including the chairman, directors, president, CEO, CFO, and senior vice presidents

Seniority Rank and status gained on the basis of longer chronological service, irrespective of merit.

Sense of mission marketing Definition of a company's raison d'etre, in broad terms encompassing its rationale rather than in terms of the product or service that it creates.

Sensitive market In finance, an unstable market in which the prices and volume of trading fluctuate wildly because of the potential for unforeseeable events.

Sensitivity analysis Method of judging the validity of a decision by fine-tuning the assumptions and premises on which it is based. By altering one or more of these premises, the analysis tests the strength of each assumption.

Sensitivity training Developed by psychologist KURT LEWIN in 1947, training designed to ensure the quality of interpersonal relationships in an organization by open and honest discussion that exposes weaknesses, residual prejudices, and biases.

Sequence arrow Part of a diagram showing the sequence of events in a network.

Sequencing Establishing the priorities and order of work to be done, taking into account queuing times and job interference.

Sequential product development Approach to NEW PRODUCT DEVELOPMENT in which one stage is completed before the next one is begun.

Serendipity Unanticipated happy experience of finding something new while searching for something else. Term coined by Horace Walpole and drawn from the Isle of Serendip (or Ceylon, now Sri Lanka), which was discovered in the story *The Three Princes of Serendip.*

Serial organization Type of organization in which the entire task is assigned to a particular department, division, or unit.

Served market Segment of the total market that a firm is actively trying to serve and that is always on the firm's radar. A firm obviously knows more about its served market than about other segments, and is therefore poised to target it more effectively.

Service economy Sector of an economy that provides direct services to the consumer, especially in four categories: (1) finance, insurance, and real estate; (2) transport; (3) professional, as in accountants, lawyers, doctors, and architects; (4) consumer services, as in restaurants, cleaners, and mechanics. The service sector is characterized by (1) intangibility, because there is no transfer of ownership, and the product is experiential rather than concrete and the assessment of quality is subjective; (2) consumer participation, because the consumer is an active participant in the transaction; (3) simultaneity, because production and consumption are simultaneous; (4) interaction, because it is a unique experience and may not be replicated exactly at another time; (5) seamless, because the provider also sells and delivers the service; and (6) geo-graphical proximity, because services providers must be close to the consumer geographically and therefore tend to be local.

Service factory Term coined by business consultants Richard Chase and Warren Erikson, designating a factory that also serves as a showroom, customer service facility, and laboratory.

Service industry Sector of the economy outside of agriculture and manufacturing, including financial services, personal services, business services, sales, distribution, entertainment, health care, legal services, and education. In the United States, it has been the fastest-growing sector since the 1980s.

Servqual Combination of high-quality products and high-quality customer service, an ingredient in customer satisfaction. Servqual is based on a number of factors: tangibles, reliability, consistency, dependability, responsiveness, promptness, assurance, credibility, competence, access, and empathy.

Set-up time Period of time used for preparation and start-up of a machine or operation.

Sexism Prejudicial actions or beliefs against members of the opposite sex, especially in recruitment and promotion.

Sexual harassment Physical or verbal abuse directed against others in the workplace, especially sexual advances and sexually oriented communications, which are prohibited by law; often manipulative, reflecting an unequal power relationship.

Shadow pricing Best price estimate for a product that has not reached the market and therefore lacks the demand on which to base an actual price.

Shakeout Change in the traditional structure of an industry or market that drives the weaker players to leave the market or go bankrupt.

Shamrock organization Described by psychologist CHARLES HANDY, an organizational structure consisting of four levels: professional; labor, including flexible-time workers; contractors; and consumers. Only professional workers are on the payroll.

Share Portion of the title to a company, as evidenced by a share certificate. Shares are divided into ORDINARY SHARES with voting rights and PREFERERED SHARES without voting rights. Shares in a public company are bought and sold in an open market, as in a STOCK EXCHANGE. Also termed STOCK.

Share index Average of a selected number of prominent stocks traded on an exchange, compared to a baseline, such as their relative value at the beginning of a year. Also *stock market index.*

Share option Right of employees to buy shares in their company at a favorable fixed price or at a stated discount over the market price.

Shared value Value held in common by a group, making the group more cohesive than otherwise.

Shareholder Person who holds a SHARE in a company. Also a *stockholder.*

Shareholder value Worth of a company's stock, in terms of dividends, price, and potential. A common corporate outlook today regards maximizing the value of its shares as a high priority. Thus, shareholder value may be increased through greater dividend payments, appreciation in the value of the share, and better performance results.

Shareholder value analysis Method for valuing EQUITY in a company, using the formula: shareholder value equals value of business debt.

Shark repellent See PORCUPINE PROVISION

Shark watcher Business consultant who specializes in helping companies identify raiders and provides early warning of stock warehousing that would be preliminary to a takeover attempt.

Sharpbender Firm that has been underperforming its rivals in an industry but suddenly takes off and joins the overachievers, often as a result of a new management team, a new product, or a new strategy.

SHEEP SKY-HIGH EARNINGS EXPECTATIONS

Shelf life Longevity of a product, especially a perishable commodity.

Shell company Nontrading company with or without a stock exchange listing, used as a cover for illegal activities, such as money Laundering.

Shewhart, Walter A. (1891–1967) Originator of the *Shewhart cycle*, formulated in his *Economic Control of Quality of Manufactured Product* (1931). He is also credited with the development of theories of Process control and the *Shewhart transformation process*.

Shigeo Shingo (1919–1990) One of the pioneers of Just-in-time and one of the world's leading experts on the manufacturing process. Author of *A Study of the Toyota Production System from an Industrial Engineering Viewpoint* (1989), *Revolution in Manufacturing: The SMED (Single Minute Exchange of Die) System* (1985), and *Zero Quality Control: Source Inspection and the Poka Yoke System* (1986).

Shop floor Area of a factory where production takes place, as distinguished from an office or retail space.

Shop steward Employee who represents a trade union and who is charged with negotiations of labor contracts.

Short position Speculative selling of securities, commodities, or currencies before they are purchased, in anticipation of a decline in price. The securities are usually "borrowed" from a broker and then returned when purchased. Also termed *selling short* or *shorting*. Opposite of Long

position, which is the conventional purchase of shares in anticipation of a price rise.

Short-termism Policy that maximizes current or short-term profits at the expense of long-term development and investments.

Show stopper In business, legal action in which the target firm in a hostile takeover seeks a permanent court injunction against the other party, citing potential injury to its business.

Shunto In Japan, annual wage negotiations every spring.

Shut-down cost Expense incurred in closing down an operation or company.

SIC Standard industrial classification

Sick building syndrome Widespread and simultaneous illnesses claimed by occupants of a building where there is suspected pollutants, poor ventilation, ill-cleaned air conditioners, or pathogens in the air.

Signaling Transferring information from one party to another, as a form of communication that is less overt than a formal notification.

Signaling hypothesis Principle that actions by economic agents are motivated by the desire to send a positive signal rather than the stated purpose. It explains the mismatch or asymmetry between the investment on an advertising or production budget and the anticipated benefits. Every action is interpreted as a message to the wider market that the company is doing well and is standing by its commitments.

Silver bullet Magic, quick solution to a difficult and persistent problem; from the popular radio and TV series *The Lone Ranger,* who used silver bullets in pursuit of outlaws.

Simo chart Basic motion-time chart used to show the simultaneous nature of motions, commonly a THERBLIG chart with motion symbols plotted vertically with respect to time. Also *motion-cycle chart.*

Simon, Herbert A. (1916–2001) American social scientist, one of the most influential in the 20th century, His research ranged across cognitive psychology, cognitive science, computer science, public administration, economics, management, sociology, and political science. He was a professor at Carnegie Mellon University. He was the founding father of several of the frontier sciences including information processing, artificial intelligence, decision making, problem solving, attention economics, organization theory, and complex systems. He coined the terms "bounded rationality" and "satisficing." He won the Nobel Prize in Economics in 1975.

Simulated market test Market research technique to forecast and measure repurchase rates and numbers of repeat customers. Also called *Hall's test.*

Simulation Recreating or modeling a hypothetical situation through the use of random numbers in order to preview likely outcomes and develop problem-solving strategies. The best-known method is the MONTE CARLO SIMULATION, which measures uncertainty.

Sin tax Tax levied on undesirable activities and products, such as cigarettes and liquor.

Sinecure Job or position that involves little work but is a reward for past favors.

Singer, Peter Albert David (1946–) Australian moral philosopher. He is the Ira W. DeCamp Professor of Bioethics at Princeton University and a Laureate Professor at the Centre for Applied Philosophy and Public Ethics at the University of Melbourne. He is a humanist concerned with human and animal rights.

Single business strategy Industry in which 90% or more of sales come from one buyer, product, or business. There is no attempt at diversification and management concentrates on traditional strengths.

Single loop learning Concept in organizational learning where the effects of feedback from previous learning are used to change present behavior.

Single sourcing Purchasing policy of using only one supplier for a component or service.

Single status Japanese concept under

which all employees have the same standing in nonfunctional roles, thus all employees wear the same uniform and use the same canteen.

Sit-in Industrial action involving workers who physically occupy a company's premises and refuse to leave in an effort to forestall LOCKOUT.

Situational analysis Process of analyzing past and present situations facing an organization in order to prioritize them by degree of complexity.

Six-markets framework Model showing a firm's six constituent markets: internal, referral, influence, recruitment, supplier, and customer.

Six-Sigma Data-driven method for achieving faultless perfection and quality without defect. Sigma is the Greek letter used to denote standard deviation. The greater the number of sigmas, the fewer the defects; six sigmas indicate a defect level of 3.4 per million.

Skewness Asymmetrical nature of a statistical distribution curve.

Skillware Blend of hardware and software.

Skinner, Burrhus Frederick (1904–1990) American psychologist and professor of psychology at Harvard University until 1974. He founded his own school of experimental research psychology, invented the operant conditioning chamber, and founded the branch of philosophy known as radical behaviorism. His analysis of human behavior culminated in the work *Verbal Behavior* (1957). He identified the rate of response as a dependent variable in psychological research and devised schedules of reinforcement. His other major works are *Walden Two* (1948) and *Beyond Freedom and Dignity* (1971).

Skunkworks Special operations division of a corporation engaged in or charged with radical innovation, operating outside the hierarchical structure.

Sky-high earnings expectations (SHEEP) Describing investments that promise unrealistically high returns.

Sleeper Product or service for which there is a steady demand and that takes off to become a bestseller.

Sleeper effect Gap between discover and application, or other types of time lapses between conception and execution, usually relating to research.

Sloane, Alfred P. (1875–1966) American industrialist and long-time president of General Motors in its heyday. Sloane introduced the concept of a professional management style, in contrast with the personal and highly autocratic style of HENRY FORD, his competitor.

Slumpflation Economic downturn characterized by declining output and rising prices.

Slush fund Clandestine fund set apart for promoting illegal activities and not reported to the authorities.

Small business Privately owned corporation, partnership, or sole partnership with typically fewer than 500 employees. They fall under the purview of the Small Business Administration.

Small office, home office (SOHO) Place where many self-employed workers conduct their business.

Small print Conditions and obligations of parties to a contract or agreement, printed in small letters and usually in legalese, in the hope of avoiding closer scrutiny.

Smart money Knowledgeable investors who avoid common pitfalls and have inside information on better opportunities.

Smartsizing Alternative to DOWNSIZING, involving laying off only incompetent employees and eliminating highly wasteful expenditures.

Smith, Adam (1723–1790) Scottish economist and philosopher, author of *The Wealth of Nations* and other works, whose theories on the FREE MARKET and rational economy undergird CAPITALISM. Smith argued that all human activities are driven by self-interest, and the cumulative effect of self-interest works toward the good of all members of society. He also argued for the division of labor and specialization in manufacturing.

Smokestack industries Traditional manufacturing industries, such as steel.

Smurfing Dividing a large financial transaction into smaller ones that then fall below the threshold for reporting to regulatory agencies.

Social accounting Record keeping that emphasizes charitable contributions, community involvement, environmental and health causes, advocacy, education, product safety, and other nontraditional expenditures.

Social audit Assessment of the nonfinancial impact of a corporation on society, the environment, public welfare, political advocacy, and education and training.

Social capital Cumulative social skills of employees considered as a company asset, enhancing teamwork, encouraging democratic decision making, and helping develop a sense of community.

Social control Control exerted by societal norms on individual opinions and attitudes.

Social costs Financial effects of a project on society and the environment. Also *social opportunity costs.*

Social Darwinism Charles Darwin's theory of evolution applied to economic and social situations. Generally disregarded today, but some previously applied a "survival of the fittest" view to show that the strong get stronger at the expense of the weak, and the rich get richer at the expense of the poor;

the implication was that this inequality is legitimate because it is nature's pattern.

Social loafing Tendency of people to expend less effort on a task when working as part of a group than when working individually.

Social media Various forms of electronic communication, including Facebook and Twitter. Also termed *social network*.

Social responsibility Fashionable concern for nonmonetary and societal issues by corporations, as expressed in annual statements detailing financial contributions to social causes, health projects, charities, and educational scholarships, as well as community involvement designed to boost corporate image. Also termed *social responsiveness*.

Social status Rank in a classification based on social standing, educational and professional attainment, and contributions to social welfare.

Societal marketing Linkage of marketing programs with popular social goals, such as the environment, antismoking, fitness, medical research, literacy, safety, and child welfare, mostly to create a favorable public image. Societal marketing operates at the intersection of public relations and merchandising. Also termed *social marketing*.

Sociotechnical system Term coined by Eric Trist, Ken Bamforth, and Frederick Emory to describe the interaction between people and technology in the workplace as well as between human behavior and social infrastructure. The focus is on procedures and structures and the knowledge that governs their mutual growth.

Soft core Unaggressive, unsophisticated, or elementary.

Soft landing Downward economic spiral, slowing down without going into a Recession.

Soft sell Sales pitch characterized by gentle and nonaggressive tactics, with respect to the customer's wishes.

Soga shosha Massive international trading companies, such as Mitsubishi and Mitsui, created in Japan during the Meiji restoration. Other major *soga shosha* include Itochu, Mayuberi, Sumotomo, Nisho Iwai, Tomen, Nichimen, and Kanematsu. *Soga shosha* operate in a number of ways: as pure traders, as project organizers and managers for complex projects, as market intelligence coordinators, as enablers of Japanese companies who want to enter foreign markets, as brokers for strategic raw materials, and as sources of trade finance.

SOHO Small office, home office

Solvency ratio Accounting measure used to judge a company's long-term solvency, measuring a company's after-tax income against its total debt obligations.

SORC Stimulus, organism, response, consequence

Sore thumbing Technique in job evaluation of identifying people who stand out as odd, and therefore are a distraction to others.

South Popular but imprecise term for underdeveloped countries, which are found mostly in the Southern Hemisphere. Contrast with NORTH, or the industrialized world.

Sovereign wealth fund Investment fund owned by a sovereign nation.

Span of control Number of subordinates who report directly to a given manager in a CHAIN OF COMMAND. The concept affects ORGANIZATIONAL DESIGN, including speed of communications, employee motivation, reporting relationships, and administrative overhead.

Spear carrier Loyal official in a second tier of command, charged with carrying out orders and ensuring the compliance of subordinates.

Special drawing rights (SDR) Standard unit of account used by the INTERNATIONAL MONETARY FUND.

Specialization Segment of a larger task, handled by a worker who is a specialist in that segment. The smaller the segment, the greater the specialization.

Specific risk In finance, a risk associated with an individual asset in a portfolio, as opposed to a systematic risk associated with the market as a whole; a specific risk can be corrected by DIVERSIFICATION.

Speculation Practice of engaging in risky financial transactions, especially in a stock market, in an attempt to profit from short- or medium-term fluctuations in their market value. It absorbs excess risks, which may be offset by larger profits in the future.

Spend management Systematic effort to maximize corporate expenditures by achieving best value for every dollar spent. Unlike simple cost-cutting, this analyzes spending behavior patterns in all areas, especially procurement, contract management, supply chain logistics, and invoicing.

Spinoff Less profitable division or subsidiary that is divested by a corporation; the resulting smaller entity sometimes becomes more valuable in the process.

Spokesperson Representative of a group or organization charged with expressing its position on issues or problems.

Spondulik Physical unit of money, such as coins.

Sponsor In finance, an institution, such as an INVESTMENT BANK, that handles new issues of stock.

Spot contract Contract for buying or selling a commodity, security, or currency for payment and delivery and settlement on the spot date, which is normally two business days after the trade date. The settlement price is called the spot price or spot rate. Contrast with FORWARD CONTRACT or FUTURES CONTRACT. Also *spot transaction*.

Squeeze Controls imposed by a government to control the rate of INFLATION, such as limits on lending or increases in wages and salaries.

Staff Full-time WHITE-COLLAR workers, whose conditions of work, pay grades, and fringe benefits are different from those of BLUE-COLLAR workers.

Staff management Personnel having a specialist or advisory support function, but who are not in the CHAIN OF COMMAND.

Stagflation Blend of terms STAGNATION and INFLATION, reflecting an economic downturn where income and output are declining while prices are rising.

Staggered directorship When election of members of the BOARD OF DIRECTORS is spread over a couple of years, so that they don't all begin and end their terms simultaneously; this has the effect of prolonging any attempts at a hostile takeover, as only a fraction of directors can be replaced during a single election.

Stagnation Stage in economic development when there is little forward activity.

Stakeholder Member of a community with interest in the fortunes of a company or organization, and who possibly benefits from its success and profits, including employees, shareholders, suppliers and distributors, and all other persons affected by a firm's decisions and actions.

Stakeholder analysis Study of the divergent interests of all those who have a stake in the operation of an organization and therefore its management decisions.

Stale bull Trader or speculator who has a LONG POSITION on a commodity that shows a paper profit, which cannot be translated into actual profits because there is no demand for it.

Stalemate industry Industry in which there are few opportunities to create competitive advantages against existing products. ECONOMIES OF SCALE do not produce significant cost advantages. Such industries are high in capital intensity and have large fixed capital. This makes exit from such businesses difficult, as the assets are difficult to resell and environmental legislation requiring cleanup after closure forces them to continue production despite losses.

Standard and Poor's 500 Stock Index (S&P 500) General market index of leading U.S. stocks, produced by Standard and Poor's, a McGraw-Hill company.

Standard costing System of cost control that sets predetermined standards and then compares them with actual costs to establish the variance.

Standard industrial classification (SIC) Codified classification system used to describe different types of industries.

Standard performance Concept used in work measurement to achieve comparability of data or range of observations and to provide a basis for calculating wok-related bonuses.

Standardization Setting of acceptable standards in production and quality of products, or of uniform measurements and specifications for products in the manufacturing process.

Standby credit Letter of credit that guarantees a loan or a third-party guarantee to honor a loan to an investor who has a low credit rating.

Star In the BOSTON MATRIX, an investment opportunity with high growth potential.

Start-up costs Preliminary expenses associated with the launch of a project or operation, usually until it becomes self-supporting.

State of the art Exhibiting the most advanced techniques and expertise, and representative of the best knowledge on the subject.

Stateless globalism Borderless multinational business activity that is under so many jurisdictions that it is virtually under none and can thus flout local ordinances.

Statistical demand analysis Set of statistical procedures used to examine major influences on sales, such as prices, promotion, and product quality.

Statistical process control Technique for determining, by sampling, whether a product or service is conforming to its original specifications.

Statistical quality control Statistical inference to determine tolerance levels for inspection of process output on which to base decisions to accept or reject.

Status Position and rank within a hierarchy of persons or products and the respect accorded.

Status consensus Agreement among members of a group regarding the relative position of each member. Also termed *status consequence*.

Status symbol Representation of someone's importance; in business, traditionally the corner office, perquisites, and other signs of importance.

Steady state Stable organizational cycle in which routine activities predominate the calendar.

Stealth marketing Subtle form of marketing that utilizes noncommercial outlets where promoters do not reveal their identities. Also termed *buzz marketing*.

Stealth tax Tax obligation, the incidence of which may be concealed under various rubrics through the abolition of allowances and adjustment of thresholds.

Steamroller tactics Rough and ruthless pressure tactics designed to intimidate and smother opposition and achieve a given goal without regard to its human cost.

Step change Discontinuous change in which there is a quantum but orderly leap from one stage to another.

Stepped cost Operating costs calibrated for a certain range of output and then allowed to rise by steps upon the addition of more elements.

Stereotyping Making blanket assumptions about individuals or groups, based on prejudices and folk beliefs.

Stewardship accounting Recording and monitoring of business transactions for the purpose of oversight rather than analysis.

Stewart, Rosemary Gordon British management guru respected for her research on managerial behavior. Author of *The Reality of Management* (1963).

Stewart, Thomas A. Editor of the *Harvard Business Review.* He pioneered the field of intellectual capital in his book *Intellectual Capital: The New Wealth of Organizations* (1997). He expanded the concept in his second book, *Wealth of Knowledge: Intellectual Capital and the Twenty First Century Organization.*

Stickiness Tendency of certain economic indicators and variables to pause at or near their existing levels, despite changes in supply and demand. Stickiness is related to limited information, the existence of long-term contracts, and the hidden costs of repricing.

Stimulus, organism, response, consequence (SORC) Behavioral model used in ORGANIZATIONAL DEVELOPMENT.

Stock 1. Share. 2. Inventory.

Stock exchange Market in which securities are bought and sold; its primary function is to raise capital.

Stock watering Practice by which a company inflates the value of its assets and exaggerates its profits as a pretext for issuing new shares and thus diluting the equity.

Stockpile Hoarding of products or raw materials as a hedge against shortages or price increases, or as a means of profiting from subsequent shortages.

Stop-go In the United Kingdom, fiscal policy that vacillates between growth and slowdown.

Stop-loss order Directions placed with a broker to sell shares when they drop to a specified price; used in a volatile market by speculators.

Straight-line method Calculation of the amount by which a fixed asset is to be appreciated, in which the depreciation is based on the original cost or valuation less the asset's net residual value, divided by its estimated life in years—in effect, depreciating the charges against profits annually.

Strategic alliance Friendly effort of two or more companies to build on their mutual strengths and expertise for a specified time to reach a particular goal. Such alliances are less far-reaching than JOINT VENTURES. As a strategy, alliances enable companies to gain access to markets, exchange technologies, form defensive shareholding blocs, and share expenses. They are easily formed and disbanded. Despite these advantages, the alliances also pose risks, especially cultural clashes with firms based in different nations with different cultural values.

Strategic asset Source of competitive advantage, based on exogenous factors rather than internal core strengths, such as access to new government subsidies.

Strategic behavior Corporate behavior designed to influence the structure of the market positively, especially by diluting the FREE MARKET or restricting consumer choice and regulating the supply of goods.

Strategic business unit (SBU) Autonomous division of a large company, responsible for a particular range or mix of products, with a specific set of strategic objectives and investment policy.

Strategic choice Alternatives available to decision makers for using available resources and manipulating a competitive edge.

Strategic core competences Combination of competences required by an organization to dominate existing markets or create new ones.

Strategic drift Self-imposed limitations on strategic choices driven by past assump-

tions and the experience gained in past successes and failures. It makes corporations more conservative by discouraging forays into untried areas.

Strategic fit 1. Extent to which diversification into another field harmonizes with plans for growth in terms of costs and product mix. A good fit measures the synergy that results from mergers involving a fusion of skills and know-how, as well as cost reductions from ECONOMIES OF SCALE. 2. When two businesses reach the same consumers through different distribution channels or are marketed and promoted through the same channels; the cost sharing can take place in procurement, R&D, and administration.

Strategic gap analysis Examination of a business strategy to determine how it advances the company's overall standing and position in the market. If there are gaps, they need to be closed before the STRATEGIC PLAN can be adopted.

Strategic group Group of firms in a market or industry that hold a controlling position in regard to range, coverage, and distribution; comparison of members of the group can help identify the closest competitors and potential challenges and opportunities.

Strategic inflection point The point at which an organization decides to change its corporate direction and pursue a different strategy of growth.

Strategic intent Clear statement of the

overall direction of a company's growth and the paths it intends to take to get there; in essence, this is a manifesto that brings the team together in pursuit of a common goal and vision.

Strategic management Philosophy that focuses on long-term objectives and develops policies designed to achieve them through concrete steps that harness the resources of the organization. The process begins with a POSITION AUDIT that analyzes SWOT. This leads to a statement of STRATEGIC INTENT and a STRATEGIC PLAN. Implementation of the plan will require the allocation of sufficient financial, human, and technical resources; establishment of appropriate mechanisms and structures; and continuous monitoring and analysis of results and performance. The plan must also allow a process of constant reevaluation and reassessment of the plan as new opportunities and challenges emerge either internally or externally.

Strategic management consists of both decision making and implementation. The decision-making process comprises a series of nine steps: (1) determination of the mission of the corporation; (2) assessment of the internal environment and corporate culture; (3) analysis of the firm's external environment through PEST analysis; (4) use of SWOT analysis to match external environments with internal strengths and weaknesses; (5) identification of management options in navigating the maze of problems and opportunities; (6) choice of relevant strategies and policies to address

the options; (7) development of two sets of strategies, one long term and the other short term; (8) budgeting of allocations and drawing up of implementation schedules; and (9) review and evaluation.

Strategic management occurs at three hierarchical levels: (1) the corporate level, where the parameters are defined; (2) the business-unit level, or cluster of business units, where the plans are drawn up and portfolio models are adopted determining growth, life cycle, competitive position, and direction; and (3) the business level. Companies evolve by stages toward strategic management, not at one quantum leap. According to McKinsey and Company, they proceed through four stages: (1) financial planning, (2) forecast-based plannings, (3) externally oriented planning, and (4) strategic management. Leading companies go into decline because they fall into any one of three traps: (1) they use unrealistic or obsolete criteria to assess strengths and weaknesses; (2) they become complacent and thus inflexible; and (3) they fail to recognize industry changes and respond.

Strategic management accounting System that provides results-oriented information, not merely mathematical calculations; the method is not static but dynamic.

Strategic misrepresentation In planning and budgeting, the tendency to deliberately minimize the negative and accentuate the positive, or to understate costs and overstate benefits. Planners tend to acquire a personal bias in pushing the projects that they direct and therefore they tailor the data to fit their conclusions.

Strategic plan Future-oriented statement that presents all the information and data needed to determine the direction of a company or project. There are several elements that go into a corporate plan: vision, assumptions, objectives, information, analysis, measurement, evaluation, and opportunity.

Strategic style Ways in which a parent company directs the growth of a subsidiary through full control, financial control, or strategic control, the last allowing some leeway for the subsidiary to have input into strategic decisions.

Straw boss In a workplace, a foreman with no formal title or status.

Straw man, building Forming an initial, somewhat tenuous plan to solve a problem, thereby providing a starting point for further development.

Street, the Wall Street, as in "heard on the street."

Strengths, weaknesses, opportunities, and threats (SWOT) Analysis and audit procedure of internal or external elements in consideration of a proposed undertaking. Strengths and weaknesses are internal while threats and opportunities are external, and both are weighed before approval. *Internal strengths* are a good distribution system and good cash flow, while *weakness* could be an extended product line and poor servicing capabilities. *Opportunities* could be an opening for a new product or the failure or vulnerability of a competitor while *threats* might come from plans for a similar venture by a competitor or new government regulation. SWOT is also used for POSITION AUDITS.

Stress In human beings as well as institutions, structures, and machines, the cumulative effect of wear and tear and the weakness of constituent parts brought about by structural defects or breakdown, which may in time affect the integrity of the entity.

Stress audit Review of the stress factors identifiable through an analysis of vulnerabilities in a corporate environment.

Stress interview Meeting with a prospective employee, conducted in a hostile manner with the intention of testing the interviewee's ability to cope with stress.

Stress testing Method of risk analysis in which simulations are used to estimate the impact of worst-case situations.

Strike price Fixed price at which the owner of an option can purchase (in the case of a call) or sell (in the case of a put) a security or commodity. Strike price is the key variable in a derivatives contract between two parties. Also EXERCISE PRICE.

Stroking In transactional analysis, giving another person a sense of recognition and support.

Structural capital Supportive infrastructure, processes, and databases that enable human capital to function. It includes organizational capital, such as buildings, hardware, software, patents, and brands. Process capital includes techniques, procedures, and programs that enhance delivery of goods and services. Innovation capital includes intellectual properties and intangible assets.

Structural unemployment Long-term unemployment resulting from the changing nature of an industry and not the result of seasonal variations in production.

Structure-conduct-performance model Common paradigm in INDUSTRIAL ORGANIZATION ECONOMICS that states that the structure or form of a particular market (the ease of entry versus barriers to entry) will determine the conduct or strategic behavior of buyers and sellers, and the overall performance and social efficiency of that market. As the number of players increases or decreases, the ability of any one firm or group to influence prices also changes, thereby affecting overall efficiency.

Structured finance Creation of complex debt instruments by SECURITIZATION or the addition of DERIVATIVES. It involves pooling of assets, TRANCHING of liabilities, and reduction or dilution of risk.

Structured interview Quantitative research method employed in survey research in which each interviewee is presented with the same questions in the same order. The choice of answers is often fixed or close-ended. Also *standard interview*.

Structured investment vehicle ARBITRAGE fund that raises money by selling asset-backed commercial paper and medium-term notes, and invests the money in asset-backed securities.

Structure of organizations Five base levels make up an organizational structure: (1) operating core or persons in production and distribution; (2) strategic apex, or supervisors and managers responsible for overall direction; (3) middle line, or managers who connect the apex with the operating core; (4) support staff, social, legal, human relations, and accounting; (5) technostructure, or people who monitor and supervise others.

Subculture Specialized group within a larger corporate culture, subject to the societal influences of the larger culture.

Subjective goodwill Accounting of company assets, calculated by deducting its net tangible assets from the net present value of its estimated future cash flows.

Submarginal Relating to a yield less than the cost of production.

Suboptimization Failure of individual components of a system to work together to achieve desired SYNERGY. This may result from the failure of any component to meet the output goals, poor communications and inadequate information, or growth of contradictory SUBCULTURES that deviate from the common direction.

Subprime Categorization of loans to borrowers with poor credit ratings, usually entailing greater risk, thus requiring Securitization with high-risk, Off-balance sheet instruments.

Subsidiary Enterprise owned and controlled by another, usually larger one.

Subsistence agriculture Self-sufficiency farming in which farmers grow enough food to feed themselves and have little left over for the markets.

Subsistence crop Crop grown by a farmer to feed his family and not intended for sale in the market.

Subsistence theory of wages In classical economics, the theory that personal earnings are always influenced by a person's level of minimum subsistence.

Substance over form Accounting principle that transactions are governed more by their commercial rationale than their legal form, especially as applied to creative and Off-balance sheet accounting.

Substitution awareness effect Consumer resistance and sensitivity to prices as determined by the existence of alternative choices.

Succession management Human resources effort concerned with ensuring that there are qualified candidates available to take positions as they become vacant through retirement or attrition. It requires a forecasting technique that matches future needs in personnel with available resources.

Successive approximation Method of estimation that begins with a rough approximation and is refined with additional data.

Sucker effect Reluctance to appear gullible when in a team, contributing more than the minimum effort.

Suggestion scheme Attempt to encourage employees to share with management their ideas on improving quality and productivity, and making monetary awards or offering other inducements to do so.

Sugging Short for "survey under the guise of research," a marketing ploy by which telemarketers masquerade as researchers to gather valuable information on consumer preferences.

Sumptuary law Legislation that minimizes the sale and consumption of goods believed to be harmful to human beings or society.

Sunk costs Expenditures that have already been incurred and cannot be recovered.

Sunlighting Continuing in full-time employment after retirement.

Sunrise industry Industry in the early stages of its life cycle that experiences growth as a result of a wave of technological advances.

Sunset industry Industry in decline or in the later stages of its life cycle, unable to meet competition because of poor planning, redundant products, or unprofitability.

Sunset law Law that expires on a certain date unless it is renewed.

Superordinate goal Principle that when people cooperate on reaching a goal of equal importance to them all, the effort will bring them closer together. Used in business to encourage teamwork.

Supervisor First-level manager who controls workers and takes full responsibility for their conduct and performance.

Supply and demand Economic model of price determination in which the price for a good will vary until it settles at a point where the quantity demanded by consumers at current price will equal the quantity supplied by producers.

Supply chain Series of linked stages in a supply network, along which flow goods and services in an orderly fashion.

Supply chain management Management of the links in a SUPPLY CHAIN to maximize the orderly flow of materials and inventory of stock. It includes logistics, the timing of purchases, quality of supplies, and information on suppliers.

Supply-side economics MACROECONOMIC policy based on the idea that stimulating growth by producers (manufacturers, servic-

es) will increase the supply of goods, thereby lowering prices and benefiting consumers as well as encouraging overall economic growth; this is usually achieved through tax cuts to businesses, and it's a concept usually associated with conservative ideology, the opposite of KEYNESIAN ECONOMICS. See also TRICKLE-DOWN ECONOMICS.

Surface bargaining Negotiation in which there is a hidden agenda and stated issues are secondary.

Survey research Form of market research in which data are gathered through face-to-face and telephone interviews and by mailed questionnaires.

Sustainable development In the developing world, economic policies designed to promote growth without depleting or undermining the country's ecology or resource base.

Sustainable growth Rate at which a company can achieve a healthy growth rate while not depleting funds.

Swap See CREDIT-DEFAULT SWAP.

Sweatshop Factory employing cheap labor, for long hours and under unsafe conditions, so as to mass-produce goods. Though largely produced for the developed world, today these goods are made in underdeveloped countries where there are few laws protecting workers. The term, however, dates back to early U.S. factories, especially the garment industry.

Sweep Banking facility that automatically transfers funds from one account to a higher or lower interest-earning account when a threshold is reached.

Sweetheart contract Agreement between a manufacturer and a supplier, not based on the lowest bid received but on special relationships, favoritism, or nepotism.

Swing shift Flexible work schedule by which workers have variable hours of work but are required to work for a certain number of hours per week at their convenience.

SWOT Strengths, Weaknesses, Opportunities, and Threats

Symbolic information Data processed by computer, involving numbers, names, and words that can be handled in a binary manner.

Syndicate Group that pools its resources in an enterprise in which all members have a stake.

Synectics Problem-solving methodology that simulates thought processes of which the subject may be unaware. It was developed by George M. Price and W. J. Gordon, originating in the Arthur D. Little Invention Design Unit in the 1950s.

Synergy Added value that results when two or more entities join forces to realize more than can be achieved singularly. The effect is based on the principle that the result is greater than the sum of its parts. It is used as rationale for corporate mergers, but may occur in sales, operations, investment, and management.

System Integration of components into a harmonious whole that works seamlessly and therefore can be understood and studied as a single unit.

System Four Form of Organizational development designed by organizational psychologist Rensis Likert, which emphasizes participation, employee-centered leadership, open communication, and group decision making and goal setting.

Systems analysis Study of systems, especially in technology and management, for ensuring that the parts work in conjunction to produce the desired outcome. It studies the feasibility of the system, the choke points, the risk and liability of failure, the technological imperatives, and the costs of maintenance.

Systems dynamics Computer-based system developed by the Massachusetts Institute of Technology for modeling the behavior of transient systems. It determines the adequacy of the systems by interjecting the question, "What if?" at every junction.

Tactical asset allocation In finance, enhancing the portfolio returns by altering the asset composition and mix.

Taguchi, Genichi (1924–2012) Japanese management consultant who developed the concept of quality engineering through his TAGUCHI METHOD and author of *Introduction to Quality Engineering*. He is credited with such concepts as *robust design* and *Taguchi loss function,* designed to improve engineering quality and productivity. He introduced three stages in production: system design, parameter stage (in which the product is defined under several parameters), and tolerance design.

Taguchi method Devised by management consultant GENICHI TAGUCHI, a method of testing the design of a new product under the most adverse circumstances, through a battery of permutations and combinations and statistical analysis.

Take-off stage Period of development marked by rapid development, stage 3 in economist W. W. ROSTOW's stages of growth. It follows the *traditional society stage* and *preconditions for take-off stage*

and is followed by the *drive to maturity stage* and then the *age of high mass consumption stage.*

Takeover bid Offer to the shareholders of a company, over the heads of its management, to buy their shares at a specified price and thus gain control. Such a bid may be with the blessing of management or it may be a HOSTILE BID. In the case of an *unconditional bid*, the bidder pays the offered price irrespective of the number of shares acquired, while in the case of a *conditional bid,* the offer is good only if sufficient shares are acquired to gain a controlling interest.

Tall organization Pyramid framework for management of an organization, with a relatively large number of intermediate levels. Compare FLAT ORGANIZATION.

Tannenbaum-Schmidt continuum Model of leadership that sees the role as a continuum stretching from autocratic to democratic. In any given situation, the impact of leadership will be judged by three criteria: (1) the leader's self-confidence, charisma, and philosophy of management; (2) the complementary qualities of the followers or employees, such as experience, sense of responsibility, and responsiveness; and (3) the nature and complexity of the circumstances and problems addressed.

Target costing Method of costing products or services to reflect the price that customers are willing to pay and the price charged by competitors. The target cost must include a specified profit margin. It differs from the actual cost, which may be based on the cost of raw materials and production. Target costing was popularized by the Japanese, who used techniques such as JUST-IN-TIME, KAIZEN, TEAR DOWN, TOTAL QUALITY MANAGEMENT, VALUE ENGINEERING, ACTIVITY-BASED COSTING, and BENCHMARKING to achieve target costs.

Target marketing Marketing aimed at meeting the needs of a specific group of customers. See also NICHE MARKET.

Task Unit of work; one of the elements of a job.

Task analysis Disaggregation of the elements of a task to identify the skills required. It assesses what people, machines, or a combination thereof are needed and why.

Task culture Term coined by management consultant CHARLES HANDY to describe corporate behavior focused on the completion of tasks.

Task orientation Leadership style concerned with setting goals, structured tasks, and measured performance. It involves planning feedback from participants and concern with the quality of outcome.

Task roles People with discrete capabilities, assigned to problem solution and decision making, as initiator, opinion seeker, and summarizer.

Taskforce Group of people charged with the execution of a specific plan or program.

Tax haven Country with a low tax rate, used by wealthy investors and companies to relieve themselves from a high tax burden. Often requires residence for a given part of a year, citizenship, or corporate headquarters. Four of the most popular tax havens are the Bahamas, Cayman Islands, Monaco, and Liechtenstein.

Tax treaty Agreement between two countries for providing relief from double taxation, applied to income earned in both countries.

Tavistock method Approach to management and management studies initiated by the Tavistock Institute for Human Relations in London.

Taylor, F. W. (1856–1915) American engineer who invented WORK STUDY and pioneered scientific management, sometimes known as *Taylorism*. He emphasized TASK ANALYSIS and stressed the importance of good communications, recruitment, and training. Taylor was the author of *Principles of Scientific Management* (1911) and *Shop*

Management (1903). He developed many management concepts, such as *functional authority*, which stated that all authority was based on knowledge and not position.

Teaching company Corporation in which each employee is expected to both learn and teach others.

Team Group of employees organized to accomplish a common purpose. There are six major types of teams: informal, traditional, problem solving, leadership, self-directed, and virtual.

Team building Relating to exercises or programs designed to construct group functions and create teams that are cohesive, united, and emotionally bonded.

Team management wheel Visual aid for the efficient coordination of teamwork and for TEAM BUILDING and training, devised by management consultants CHARLES MARGERISON and DICK MCCANN. It helps team members to choose the work they prefer to do

Team role Position on a team and the nature of the participation. There are 11 distinct roles played by members of a team: team worker, completer, shaper, monitor, evaluator, planner, resource person, investigator, coordinator, implementer, and specialist.

Tear down Method of comparing a company's products and components with those of its competitors. Originally devised by General Motors, it was adapted by the Japa-

nese, who expanded it to include eight different steps: (1) *dynamic tear down*, which reduces the number of assembly operations; (2) *cost tear down*, which reduces the cost of the components vis-à-vis those used by competitors; (3) *material tear down*, of materials used in surface treatments; (4) *static tear down*, by disassembling competing products; (5) *process tear down*, by comparing manufacturing processes for similar parts; (6) *matrix tear down*, by identifying the volume of each component used by a model per month; (7) *unit-kilogram price tear down*, which plots the value per kilo for all the products in the same group against their weight; and (8) *group estimate tear down*, which combines basic VALUE REENGINEERING and tear-down methods.

Teaser rate Low interest rate designed to attract new customers, available for only a short period.

Technical analysis Method used to forecast the direction of prices through the study of past market data, especially prices and volume.

Technocrat Technical expert alternating as a manager, who brings technical skills to management problem solving.

Technological change Improvement in the ratio of productivity and output to labor brought about by inventions, automation, and computerized methods of production.

Technological risk Chance that a business may be overtaken by technological advances, making certain of its products and services obsolete.

Technological unemployment Reduction in the labor force and loss of employment, brought about by automation and computerized production.

Technology assessment Collection of data on a firm's utilization of currently available technology and potential use of technological breakthroughs.

Technology management Science that links engineering, science, and management to plan, develop, and implement technological capabilities that can shape the strategic and operational objectives of an organization.

Technology transfer Transfer of technological know-how, mostly through licensing, usually across borders and especially from industrially advanced countries to underdeveloped countries.

Telecommuting Nontraditional employment pattern in which employees work from home and communicate with employers via telephone and Internet.

Teleconference Discussion or meeting in which participants are geographically separated but are linked via telecommunication.

Telemarketing Direct sales of products or services via phone calls by trained representatives.

Tenor In finance, the period between issuance of a security and its maturity, or the period of a loan or contract.

Terms of trade Formula that measures the trading position of a country by dividing export prices by import prices. When the former is stronger, a country's trading position is favorable.

Terotechnology Branch of technology dealing with the use of management, engineering, and financial skills in the operation of a factory.

Test marketing Pilot marketing attempt that assesses consumer reactions in a limited market and extrapolates the results to cover the broader market.

T-group Training group that uses informal roles to help participants enhance their interpersonal skills and relationships.

Theory Set of integrated ideas, conclusions, hypotheses, and concepts used to describe a phenomenon or investigate patterns, and whose validity has been tested in a scientific setting.

Theory E Orienting an organization to focus primarily on the creation of shareholder value, through the actions of its top managers.

Theory J Japanese approach to management developed by management professor William Ouchi.

Theory O Model of organizational change based on a corporate culture that includes human development, empowerment of employees, and organizational learning.

Theory of constraints Approach to production that focuses on potential bottlenecks, as well as the refinement of process and redesign of products to maximize output. The theory was developed by management guru ELIYAHU GOLDRATT to identify constraints that block success in any system and how to remove such constraints.

Theory of the firm Branch of management concerned with the nature of the corporation, rather than the nature of the market. It incorporates insights from psychology, sociology, and GAME THEORY, and focuses on reducing transaction costs. It asks the questions: (1) What is the rationale for a corporation as the most efficient agent for economic transactions? (2) Why do some firms change while others collapse? (3) What are the external and internal forces that shape a corporation? and (4) How does an organizational culture emerge in a corporation and what are its distinguishing hallmarks?

Theory of the horizontal fast track Principles developed by management guru CHARLES HANDY for developing company versatility by moving people from job to job to test and hone their capabilities.

Theory W Variation of THEORY X.

Theory X Concept of human motivation put forward by management professor DOUGLAS MCGREGOR, which states that human beings are inherently lazy, unmotivated, and irresponsible. They prefer being led and directed, rather than being autonomous, and the only time they are creative is when they find ways to circumvent the system. Their only motivators are money and coercion.

Theory Y Concept of human motivation put forward by management professor DOUGLAS MCGREGOR, which states that human beings are capable of genuine altruism and pursuit of excellence, and may be inspired by creativity and ingenuity given the right incentives. They are capable of being responsible and disciplined and enjoy recognition and encouragement.

Theory Z Alternative theory of human motivation borrowed from Japan, put forward by management professor William Ouchi. It proposed that employees seek better career prospects, more secure employment, greater participation in decision making, greater emphasis on team spirit and camaraderie, and greater mutual respect.

Therblig Reverse spelling of Gilbreth, after FRANK and LILLIAN GILBRETH, pioneers in motion study. It is a unit of measurement used in motion economics, one of 18 fundamental units of every operation, whose configuration is essential for the successful completion of a task.

Thin market Demand for a security, commodity, or currency with few transactions, where the spread between bid and offer is wide and where even small transactions have a large impact.

Think tank Research organization that assembles experts in a given field, with the goal of stimulating fresh thinking.

Third sector Nonprofit and charitable organizations, a group of businesses that constitute a powerful and influential voting bloc.

Third wave From futurist ALVIN TOFFLER's description of society's development as a series of waves. The first wave is agricultural, the second is industrial, and the third is postindustrial, or basically the INFORMATION AGE.

Third world Term used during the cold war to describe nonaligned countries (vs. Soviet or Western world), then extended to mean the underdeveloped countries in contrast to the industrialized countries of the West. It was a translation of the French term *tiers monde,* even extending back to references to the Third Estate, meaning the peasant class during the French Revolution. The term has been replaced by other descriptors, such as the SOUTH and *three-fourths world.* See also FOURTH WORLD.

360-degree evaluation Technique used in personnel management, in which opinions regarding an employee's performance is obtained from superiors as well as peers.

Three-dimensional management Theory

outlining a management style developed by management experts WILLIAM REDDIN, ROBERT BLAKE, and JANE MOUTON.

Three Ss Strategy, structure, and systems—three classes of decision making.

Tichy, Noel U.S. business guru known for his research on TRANSFORMATIONAL LEADERSHIP; author of *The Transformational Leader* (1997).

Tiger market Group of Asian countries—Singapore, Taiwan, South Korea, and Hong Kong—seen as emerging markets in the 1990s. Compare DRAGON MARKETS.

Time and motion study Business efficiency technique combining the time study of F. W. TAYLOR and motion study of FRANK and LILLIAN GILBRETH. It is an element of scientific management or Taylorism. The integrated system is also known as methods engineering.

Time-based competition Analysis of the time elapsed between order receipt to delivery, as a way of compressing the process. It also adds value by aligning promised lead times with actual lead times, promised quality with actual quality, and promised quality with actual quality. It is an extension of JUST-IN-TIME to every aspect of the product delivery cycle.

Time budget Detailed timetable assigning times for each unit of work.

Time fence Period during which a master

production schedule may not be changed, lest it destabilize the production schedule.

Time horizon Time frame for completing a task as it extends into the future.

Time management Efficient use of time through prioritization of tasks and elimination of unimportant or unproductive tasks.

Time pacing Practice of producing or introducing new products according to a given schedule.

Time-series analysis Market research technique for forecasting sales by breaking down trends, cycles, seasons, and other variables.

Time sovereignty Control over the way a person spends his or her work time, especially the ability to manage time without reference to the clock.

Time span of discretion Setting salary scales and differentials on the basis of a formal evaluation of performance, especially the way an employee handles responsibilities without supervision. Term coined by economist ELLIOTT JAQUES.

Time to market Period between initial concept and finished product, including its introduction in the market.

Tipping point Point at which a new idea or product attains the CRITICAL MASS to become commercially feasible and reproducible.

Tire kicker Consumer who superficially checks out merchandise, without any real intention of buying it.

Title inflation Practice of giving employees high-sounding titles without the accompanying increase in authority, pay, or status.

Tobin, James (1918–2002) American economist who served on the Council of Economic Advisers taught at Harvard and Yale universities. He was a Keynesian who advocated government intervention in the economy. He pioneered contributions to the study of investment, monetary and fiscal policy, and financial markets. He received the Nobel Prize in Economic Sciences in 1981. His book, *Is Growth Obsolete?* (1972), introduced the Measure of Economic Welfare for economic sustainability assessment.

Toehold Initial stake in a company, acquired as preliminary to a formal TAKEOVER BID.

Toffler, Alvin (1928–) American futurist, author of *The Future Shock* and *The Third Wave*. His work studied the digital revolution, communication revolution, and technological singularity.

Tokenism In human resources, a superficial effort at diversity by having a nominal minority representation, without assigning real power to the employees.

Tolerance Defined limits within which

deviation or a departure from the norm may be tolerated, as in quality control or engineering.

Tolerance for ambiguity Ability to handle complexity or lack of clarity in situations and to welcome conflicting interpretations and perspectives.

Too big to fail Notion developed during the financial crisis of 2008 that some financial institutions have such a decisive influence on the economy that their failure would cause massive losses and bring great disruption. This notion carried the implication that CENTRAL BANKS and governments would bail out such institutions even if they failed because of their own greed or improprieties. The principle creates a MORAL HAZARD by suggesting that there will be no consequences for illegal or very risky actions.

Top-down Originating and proceeding from the top echelons and percolating to the bottom, as opposed to BOTTOM-UP.

Top-down design Approach to product design based on general principles or deductive reasoning, rather than empirical research or user feedback. Compare BOTTOM-UP DESIGN.

Top-down or Bottom-up design Strategies of information processing and knowledge ordering mostly concerned with software. Top-down (also called step-wise design) involves analysis, decomposition, and synthesis and begins with the big pic-

ture. Bottom-up assembles or links smaller subunits to create the grand picture or form a complex whole.

Top management Highest echelon in a corporate organization.

Total market demand Total volume of the potential demand for a product or service by a defined group, in a defined area, and during a defined period.

Total productive management (TPM) Management approach that empowers employees operating equipment to take responsibility for routine maintenance and to develop a proactive schedule of failure prevention.Considered an integral part of JUST-IN-TIME and TOTAL QUALITY MANAGEMENT. TPM eliminates downtime and thus increases productivity.

Total Quality Management (TQM) Holistic approach to management that integrates all elements of production to achieve quality and efficiency. The approach was pioneered by management experts including W. EDWARDS DEMING, ARMAND V. FEIGENBAUM, KAORU ISHIKAWA, JOSEPH M. JURAN, and GENICHI TAGUCHI. Also termed *total quality control.*

TQM ensures that all parts of an organization are working in unison and have a part in the success of the program. The principal elements of TQM are (1) long-term commitment by management; (2) commitment to getting things right the first time; (3) commitment to continuous improvement; (4) understanding of the relationships that sustain quality, especially between producers and consumers; (5) understanding that costs are defined not merely in terms of money but also as quality, that monetary savings may not always be quality-friendly; (6) aligning systems to organizational needs, and where they are not so aligned, work processes are redesigned; (7) streamlining communications between staff and management with appropriate training; (8) empowering and enabling workers; and (9) constantly measuring, evaluating, commending, and rewarding performance. The primary responsibility for TQM is assigned to production workers rather than a department.

The principal TQM concepts and categories are:

Goals

1. Habits of improvement are based on CONTINUOUS IMPROVEMENT or KAIZEN.

2. Perfection is based on zero defects and continuous cost reduction.

Basic Principles

1. PROCESS CONTROL is based on continuous inspection by the workforce rather than supervisors.

2. It should involve measurable and easy-to-see quality through display boards and signs monitoring achievements.

3. Insistence on compliance and quality takes precedence over meeting quotas.

4. Each production worker has the ability to stop production if work is substandard.

5. Workers assume full responsibility for all shortfalls in quality. The workforce is expected to work late to make necessary corrections.

6. Every item of output is inspected, not merely random samples.

7. Achievement is for project-by-project improvement.

Facilitating Concepts

1. Responsibility for quality rests with line workers and not the department. It also rests with the suppliers, who receive appropriate training.

2. Small lot sizes make inspection easier.

3. Factories are keep immaculate.

4. Machines are checked daily, not by specialists but also by workers themselves with the help of checklists.

Techniques and Aids

1. Problems are exposed early.

2. Work process is redesigned to avoid mistakes. Machines are fitted in Japan with *bakayoke*, which checks automatically for abnormal functions.

3. Manual inspection is required for lower volumes. 100% of production is inspected in the case of unstable

processes, but in the case of stable processes, sample inspection may be used, restricted to the first and last pieces of a production run.

4. Statistical tools are used, such as CAUSE-EFFECT DIAGRAM.

5. Every corporation has QUALITY CIRCLES to which all employees belong.

Towne, Henry (1844–1924) Pioneer of SCIENTIFIC MANAGEMENT who inspired American engineer F. W. TAYLOR. His best-known work is *The Engineer as an Economist* (1886). He coined the term GAIN SHARING as part of an attempt to increase worker productivity.

Toyota Production System Manufacturing system developed by Toyota that increases productivity and efficiency by avoiding waste, such as waiting time, over-production, transportation bottlenecks, and unnecessary inventory, It was developed by Japanese businessman TAIICHI OHNO. It integrates such methods as LEAN production, JUST-IN-TIME, KANBAN, and *production smoothing.*

TPM TOTAL PRODUCTIVE MANAGEMENT

TQM TOTAL QUALITY MANAGEMENT

Trade Economic activity oriented toward the selling of products and services for a profit.

Trade association Professional group of companies engaged in the same business to further their common interests.

Trade description Principal characteristics of a product, designed to inform consumers of exactly what they are getting for their money.

Trade dispute See INDUSTRIAL DISPUTE.

Trade fair Exhibition of products in a special category, bringing together manufacturers, distributors, and consumers.

Trade name Informal name used by a company.

Trade secret Proprietary formula for a product or process, integral to its success and appeal, the disclosure of which is a criminal offense.

Trade union Labor union.

Trademark Distinctive symbol that identifies a product, producer, or trader. It is usually registered with the government and unauthorized use is an infringement that carries penalties.

Tradeoff Compromise based on a balance of advantages and disadvantages or a number of options.

Trading down Reduction of prices and services to customers for increased sales volume.

Trading halt Cessation of trading in a

financial market when the price reaches a threshold, or on the basis of a development affecting the stability of the institution.

Trading stamp Stamp or coupon once popular with consumers that can be collected, traded, or redeemed with certain participating retailers for goods of choice.

Trading up Introduction of a product in a new market or in a more exclusive market, without raising prices to compensate for the additional costs.

Training loop Process that assesses, delivers, and reviews training needs.

Trait theory Related to the great man theory, a belief that all leaders display the same key personality traits.

Tranche 1. Part or installment of a large sum of money available to the borrower on reaching a milestone. 2. In a securitization, any of several classes of debt instruments created from the same pool of assets but with different risk ratios to attract different classes of investors.

Transaction costs All aspects of a transaction, including negotiations, monitoring, and enforcement, with two main components: transaction uncertainty and performance ambiguity. The basis for an economic theory developed by economist RICHARD COASE, which stresses the influence of these transaction costs on economic behavior. High transaction costs add to allocative in-

efficiencies, increase the hierarchical levels through which they have to pass, and affect the quality and quantity of the information transmitted.

Transactional leadership Introduced by management guru JAMES M. BURNS, a term to describe a manager who pursues the achievement of goals without being stymied by a concern for the nature of these goals. Contrast with TRANSFORMATIONAL LEADERSHIP.

Transfer of training Continued application of skills and learning gained during training to the actual work environment.

Transfer price Price at which goods and services are bought and sold between divisions or subsidiaries within a group of companies.

Transformational leadership Visionary leadership style that inspires loyalty and confidence among followers and motivates them to do more than they are required to do. Transformational leadership acknowledges the individual contributions of team members, encourages free exchange of ideas, shares credit for achievements, and takes responsibility for failures. See also TRANSACTIONAL LEADERSHIP.

Transnational organization See MULTINATIONAL COMPANY.

Transparency In business, the quality of being open about goals and methods and sharing positive as well as negative developments, as well as in compliance with legal and moral requirements.

Tribology In engineering, the interaction of surfaces through friction, including design of bearings and the application of lubricants.

Trickle-down economics Belief that wealth earned at the top, by large corporations and wealthy individuals, makes its way down slowly but surely to the underclasses.

Triple I organization Identified by management guru CHARLES HANDY, a corporate culture in which the focus is on three areas—information, intelligence, and ideas—contrasted with a hierarchical culture.

Triple witching hour Third Friday in March, June, September, and December (quarters) when stock index OPTIONS, FUTURES, and individual stock options all expire at the same time, adding potential of volatility to the markets.

Troubleshooting Dealing with unexpected problems in production, distribution, or personnel.

Trist, Eric (1909–1993) British pioneer in the field of organizational development and founder of the Tavistock Institute for Social Research in London.

True and fair view Accounting term to indicate that a set of accounts is a fair presentation and complies with all legal requirements.

Trust 1. Form of monopoly in which the owners of merging corporations yield their stock to a board of trustees empowered to act on their behalf. It is outlawed under ANTITRUST LAWS. 2. Arrangement under which property is held by an appointed person (*trustee*) on behalf of the beneficiaries.

Trust-control dilemma Problem confronting managers regarding how much to delegate to employees, how much to trust them to do the work, and how much to control that work.

Turbulence In business, unpredictable and swift changes in the organizational environment and structure, leading to a shakedown in the functions and authority of the employees.

Turkey farm Part of the organization to which the most inefficient employees are assigned or exiled, so that they do not affect the morale of the remaining employees.

Turnaround Strategy to reverse a decline in profitability or sales, thereby putting the company back on the road to recovery. This may be achieved through DOWNSIZING, divesting the company of all but its core operations, and managerial changes. The areas where turnaround strategies focus are (1) management vision; (2) leadership role of CEO and chairman; (3) board of directors; (4) core businesses; (5) diversification; (6) financial control; (7) organizational structure; (8) competition, price, and product; (9) cost structure and disadvantages; (10) operating inefficiencies; (11) changes in market demand; (12) adverse movement in commodity prices; (13) lack of marketing effort; (14) underestimates of capital requirements; (15) capacity expansion; (16) failed acquisitions; (17) high debt/equity ratio; (18) financial policies; and (19) overtrading. Successful turnaround strategies include: (1) change in management, (2) strong financial control, (3) decentralization, (4) new product focus, (5) improved marketing, (6) growth through acquisition, (7) asset reduction, (8) cost reduction, and (9) debt restructuring.

Turnover Total sales of a company for a stated period.

Tversky, Amos Nathan (1937–1996) Israeli psychologist. Much of his early work was concerned with measurement. He co-authored *Foundations of Measurement*. Together with DANIEL KAHNEMANN he developed PROSPECT THEORY, which explains irrational economic choices. It is one of the seminal theories in behavioral economics.

Twinning Partnership of companies and universities, especially in R&D.

Two faces of power Duality in the exercise of power, one benign and the other self-aggrandizing; inherent in the control functions of authority.

Two-factor theory Concept of work-study engineer FREDERICK HERZBERG that job performance is driven by motivators in what he termed "hygiene factors."

Type A personality Person with hyperactive personality traits, who is impatient with delays, dictatorial in dealing with associates, hard-driving, and aversive to leisure.

Type B personality Person who is easy going, a good listener, slow and deliberate in manner and speech, has extensive interests outside of work, and is articulate.

Type T personality Person who deliberately enjoys taking risks and does not consider consequences in adopting a course of action.

Uniform Commercial Code (UCC) Collection of laws and statutes relating to business and commerce, as regards contracts, leases, negotiable instruments, and letters of credit.

Ultimate holding company Parent company or group that, through an interlocking system of directorships, controls and owns subsidiaries, each of which operates under its own name and with its own management.

Ultra vires (Latin, "beyond the powers") Denoting the act of an official or corporation for which there is no authority in law or the memorandum of association.

Unbundling Separation of a business into its constituent parts, with the purpose of selling off some of them.

Uncontrollable costs Expenditures that are beyond the discretionary powers of management to restrict or check.

Undermanning Deliberately using fewer workers to do a job and thus overworking them.

Understandability Accounting principle that financial information presented in a report is both in language and content easily grasped by a reasonably intelligent layperson. It should not be so dense that it overwhelms the reader, and it should not be so perfunctory that it leaves out important facts.

Undifferentiated marketing Advertising and selling a product for the widest possible base of users, with the broadest range of interests, tastes, and needs.

Undue influence Applying unfair pressure on a person to sign a document or advocate for an outcome that is to the advantage of the person wielding the pressure.

Unemployment Inability to find employment, even when actively sought; usually a reflection of employers not hiring, often because of a drop in demand.

Unfreezing First of psychologist KURT LEWIN's three-step process of change in an organization, the others being *transition* and *refreezing*. It requires management to force a revision of ideas and practices before introducing new ideas.

Ungluing Breakup of the traditional supply chains by removing the nexus of interest or the rationale for partnership.

Unique selling point (USP) The most distinctive feature of a product, advertised in its promotion.

Unit pricing Display of the price of a single unit in a multipack bundled product, useful for comparison shopping.

Unitary firm Organization without internal divisions, where all management functions are centralized or where only a single product is manufactured.

Unity of management Management expert HENRI FAYOL's classic principle, calling for a direction by one manager, with undivided authority and single vision. Also termed *unity of direction*.

Unorganization Organizational design that dismantles traditional structures and processes by DELAYERING management, OUTSOURCING projects, and encouraging *teleworking*.

Unstructured interview Discussion with an applicant for employment that does not follow a routine and is free-flowing, emphasizing flexibility for the interviewer and scope of expression for the interviewee.

Upselling Sales technique of encouraging consumers to buy add-ons to a product, such as a warranty for an appliance or a carry-on case for a cell phone.

Upset price Minimum sale price at an auction.

Upstream Denoting a short-term loan from a subsidiary company to a parent company.

Upstream progress In marketing, advancement made against competition.

Upward communication Process of information flowing from the lower levels of a hierarchic organization to the upper levels. It is more democratic than traditional forms of communication.

Ure, Andre (1778–1857) Scottish doctor and chemist, an early pioneer of management science who published one of the earliest textbooks on manufacturing in the textile industry. Ure was a defender of the emerging factory system.

Urwick, Lyndall (1891–1983) British business management expert. He formulated a comprehensive theory of management drawing from the work of HENRI FAYOL, F. W. TAYLOR, MARY PARKER FOLLETT, and others. His best-known work is *The Elements of Business Administration* (1943).

USP UNIQUE SELLING POINT

Usufruct Right of enjoyment that enables a holder to derive profit or benefit from a property owned by another or is under common ownership.

Utility theory View of behavior, strategies,

and processes to deal with risky choices and decisions, stressing the subjective value attached to a particular course of action or outcome.

Utilization Regarding an operating system, the proportion of output to design capacity.

Utilization management Techniques used by efficiency experts for analyzing and improving productivity.

V

Valorization Stabilization of a currency or commodity by artificial means, such as state intervention.

Value Agreed-upon worth of a product or service, as distinct from its retail price or cost to produce.

Value added Greater worth added to goods and services at each stage or step in the chain of production, which becomes the basis for levying a VALUE-ADDED TAX.

Value-added tax Form of consumption tax or excise added incrementally on the value added at each stage of processing or the production and distribution of a commodity and is ultimately passed on to the consumer. Unlike a sales tax, it occurs each time a business in the supply chain purchases products.

Value analysis Technique developed by educator and engineer LAWRENCE D. MILES to maximize the utility provided by a product or service and to minimize or eliminate waste. It measures the value-added and non-value-added elements in a production

and delivery process in order to reengineer the design more efficiently.

Value chain Series of activities that directly create value, by which a good or service is produced, distributed, and marketed. Each step contributes different values and incurs different costs. As VALUE is the amount that buyers are willing to pay for a product or service, PROFIT is the differential between value and the costs incurred. The activities include outbound logistics, operations and production, marketing and sales, and service, as well as support activities such as human resources, technology, and infrastructure.

Value dimensions Dutch researcher GEERT HOFSTEDE's classification of values as they impinge on behavior: (1) power distance; (2) uncertainty avoidance; (3) individualism; and (4) masculinity. Hofstede's values are learned qualities imparted by a culture.

Value engineering Design of a product to eliminate costs that do not contribute to the VALUE of the product. It has three aspects: (1) value target; (2) development of new products from concepts and increasing functionality without a corresponding increase in cost; and (3) manufacturing value engineering, which identifies the best method to produce a part with the trade-off between cost and quality.

Value-instrumentality-expectancy theory Proposed by business professor VICTOR H. VROOM, a theory of motivation that the level of effort exerted by an individual on any task is based on three variables: (1) instrumentality, or the belief that the action will be successful; (2) confidence that success will bring rewards; and (3) valence, or the desirability of the reward.

Value migration Flow of VALUE and PROFIT away from companies with outmoded business models and toward those with more efficient models. Companies that are more flexible thus gain COMPETITIVE ADVANTAGE. The value stabilizes as a competitive equilibrium is reached.

Value planning Planning designed to maximize the value of a corporation to its shareholders, with value being the present worth or estimation of future cash flow.

Value reengineering Radical redesign of processes to achieve a dramatic improvement in performance, such as cost, quality, speed, and service.

Variety wars Competition based on the introduction of new products, aimed at overwhelming competitors' productive capacity and displacing their products on the shelves.

Veblen, Thorstein Bunde (1857–1929) American sociologist and founder of the institutional economics movement. He was a critic of capitalism, which he lambasted in *The Theory of the Leisure Class* (1899). He combined a evolutionary and Darwinian approach to economics with an institutionalist approach to economic analysis. He discredited the conspicuous consumption and waste of capitalists, whom he equated with parasites.

Veblen effect Economic phenomenon first noted by American sociologist THORSTEN VEBLEN, where high levels of consumption lead to increased demand or higher prices.

Velocity of circulation Average number of times a unit of money is used in a specified period, equal to the total amount of money spent during that period divided by the total amount of money in circulation.

Venture capital Money loaned to start up businesses, usually by venture capital funds, which then own equity in the start-up. This is private equity funding that is considered high risk but can also give high yields. Also *venture capitalist*, a person involved in venture capitalization.

Vertical integration Process whereby a company extends its business interests into all stages of its production and distribution. Vertical integration may be achieved through BACKWARD or FORWARD INTEGRATION at any stage of a company's history. Vertical integration adds to the capital investment, includes additional risk to a firm's position in the industry, makes it more difficult to exit, and may require careful coordination. See also HORIZONTAL INTEGRATION.

Vertical linkage analysis Tool for analyzing the VALUE CHAIN to determine where opportunities exist for enhancing competitive advantage.

Vertical marketing system CHANNEL structure of distribution in which producers, wholesalers, and retailers act as a single system.

Vested interest Involvement in an enterprise or business in anticipation of personal gain.

Vestibule training Education of future employees in which they learn a job skill in a simulated environment.

Vineyard organization Model structure in which the parent group is viewed as the vine and the subsidiaries or employees as clusters of grapes. The clusters are relatively autonomous, but are dependent on the vine for sustaining power.

Viral marketing Strategy that relies on the Internet, social media, and word of mouth to promote products and services.

Virement System of budgetary controls in which funds may be transferred from one part of the budget to another during a financial year, usually to make up for a shortfall.

Virtual organization Business form without physical properties, such as a defined location or full-time employees, and that provides products or services through third parties or by OUTSOURCING.

Virtuous cycle Cycle of company growth that replicates itself by producing positive returns at every turn. Opposite of *vicious cycle*.

Visible management Philosophy that top managers should not hide behind their desks but instead make themselves accessible to their subordinates.

Visibles Earnings from exports and payments for imports of goods, as opposed to services such as banking.

Vision Leadership quality of formulating ideas, plans, or dreams that help shape the future and ability to persuade colleagues and associates to share those dreams.

Vision statement See MISSION STATEMENT.

Vital statistics In business, data relating to demographics that can influence marketing strategies.

Vitalist theory Management principle that the entire organization needs to be designed before the parts are put into place.

Vitamin model Eight factors that affect job satisfaction: money, security, social position, clarity, variety, control, use of skills, and contact with peers.

Vroom, Victor Herald Canadian authority on management who explored motivation, leadership, and decision making in his *Work and Motivation* (1964). See also VROOM-YETTON-JAGO MODEL.

Vroom-Yetton-Jago model Theory of leadership that leaders should vary the extent to which they allow followers to participate in decision making, according to certain factors constructed in a DECISION TREE: the nature of the task, the extent of possible disagreement, and the willingness of followers to accept the ultimate decision.

Vulnerability analysis Method of evaluating threats to a company in different areas and functions: resources and assets, customer needs, cost position, consumer base, technology, corporate identity, regulations, social values, customer goodwill, and complementary products and services. Vulnerability analysis identifies the threats, ranks them on a scale, estimates their probability, and determines the firm's capability to deal with them.

Vulture capital Investment in firms or properties that are facing liquidation, then turning them around in order to sell them at a profit.

W

Wa *Japanese* Term for a situation in which there is complete harmony, with no possibility of conflict.

Wage compression Reduction in the gap between the higher salary scales and the lower ones so as to make compensation more equitable.

Wage differential Difference in earnings between workers with similar skills in different industries, or between workers with different skills in the same industry.

Wage freeze Government-imposed prohibition of wage increases for a specified time, usually an effort to curb INFLATION. Distinguished from *wage restraint*, which is a recommendation for freezing salaries.

Waiver A formal setting-aside of a requirement; nonenforcement of a right.

Wall Street In lower Manhattan, the street on which the New York Stock Exchange is located; however, generally a reference to the entire U.S. financial system, including the stock exchanges.

Warranty Clearly defined guarantee of performance or quality, often with clauses ensuring the repair or replacement in the event of defects or shortcomings, in a contract, usually covering a specified period of time. The warranty may be expressed (clearly stated) or implied (mutually understood).

Wasting asset Resource that has a finite life and is consumed when used, such as coal or oil.

Waterman, Robert H. Business guru and associate of TOM PETERS, with whom he coauthored *In Search of Excellence* (1982).

Watt, James (1736–1819) Scottish inventor and mechanical engineer who was one of the pioneers of the INDUSTRIAL REVOLUTION. He developed the concept of horsepower and the SI unit, the watt, is named after him.

Weakest link Descriptive of the least efficient or least durable component of a machine or organization, which determines the longevity of the whole, as in the weakest link of a chain.

Wear and tear Diminution in the value of a physical asset from use or age, one of the elements of DEPRECIATION.

Weber, Max (1864–1920) German sociologist and philosopher who also wrote on INDUSTRIAL ORGANIZATION and is considered the father of INDUSTRIAL SOCIOLOGY. He held that managers should not be managers, and that management should be based on a CHAIN OF COMMAND.

Welfare function Management's responsibility for the physical and mental welfare of employees, including health and safety, AFFIRMATIVE ACTION, maternity leave, sick leave, and other benefits mostly also required by law.

Wheel of retailing Concept that retailers begin as low-margin and low-price operations, and then evolve into higher-priced stores as they move up the status scale.

Wheelwright, Steven C. Emeritus professor at Harvard Business School and president of Brigham Young University. He is author of *Strategic Management of Technology and Innovation*.

Whipsawing Pitting one group against another in order to gain a bargaining advantage, as for teams of employees or labor unions in an industry with different employers.

Whisper stock Share in a company about which there are whispers in the market about a change in value or a takeover.

Whistle blowing Public exposure of illegal, corrupt, unethical, criminal, or antisocial activities in an organization, reported by one of its members.

White collar Relating to office employees, in contrast to manual workers or BLUE-COLLAR workers.

White-collar crime Criminal offense associated with corrupt business actions, including embezzlement, fraud, and INSIDER TRADING.

White elephant Asset whose maintenance costs are greater than the possible benefit or profit.

White goods Consumer durable goods such as refrigerators and washing machines, which are traditionally painted white. Compare BROWN GOODS.

White knight Friendly person or business that makes a bid to take over a company under favorable terms, often to offset a HOSTILE BID.

Whyte, William Hollingsworth (1917–1999) U.S. sociologist and, author of *The Organization Man* (1956), a study of the impact of corporate culture on society.

Wildcat strike Local strike, often without formal notice, by a local union without official union backing.

Willie Sutton rule Maxim that business should focus on its most profitable areas, based on Willie Sutton's statement that he robbed banks because that was where the money was.

Win-win Situation in which both parties to a dispute or a negotiation gain something and lose less.

Window dressing Practice of making an offer or situation appear better than it really is, often through addition of frills or by disguising negative factors.

Woodward, Joan (1916–1971) British authority on organizational sociology. She was a pioneer in empirical research in organizational structures that established the link between technology and production. She is associated particularly with CONTINGENCY THEORY. In 1970 she published *Industrial Organization: Behavior and Control.*

Word of mouse Internet-driven publicity.

Word of mouth Favorable or unfavorable reviews or comments conveyed orally by customers and users and considered influential in sales because it is based on experience.

Work ethic Driving force that makes work enjoyable and fulfilling. Usually, PROTESTANT ETHIC.

Work-in-progress Project that has been begun but is not yet completed.

Work-life balance Relationship between meeting the demands of work and maintaining a healthy home environment; a healthy balance is said to neutralize stress.

Work permit Issued by a local government, a permit that allows underage employment, construction, or other applications, usually with stipulated controls; a license granted to a foreign national to work for a limited period within a country.

Work simplification Idea pioneered by work-study team FRANK and LILLIAN GILBRETH as part of SCIENTIFIC MANAGEMENT, in which work that does not add VALUE to a process is wasteful and therefore expendable. The goal is to eliminate complexity altogether or at least reduce it to the bare minimum.

Work study Measurement and analysis of the flow of work and other parameters and processes, with a view to identifying their effectiveness and efficiencies. The study is associated with TIME MANAGEMENT, MOTION STUDY, SCIENTIFIC MANAGEMENT, and TOTAL QUALITY MANAGEMENT.

Work-to-rule Form of industrial action, short of a strike, in which workers do not walk off the job but limit their work strictly to the minimum requirements under law. It is the same as GO SLOW.

Workaholic Person who is addicted to work, sign of a TYPE A PERSONALITY.

Workfare Social program that replaced welfare, by which applicants perform useful work in order to be eligible for government assistance.

Working capital Part of the capital of a company employed in day-to-day operations.

Worksharing Act of spreading work among several people; often a solution to labor redundancy, elimination of overtime, or reduced working hours.

World Bank. See INTERNATIONAL BANK FOR RECONSTRUCTION AND DEVELOPMENT.

World Trade Organization (WTO) UN agency charged with monitoring international trade. Under its auspices are held discussions known as *rounds*, which set conditions for free trade and also determine tariffs.

Wren, Daniel Expert on management history and author of *The Evolution of Management Thought,* in its 6th edition in 2011.

Write off To reduce the value of an asset or debt to zero, and thus take it off the books.

Writer In ROSEMARY STEWART's taxonomy, a manager who spends most of his or her time on paperwork.

WTO WORLD TRADE ORGANIZATION

WYSWYG "What you see is what you get," referring to computer displays of intended printed items.

X

Xenophobic (From Greek, Xenos, stranger, and phobia, fear) Fear of foreigners, one of the main drivers of extreme nationalism.

Yield curve Line on a graph showing the yield for deposits or fixed-interest securities, plotted against the length of time they have to run to maturity. An upward curve indicates a strong market, a downward curve indicates a falling market, and a flat or humped curve indicates market uncertainty.

Yield gap Difference between the yield on a safe investment and that on a risky investment.

Z

Z score Multivariate formula devised by finance professor EDWARD ALTMAN that measures the susceptibility of a business to failure by applying beta-coefficients to a number of selected ratios.

Zaibatsu Japanese conglomerate or group of companies that coordinate their activities to maximize profit. Each *zaibatsu* usually includes a bank, trading company, and service company, with linked equity.

Zelenik, Abraham U.S. academic who wrote the influential article "Managers and Leaders: Are They Different?" in *Harvard Business Review* (1977).

Zero-based budgeting Record keeping that starts from scratch every year and regards all expenditures as new items, with their own rationals that need to be assessed.

Zero defect Component of TOTAL QUALITY MANAGEMENT aimed at changing worker attitudes toward quality by stressing error-free production or SIX-SIGMA.

Zero-sum game In GAME THEORY, a situation in which one person's loss is another's gain because the total remains the same.

Zone of indifference Range of authority of a superior, not questioned by subordinates and accepted as a legitimate exercise of power.